QUEER COMPANY

For Petie Poppet and Madame du Bois,
with love, for their unflagging love and support

Queer Company
The Role and Meaning of Friendship in Gay Men's Work Lives

NICK RUMENS
University of Bristol, UK

ASHGATE

Published by
Ashgate Publishing Limited
Wey Court East
Union Road
Farnham
Surrey, GU9 7PT
England

Ashgate Publishing Company
Suite 420
101 Cherry Street
Burlington
VT 05401-4405
USA

www.ashgate.com

British Library Cataloguing in Publication Data
Rumens, Nick.
  Queer company : the role and meaning of friendship in gay
  men's work lives.
  1. Homosexuality in the workplace. 2. Male friendship.
  3. Gay men--Relations with heterosexuals. 4. Quality of
  work life. 5. Industrial sociology.
  I. Title
  302.3'5'086642-dc22

Library of Congress Cataloging-in-Publication Data
Rumens, Nick.
  Queer company : the role and meaning of friendship in gay men's work lives / by Nick
Rumens.
    p. cm.
  Includes bibliographical references and index.
  ISBN 978-1-4094-0191-9 (hardback) -- ISBN 978-1-4094-0192-6 (ebook)
  1. Gay men. 2. Male friendship. 3. Men--Psychology. 4. Work environment. I. Title.
  HQ76.R86 2011
  306.76'62086642--dc22
                                                                                      2011013245

ISBN 9781409401919 (hbk)
ISBN 9781409401926 (ebk)

MIX
Paper from
responsible sources
FSC
www.fsc.org   FSC® C018575

Printed and bound in Great Britain by the
MPG Books Group, UK.

Contents

List of Tables

Acknowledgements

Over the years I have made friendships in the workplace which have, in small and large ways, enriched my life outside and at work. In the company of both male and female work friends, I've laughed until I've cried, disclosed my inner feelings, smiled, frowned, become angry and frustrated, been betrayed and felt loved. I've made some amazing friends in various places I've spent time working and although not all have remained in my life as I've changed jobs, workplaces and moved house, they have helped me to explore who I am and what I want to become. There isn't the space here to mention all these friends by name but, as I've written this book, they've never been far from my thoughts. However, particular thanks go to the following work friends whose friendship has made a lasting impression: Graham and Anne Benmore, Chris Stevens, Cathie Turner-Jones and Christine Fountain.

As I have been researching and writing this book over the last few years, I have received support and words of wisdom from colleagues and work friends within academic circles, who have commented on my work, giving me plenty to think about. Special thanks then are due to Martin Parker, Jo Brewis, Gavin Jack and, more recently, John Broomfield. Colleagues and friends at Keele University have also been supportive in that respect. Thanks then to Paul Willis and Deborah Kerfoot for helping me to get my initial ideas off the ground. Beverley Hawkins has been dependably kind and big-hearted, often lending me a sympathetic ear and supplying cake at those moments when self-doubt has taken hold. Likewise, I owe a debt of gratitude to Mihaela Kelemen for her steadfast encouragement and generosity in providing opportunities to collaborate on some fantastic projects. General thanks to not only everyone who has made Southampton Solent University such a friendly place to work but also to colleagues at Surrey University who have provided me with support and the opportunity to work on this book. Sincere thanks then to David Goss at Surrey University. Sam Warren has been pivotal here too but, as a friend, she has done a sterling job of helping me to have faith in my abilities. On a similar note, I am grateful to colleagues and newly made friends at the University of Bristol, especially for giving me a warm welcome that has been nothing short of a much needed tonic. Also, hugs to my new friend Ann Rippin for being the type of person who makes going to work feel like a very worthwhile and fun thing to do.

My thanks and love to members of my family who have displayed qualities of friendship and to friends who feel like family. Those who deserve mention here include Peter Heather and his parents, Barugh and Heather, for showing interest in what I'm doing and encouraging me to be happy. Also, thanks to Susan, Gerald and Adam Rumens for doing likewise, in spades, over the years. Furthermore, I am fortunate enough to have a regal friend in Lady Buckley, who did a splendid job of keeping me in touch with what matters in life and undertaking some administrative work not befitting of a woman of her status and title. This book is really only possible because of the amazing support and love of these people and two others: Su Holmes and Danny Macdonald.

Finally, I am enormously grateful to the men who took part in my research, since it was their openness and willingness to talk about friendship that helped to provide the data to illustrate the empirical sections of this book. Last but by no means least, copious thanks to Neil Jordan and his colleagues at Ashgate for supporting the publication of this book.

Introduction

The genesis of this book was a desire to deepen our current understanding of workplace friendships. Many of us have work friends, relying on them for a whole variety of things, from help with fixing problems and passing on information to providing a sympathetic ear and a shoulder to cry on. The work of friendship itself can be observed in many organisations: laughing and joking, snatched conversations in office corridors, exchanging knowing looks in meetings, holding hands, having lunch together in the office canteen and all the other things friends do to sustain their friendships. Despite the ubiquitous nature of workplace friendships, they have received intermittent rather than sustained interest among organisation studies scholars. The patchy coverage of the subject within academic circles strikes me as being odd. Academics, like most other people, have work friends, even those who overlook them as a serious subject for scholarly analysis. And being in friendship can make all the difference to a more enjoyable work life. I am no different in that respect.

Recalling off the top of my head some unforgettable moments with work friends, I'm reminded of the time one work friend baked a birthday cake for me. The cake had to be hidden in a filing cabinet away from the prying eyes of our overbearing line manager, who failed to see the funny side when they opened the cabinet midway through lecturing us on the virtue of filing paperwork. Other moments included the time I confided in a work friend about the bullying antics of several homophobic work colleagues. My friend responded with such tenderness and a kind heart that I still regret how we lost touch with each other, after I quit the job out of desperation and moved away from the area. Another example concerns a situation involving an employee, inconsolable with grief, who requested a period of compassionate leave after their closest friend had died unexpectedly. The request was flatly refused on the grounds that the paper policy on compassionate leave covered 'family not friends'. Yet the sorrow this employee felt appeared no less agonising than if a close family member had died. The insensitive manner in which this employee's request was dealt with vexed me deeply for a number of reasons, not the least of them being how organisational policy had reduced friendship to a second-class relationship, compared to familial relations. While workplace friendships are not important to all employees, they clearly matter a great deal to others.

In different ways, then, friends have improved the quality of my work life, for which I am enormously thankful. But more than this, they have also had a hand in shaping me as a person. Here, work friends have enabled me to see myself as more than the sum of a number of identity categories I inhabit: civil partner, lecturer, son, brother and gay man, to mention but a few. Work friends have offered up interesting perspectives on my personality, my habits (pleasant or otherwise) and the idiosyncrasies that characterise me as a person. It is in the company of work friends where I can explore who I am and what I want to become. In other words, with the help of work friends, I can make choices about which identities to use as the primary threads in fashioning a meaningful sense of self and a viable life. Despite all this, we know surprisingly little about how workplace friendships are understood and experienced from the perspectives of those who participate in them. This book is about bringing these perspectives to the fore, shedding much needed light on the human dimension to these important workplace relationships. To address this knowledge gap, I carried out an interview study, based in the UK. Thirty-three gay men were recruited into the study using a snowball sampling technique. A list of participants and their demographic characteristics is contained in Appendix 3, while the methodological design of the study is outlined in Appendix 1. The broad aim of the study was to examine how gay men understand and experience friendship in their work lives. Now, as some readers might wonder at this juncture, why should we care about gay men's workplace friendships?

Part of my response to this question is that I do not think it is any coincidence that I am one of a very large number of gay men for whom friendship has been an important source of support, acceptance and validation for living an openly gay identity and life. Saying as much is to recognise that gay men have often been constructed as culturally subversive figures, marginalised on the fringes of mainstream society. The populist and academic literature on gay men's lives has documented the deleterious effects of prejudice and discrimination based on sexual orientation, often articulated through forms of homophobia and heterosexism. This is perhaps most apparent in the 'coming out' stories told by gay men and others, which have often conveyed the sorrow, fear and rejection experienced by those who have wrestled with the dilemma of disclosing their sexual identity to family, friends and colleagues (see Nardi et al. 1994; Plummer 1999). However, for many gay men rejected by biological kin, friends have come to the rescue, providing the support, acceptance and understanding that we have come to expect from blood family. Here, then, friends have helped gay men to challenge restrictive heteronormative discourses that influence the roles played by family and, by implication, about what constitutes family life. Indeed, as Weeks et al. (2001) and others (Nardi 1999; Sullivan 1998; Weston 1991) aver, friendships often flourish when people's lives are lived against dominant cultural norms. As the reader delves deeper into the book, these debates are discussed in more detail, but suffice to say gay men, and indeed many other social groups marginalised within heteronormative cultures, have long understood and valued friendship as a supportive personal relationship. This is a key starting point for this book, which presents a study of how gay men understand the role and meaning of friendship in the workplace. Here, then, another reason emerges as to why we should be bothered with gay men's friendships within the world of work.

There is little disputing the fact that many of us spend the bulk or even the better part of our waking day engaged in paid employment. Work is a means to many ends, not the least of them being financial security. But it is also the case that many of us want our experience of paid work to be fulfilling, and it is here that workplace friendships can potentially help many of us to improve the quality of our work lives. This is perhaps an obvious point to make, but it raises a number of questions about how people can develop meaningful friendships in the workplace. After all, not all organisational settings are conducive to friendship development, just as not all jobs allow us the time and energy to get to know colleagues in terms of friendship. For some, the friendship potential of the workplace is understood from a different angle, one that views organisations as problematic arenas in which to develop and sustain meaningful identities and selves.

For example, feminist research has amply demonstrated that work organisations are sites of gender inequalities, prejudice and discrimination, often to the detriment of women's careers, identities and well being (Cockburn 1991; Halford et al. 1997; McDowell 1997). At the same time, friendship is frequently understood as an integral feature of women's lives, providing spaces to disclose personal information, display emotion and critique patriarchal definitions of themselves as the *Other* (Green 1998; Oliker 1989; Raymond 1986). Yet within cultures where patriarchal values dominate, women's friendships have often been constructed as culturally problematic, particularly when they are represented as relationships that exclude men and do not serve male interests (Hollinger 1998). For some women, this has heightened their awareness of the value of female friendship as a relationship that can nourish women's identities and selves within contexts that threaten to undermine them (Andrew and Montague 1998; Raymond 1986). Thus gay men, who have found the domain of work at times to be hostile and inhospitable, are perhaps similarly attuned to the constraints and opportunities within the workplace for developing friendships which promote identity growth, support and intimacy. Cognisant of this, throughout the book my aim is to further our understanding of how gay men's friendships are developed and understood in different work contexts, paying particular attention to the various roles they play in gay men's work lives.

Another reason for writing about gay men's workplace friendships is because the current cultural landscape against which this task is undertaken seems to be brimming with all manner of possibilities for living sexual diversity. As Jeffrey Weeks (2007: 3) puts it in *The World We Have Won*, we are living in a 'world of transition', characterised by myriad losses and gains associated with acknowledging the existence of a dazzling array of sexualities and genders. Focusing on the gains, we are witness to a blurring of sexual boundaries and an emphasis on a multiplicity of postmodern sexualities from which to choose and with which to experiment (Roseneil 2000; Simon 1996). While we should never underestimate or neglect studying the continuing influence of heteronormative discourses in shaping people's lives, it is apparent that the notion of the 'homosexual' as culturally subversive is under attack from lesbians, gay men, bisexuals and transpeople (LGBT) as well as from heterosexuals (Weeks 2007). For many men and women the underlying assumptions and meanings of the identity categories 'heterosexual' and 'homosexual' are extremely limiting, just as the meanings associated with traditional gender categories are increasingly contested. Indeed, alongside gay men other men and women have taken the lead in challenging heteronormative notions of gender and sexuality, helping to extend the menu of gendered and sexual lifestyle choices on offer.

Equally and relatedly, the cultural explosion of sexualities and genders is related to the proliferation of alternative, more fluid ways of relating. A growing number of sociologists have argued that the privileging of heteronormative family relationships is being eroded. As Weeks et al. (2001) show in regard to lesbian, gay and bisexual people in the UK, new forms of relating intimately are being invented in everyday life, blurring the borderlines between what constitutes familial and other types of human relationships. Familial relationships may involve friends, just as friendships may encompass family members or others including ex-lovers. Striking, therefore, is that these 'life experiments', as Weeks et al. (2001) dub them, are also being conducted by heterosexuals (Roseneil and Budgeon 2004). In these studies it is clear that heteronormative family relationships no longer hold sway in the way they used to, as relationships such as friendship appear to play an increasingly important role in people's lives. At this point in the book, what we can usefully take from all this is the idea that friendship is a culturally significant phenomenon, part of a fluid network of relationships enabling individuals to relate intimately in different ways with a variety of people.

Thus in a context characterised by postmodern sexualities and genders and at a time when the cultural significance of friendship appears in the ascendancy (Weeks 2007; Allan 2008; Budgeon 2006; Roseneil 2004), I envisage opportunities for gay men to negotiate workplace friendships in different ways with different people. As I explore in greater detail later on, gay men have often established supportive friendships with other gay men on the basis that a shared sexual identity can engender affinity and mutual understanding, acceptance and equality (Nardi 1999; Weeks et al. 2001). As suggested above, such friendships are likely to thrive in contexts when identities and lives are at odds with heteronormative discourse. It is certainly worth pointing out that within work cultures where heterosexuality is privileged, sexuality may suffice for providing common ground among gay men for organising gay male friendships. But amid the fluidity of contemporary sexualities and genders, we might see further opportunities opening up for friendships that span the social divisions between heterosexuals and LGBT people.

Appreciating the varied ways gay men relate to others in workplace friendship involves exploring, for example, how gay men connect with heterosexual and bisexual men and women as friends. One advantage of exploring friendships that cross identity categories that relate to sexuality is the potential for telling us something about how individuals can establish personal relationships that undermine heteronormative values. Which work contexts might support the emergence of this dimension to gay men's workplace friendships is of much interest, as is analysing the possibilities for gay men and their work friends to display conformity to heteronormative constructions of sexuality, gender and friendship. As such, this book aims to provide insights into gay men's workplace friendships as relationships where diverse meanings relating to sexuality, gender and friendship are constructed and contested. Notably, here is an opportunity to throw a different light on how men's friendships have been previously theorised, by focusing on how gay men can buck the trend of stereotyping men in friendship as emotionally stilted, reluctant to disclose feelings and reveal deeper selves (Nardi 1999; Gottlieb 2008; Weeks et al. 2001). As the book reveals, men's friendships are particularly sensitive to changes in how sexuality and gender are understood, with mixed results for how gay men are able to formulate alternative ways of relating to women and other men.

In exploring gay men's workplace friendships this book mobilises theoretical resources derived from sociology as well as feminism and poststructuralism. Sociologists and feminists especially have made vital contributions to the study of friendship, some of whom have exposed and condemned the heterosexual bias in the friendship literature for ignoring the friendship experiences of LGBT people (Rose 2000). Intriguingly, the potential of poststructuralist theories for understanding friendship has yet to be fully realised. As such, this book engages with both established and emerging theories on friendship in order to underpin the empirical analysis of gay men's friendships in the workplace. Before going any further, it is useful to expand on the term 'friendship', the key concept on which this book pivots.

What is friendship?

The frequency with which commentators have turned the spotlight on friendship has been extremely intermittent. Scholarly interest in friendship can be traced back to Aristotle's conceptualisation of friendship in the *Nicomachean Ethics*, but lengthy intervals separate some of the most provocative philosophical commentaries on the topic, such as those by Immanuel Kant, Jacques Derrida, Michel de Montaigne, Saint Thomas Aquinas and Marilyn Friedman. It is only relatively recently that anthropologists, psychologists, sociologists, feminists and other scholars have engaged with friendship as a serious subject of academic study. It is not my aim to construct an encyclopaedic account of these contributions. Such an undertaking falls outside the remit of this book and would consume oceans of ink and a similar quantity of pages – far more than is permitted here. That being said, what strongly emerges from existing research is a sense of how the meaning of friendship is historically dynamic, making it difficult to define precisely.

The conceptual slipperiness of friendship is due, in large part, to the fact that friendship means different things to different people, and that the diverse meanings ascribed to friendship vary across cultural contexts and in specific moments in time (Bell and Coleman 1999). Nonetheless, Aristotle's philosophy of friendship has promulgated a widespread and enduring understanding of friendship as a voluntary, spontaneous human relationship between equals that involves the reciprocation of goodwill. Of particular note is Aristotle's notion of virtuous or true friendship. This form of friendship involves friends who are good in themselves – those who desire the absolute betterment of the other friend. These are considered 'perfect' friends. In friendships of virtue, Aristotle sees a number of virtuous elements assembled: as its object (what friends do together) there is something good or pleasant; its base is similarity: that is, friends are alike in terms of status, gender, education, and so on. Intriguingly, friendships of virtue are considered to be rare not only because pure altruism is difficult (if not impossible) to achieve, but also because men of virtue are scarce. In describing friendships of virtue Aristotle refers to 'men of such goodness', for such friendships are exclusively associated with men. Not only do friendships of virtue involve reciprocated concern and understanding between men, they also require time and intimacy in order for friends to prove to each other that they are virtuous. As such, it is not possible to have many friends of virtue. In contrast to friendships of pleasure and utility, friendships of virtue represent the pinnacle of human friendships.

It is not hard to recognise the continuing influence of Aristotle's philosophy of friendship. As Rawlins (2008) rightly notes, many of us might think of close dyadic friendships when the term friendship is mentioned. Similarly, many of us tend to understand friendship as a relationship involving people with whom we have something in common. This can be sharing the same sense of humour, pastimes, educational or family background or from shared identifications in terms of gender, age, class, race and ethnicity, to mention but a few. Of course, what we share in common with friends changes over time, and some friendships fade when friends come to realise that they no longer share or value the same things in common. For example, we can grow apart from friends who no longer share the same interests or hobbies or when shared identifications change, such as when individuals who pass as 'straight' to their friends unexpectedly come out as gay. Although the effect of such a disclosure can help to cement existing bonds of friendship, it can also be catastrophic, in that friendship can be utterly ruined. Friends may struggle to grasp what they feel is unknown and unsettling, while others might feel betrayed and deceived if one friend is thought to have kept a part of the self disguised and hidden.

Despite this, the proverb 'birds of a feather flock together' has often been applied in popular discourse to describe the attraction of familiar similarity during the early stages of friendship development. Choosing somebody as a friend is a process of establishing what makes them eligible in terms of friendship (Fehr 1996), a process often based on singling-out certain qualities and characteristics that are found appealing. The draw of the familiar is not to be underestimated. What is familiar to us is often what we find comforting, and since friendship has an important part to play as a source of sociability and affirmational support, it is not surprising that friendships are frequently struck up between individuals who share something in common. Nevertheless, there is a danger that in befriending only those who are similar to ourselves, we risk reinforcing faulty views about human differences that can lead to the formation of stereotypes and prejudice. As this book shows, friendships between those who identify differently can be important for self-growth, understanding and acceptance. It is suggested that the workplace is one arena where people can come into contact with others who are dissimilar to themselves, with positive results for the types of friendships developed.

Gaining insights into these issues, it is no coincidence that dyadic workplace friendships are the focus of this book, particularly in the empirical chapters, but the study findings do not fully support the idea that close friendships are most likely between those who are similar. Indeed, this book sounds a cautionary note about how similarity may be understood in gay men's workplace friendships. My argument is that gay men can exhibit a strong preference for befriending heterosexual men and women. Many of the close dyadic workplace friendships described by gay men involve heterosexual men and women and not lesbians, bisexuals or other gay men. As I maintain throughout this book, the concept of 'gay friendship' can operate as a homogenous construct, one that unhelpfully conceals the diversity in how gay men identify and in the friendships gay men form between themselves and with others. Following other researchers such as Galupo (2007a, 2007b), one fruitful avenue of research is the study friendships that go against the norm of familiar similarity. For this reason, workplace friendships between gay men and heterosexual men and women figure prominently in Chapters 5 and 6, which examine the discursive dynamics of workplace friendships between friends who identify differently in terms of sexuality and gender. In view of this, an analytical framework is needed that is sensitive to the multiple meanings and roles friendships hold and play in the work lives of gay men.

Friendship as 'performative'

Insights derived from Foucauldian theories (Foucault 1979; Butler 1990, 1993, 2004; Sawicki 1991) encourage us to explore the variation in how friendship is understood and experienced. By subscribing to a Foucauldian point of view that emphasises the constitutive function of discourse, it is possible to examine how individuals establish and understand human relationships in different and sometimes contradictory ways. As theorised here, discourse is understood in a Foucauldian sense, in that it refers to a general but incoherent set of statements, ideas, beliefs, actions and symbols which provide the 'conditions of possibility' for the expressions of certain ideas and bodies of knowledge (Foucault 1979). This is exemplified beautifully in Foucault's three volumes of *The History of Sexuality*, across which discourse is shown to provide a language for variously articulating sexuality in different contexts at particular moments in time. Looked at in this way, discourses can be seen as linguistic resources that play a pivotal role in the discursive enterprises of individuals, as they strive to understand themselves, for example, as sexual subjects. Discourse has a constitutive quality, enabling subjects to construct a plurality of identities and realities. By underlining the generative quality of discourse, particularly at moments when subjects exercise power, Foucauldian writers prompt us to explore how individuals continuously make sense of and ascribe multiple meanings to aspects of their lives.

For example, friendship is often understood in relation to and distinct from kinship (Allan 1989), but studies on family and friendship ties demonstrate the importance of understanding the meanings of these terms as overlapping, contested and produced in specific historical and cultural sites (Roseneil and Budgeon 2004; Spencer and Pahl 2006; Tadmor 2001; Weston 1991). Similarly, I treat friendship not as a fixed, essential property of the interactions between individuals, but as something that is constructed through the continuous and iterative enactment of friendship norms. In this sense, and borrowing from Butler (1990), friendships are performative, constructed through an active and iterative process of meaning making. This does not mean individuals can fashion meanings of friendship, or other types of human relationship, in any way they desire. Despite the choice exercised by individuals in developing friendships that, for example, contain sexual elements (Nardi 1999; Weston 1991), discourses can have a constraining effect. For example, gay men have often experienced identity dilemmas when trying to discursively position themselves simultaneously as 'gay', 'male' and 'professional', given the contested and contradictory meanings that surround these subject positions (Rumens and Kerfoot 2009). Individuals may experience normative constraints not only in how they might wish to identify, but also in how they might wish to relate to others.

For instance, Adams (1985) developed a normative explanation for older women's lack of male friends. Cross-sex friendship is often defined as romance, and given the cultural norms inhibiting romance during old age, older women struggled to develop cross-sex friendships with men. Crucially, however, friendship discourses are not singular, uniform or hold universal appeal. As Rawlins (2008: 109) notes, the idea of men and women being friends 'occupies a roiling intersection of diverse discourses concerning friendship, romance, marriage, family, individual will, relational practices, subjectivities, sexualities, femininities, masculinities, desire, permission, and narratives of the well-lived life'. Analysing informal discussions with US college students about cross-gender friendships, Rawlins explores the widely reported instances of male-female friendships among his students, but also notes the cultural discourses that shape some students' views about the limited viability of these friendships. As such, the study of gay men's workplace friendships must consider the normative discourses that affect the very possibility of these friendships. But it is not just multiple discourses that are influential here. Social structures, organisational domains and the economic and personal circumstances of people's lives also limit and create the opportunities for friendship (Rawlins 1992; Adams and Allan 1998).

Friendships in context

As suggested already, how we make sense of the term friendship is by referring to a number of friendship norms and ideals (Pahl 2000). These ideals may be circulated in discourses that suggest friendship is a voluntary, spontaneous human relationship characterised by such qualities as intimacy, trust, equality and reciprocity. This represents an ideal-type construction, which has come under criticism from sociologists for ignoring how friendships are shaped by the contexts in which they are embedded (Adams and Allan 1998; Duck 1993). Critical of the ideal of friendship as an entirely voluntary and personalistic human relationship, sociologists have developed a notion of friendship as a relationship rooted within the social realm. Sociologists such as Graham Allan, writing in the 1980s, were perturbed by the dominance of academic perspectives on friendship that ignored the influence of context, most apparent within the field of psychology (Allan 1989).

For example, early seminal work by Wright (1969, 1978, 1984) proposed a model of friendship involving investments of self in a relationship characterised by friends' voluntary interdependence and personalised concern for one another. Wright's theorisation of friendship influenced many others studying friendship within the field of psychology (Lea 1989; Winstead et al. 1995). For some time, as Allan (1989) points out, psychologists largely shouldered the responsibility of researching friendships and other personal relationships during the period from the 1960s to the early 1980s. Studies on the attributes of individuals within friendships were particularly powerful during those decades, although attribution-based analyses continue to shape insights into how we understood the processes of friendship development (Shelton et al. 2009; King and Terrance 2006).

For Allan (1989, 1996, 1998) and other sociologists (Pahl 2000, 2002) conceptualising friendship is as much about understanding how the individual attributes of friends help constitute friendship as it is about examining how friendship dyads are embedded within wide complex social contexts. In this regard, the form friendship takes is influenced by the 'wider organization of social life' (Allan 1996: 99). While the appeal of understanding friendship as a voluntary relationship is undeniably strong, it is unwise to overstate the agency people exercise in choosing others as friends. Such things as gender, sexuality, class, age, ethnicity, education, jobs, workplaces, technology, processes of industrialisation, and so on, can constrain (and enable) the choices made by individuals in making and developing friendships at any given moment in time. Adams and Allan (1998) provide the detail concerning four levels of context (personal environment, network, community and societal) that influence how friendships are developed, the particular roles they perform and how they are given meaning. As such, it is important to examine the relationship between friendship and context, evident in the research carried out on how friendships are shaped by the effects of how society is structured economically, culturally and socially (Litwak 1989; Milardo and Wellman 1992; Duck 1993; Spencer and Pahl 2006).

The sociology of friendship is a key body of literature from which this book draws. It provides the impetus to avoid relaxing into an overly idealistic – perhaps romantic – view of friendship as a purely spontaneous and personalistic relationship. As such, we can begin to understand friendships as processes of organising. The place and role of friendship in our lives depends greatly on how they are understood in regard to other relationships. Friendships may be woven into the fabric of our lives in all manner of different ways, with some people pursuing close dyadic friendships while others seek to develop large networks of friends, some of which might be formed in cyberspace. Friendships can emerge from workplace encounters while others might develop from relationships forged through shared recreational activities. Sociologists have also been keen to point out that friendships take time to develop and highlight the practical limits on the number of close dyadic friendship we can sustain (Allan 1989). What is more, sociological research has shown that friendships may also bear the potential to effect social change (Nardi 1999; Weeks et al. 2001). As I explore in Chapter 7, workplace friendships can help gay men to cultivate and sustain identities, selves and subjectivities at odds with dominant cultural norms. One possible effect is that new norms may be set that can be transferred into other people's friendships, disturbing the coherence of heteronormative discourses on sexuality, gender and friendship. Gay men's workplace friendships might have interesting political and social consequences, in that they could extend the range of ways in which men can construct different identities, selves and relationships in and outside the workplace.

The sociology of friendship has also called attention to the influence of hierarchy. Hierarchical components in friendship are generally thought to be problematic since they are likely to give rise to doubt and suspicion about whether one friend has the best intentions of the other friend at heart. After all, it is hard to deny that perceptions of hierarchy in friendship are likely to result in friends feeling less likely to 'be themselves' in each other's company (Allan 1996). There is some validity in this assertion, but there is no reason why hierarchy, like human differences, cannot be negotiated in ways that allow friendships to develop. This idea has much salience in a work context, where hierarchy is often present. Intuitively, hierarchical arrangements of people would seem to stifle intimacy and promote instrumentality, which might lead us to imagine that such friendships are, at best, problematic. None the less, friendships can span hierarchies because individuals are not reducible to and merely defined by the roles they perform in the workplace.

In the context of friendship, hierarchy is also seen to be detrimental to the formation of intimacy. Early psychology studies on friendship show that intimacy is developed and reinforced through acts of self-disclosure, wherein one friend offers the other insights into the self through revealing inner thoughts and feelings (Altman and Taylor 1973; Hacker 1981). Hierarchy may obstruct self-disclosure, particularly if one friend feels the other is holding back. But it is hard to imagine friendship not containing intimacy – to do so would be to stand at the foot of a tall wave of philosophical literature on the importance of intimacy for helping individuals to construct a sense of being in friendship. However, I do not propose that friendships between those separated by organisational hierarchies are neither possible nor lacking in intimacy. What is more, I do not subscribe to a view that friendship is only ever made 'real' by the presence of a certain type of intimacy. As Jamieson (1998) remarks, the valorisation and privileging of disclosing intimacy has often obscured the construction of intimacies that emerge from, for example, silence or the body. Following Jamieson, I am not concerned (as many psychologists have been) with identifying people's cognitive capacities for disclosing intimacy. Rather, I am interested in exploring the variation in how gay men construct different intimacies within the context of workplace friendships. Doubtless hierarchy might be an influence here, but also sexuality and gender as Chapters 5 and 6 demonstrate.

Friendship and organisation

Lastly, it is useful to say something about how this book understands the relationship between friendship and organisation. More often than not, friendship and work have been constructed as being mutually exclusive, although there are academics, among which I include myself, who seek to collapse such a dualism (French 2007; Grey and Sturdy 2007). Workplace friendships are not, therefore, relationships that are purely individual. As Chapter 3 demonstrates, friendships are constitutive of organisation just as organisations shape the construction of friendship. Seen in this way, opportunities open up for developing analyses that allow us to explore how friendship and organisation intersect or, as Grey and Sturdy put it: 'considering the ways in which friendships and organization are linked beyond the functional concerns of organisational performance' (2007: 168). Crucially friendship and organisation are not reducible to each other but, in a discursive sense, intertwine and are mutually influencing. Looked at in this way, organisations are important discursive arenas in which workplace friendships are formed. On this point, I do not regard organisations as bounded sites in which organisational discourses are confined. As Ashcraft (2007: 11) argues, the 'container metaphor' of organisation has been shattered by research that shows how organising can take place within and outside of organisations, and that organisational boundaries are fluid and unstable. In recognising how organisational discourses can exist as wider cultural formations, I suggest has a bearing on how workplace friendships can be conceptualised.

Workplace friendships are often defined by the organisational contexts in which they are formed. While this is a plausible definition it is not an adequate one, since workplace friendships do not always develop within clearly discernible organisational 'boundaries'. Rather, workplace friendships may be discursively constructed within an array of competing discourses in, around and away from physical and virtual organisational settings and structures. Individuals may encounter a range of discursive possibilities outside and at work for the negotiation of friendships, some of which may be understood as 'workplace friendships' while others may not. For example, some workplace friendships might be understood as different from friendships outside work, on the basis that work friends share common organisational experiences that non-work friends do not (Sias and Cahill 1998). But as contexts and people's circumstances change, so too does the meaning individuals assign to friendship. Thus it is important to avoid treating workplace friendships as a distinct category of friendship, which can then become homogenous and fixed. Arguably, even invoking the term 'workplace friendship' we risk treating it in this way. It might be better to speak of friendship within people's everyday lives, rather than inadvertently (re)constructing an artificial divide between work and non-work friendships. Be that as it may, I do not want to become drawn into circuitous debates about defining different types of friendships, so I use the term 'workplace friendship' throughout this book for the sake of convenience. That said, gathering gay men's perspectives and experiences of workplace friendships reveals the fluidity and variation in how workplace friendships are understood and experienced, taking us away from organisational perspectives on how these friendships might be understood in terms of commercial gain.

Summary

There is no discursive formula for helping us to identify certain relationships as 'friendship' by reference to specific arrangements of intimacy, trust, reciprocity, equality and so on. Whatever friendship means subjectively for gay men and other individuals, it can be understood as constituted through a number of competing discourses, which makes gaining empirical insights into these matters all the more important. I do not present a preconceived idea about what friendship is. This is not to suggest that I dismiss cultural ideals and academic research that suggests friendship is often understood in relation to certain qualities. But it is to question and problematise friendship norms that restrict the possibilities for individuals to relate to others in meaningful ways. Indeed, Spencer and Pahl (2006: 34) correctly point out that friendship has 'often been described in relation to a generalized or archetypal notion of friendship, rather than necessarily applied to actual flesh-and-blood relationships'. In that regard, some of the most illuminating accounts are provided by individuals engaged in challenging normative discourses on friendship, as part of a process of experimenting in new forms of relating (Roseneil and Budgeon 2004; Weeks et al. 2001). In the rest of this book I explore these matters in both theoretical and empirical terms.

Outline of the book

Chapter 1 explores the history of men's friendships. The main argument advanced here is that in order to understand the significance of friendship in gay men's lives, the broad canvas of men's friendships must be considered. One important reason for locating gay men's friendships against the context of male friendship is that populist and scholarly research on men's friendships generally stands at odds with widely held views about the ease with which gay men develop friendships. This chapter unpacks some of the discourses that surround men's friendships, making the case for scholarly research that pays attention to the potential disparities between cultural discourses and the diverse realities of men's friendships.

Chapter 2 outlines some of the conditions that have made possible gay men's friendships. Of particular interest are cultural discourses on sexuality that have influenced how friendship has acquired a primary position in many gay men's lives. Developing this theme further, I review academic perspectives that suggest gay men are particularly inventive at breaking normative constraints to develop different identities, selves and relationships. Chapter 3 begins by arguing how many organisations are normatively heterosexual and why this makes the workplace an important context for studying gay men's friendships. This chapter reviews current research on the relationship between work organisations and friendship. Attention is drawn to the growing number of studies that focus on the potential of friendship as an organisational resource. Here, then, I argue that the increasing colonisation of workplace friendships by managerialist perspectives limits the horizon of possibilities for understanding friendship as a process of organising, and part of a process of constructing a meaningful life.

The next four chapters present the main findings of the study. Drawing upon extracts from in-depth qualitative interviews, these chapters aim to provide insights into the roles and meanings of gay men's workplace friendships. Chapter 4 focuses on how gay men organise, form and maintain friendships in the workplace. An important theme in this chapter is the influence of organisation on gay men's workplace friendships, and how it varies a great deal. Chapters 5 and 6 extend this line of analysis by examining the influence of sexuality and gender on the development of gay men's friendships in the workplace. Chapter 5 sheds light on the diversity in how gay men construct workplace friendships with other men. This chapter problematises a widely held view that gay men are more likely to experience close dyadic friendship with another gay man. Similarly, Chapter 6 explores gay men's friendships with women. In particular, this chapter addresses how gay men discursively construct the friendship potential of heterosexual women and the possibilities for close friendships that are multi-stranded in terms of support and intimacy. This chapter considers how gay men's friendships with heterosexual women can be constructed as an idealised form of cross-sex friendship.

Chapter 7 takes up the theme that has been underdeveloped in the previous two chapters: the role of friendship in generating identities and selves. Here I return to the idea that heteronormativity is a powerful and commonly used lens through which friendships, identities and selves are understood. It is suggested that workplace friendships can open up opportunities for gay men to understand themselves as 'normal' subjects. This is one reason why it is useful to consider further how gay men might use workplace friendships to embrace and contest normative constructions about what it is to be human. In the concluding chapter, I attempt to draw together some of the recurring themes and issues of the empirical chapters, by discussing the significance of gay men's workplace friendships at an individual level as well as in political and organisational terms.

Chapter 1
Understanding Men's Friendships

Introduction

In order to explore the role and meaning of friendship in gay men's work lives, the rich canvas of men's friendships must first be considered. However, men's friendships have been saddled with a bad reputation. A recurrent view emerging from a raft of scholarly research is that men are less inclined than women to value friendship in their lives and less likely than women to develop emotionally intimate friendships. This view of men's friendships has become deeply entrenched in academic and populist writing, to the extent that the problem with men's friendships is often located in men themselves. In this chapter I argue that there is good reason to problematise the blithe assumptions about men's friendships. First, we need to recognise that men's and women's friendships should not be judged by identifying the 'masculine' and feminine' determinants of each. This has encouraged stereotypes on gendered forms of friendship that privilege the expressive dimensions of personal relationships, shading out alternative perspectives on how men and women relate intimately in friendship among and between each other. A poststructuralist approach is presented as a corrective to this dichotomous understanding of gender differences in men's and women's friendships. Second, it is important to develop an understanding of the variation within men's friendships, in order to avoid treating men's friendships as a homogeneous construct. Here I draw upon feminist analyses, critical scholarship on masculinities and historical research to demonstrate how men have understood and experienced friendship in dynamic and uneven ways. Thus the overall aim of this chapter is to examine the cultural discourses that surround men's friendships, exposing the multiple meanings friendships hold for men.

Conceptualising men's friendships

Research on men's friendships has promulgated a commonly held view that men are not as intimate as women in friendship, and do not value friendship highly. As Wood and Inman (1993) assert, this stereotype of men in friendship was incubated in early academic research within the field of psychology (Bell 1981; Booth 1972; Caldwell and Peplau 1982; Lewis 1978; Rubin 1985; Weiss and Lowenthal 1975). Scholars argued that gender differences in men's and women's friendships are particularly apparent in how friendships are developed and maintained. Argyle and Henderson (1985: 75) exemplify the dominant perspective on this matter:

... pairs of female friends spend most of their time together talking, discussing personal problems, giving and receiving social support, and with a high level of self-disclosure ... men are more likely to *do* things together – to play games or to engage in other joint leisure.

Some of the most frequently cited psychology studies on men's friendships have used some vivid descriptors to depict men's friendships as relatively deficient in intimacy, compared with women's friendships. For example, Hacker (1981: 385) coins the twin-terms 'blabbermouths' and 'clams' to convey the degree to which women and men self-disclose in same-sex friendship respectively. In similar fashion, Wright (1982) suggests men's friendships operate 'side-by-side', where men are mutually focused on a shared activity. Women's friendships are described as 'face-to-face' because they are angled towards the mutual disclosure of personal information and the development of shared concern for one another.

From this body of work, it seems that men in friendship are apprehensive about self-disclosure. Of Lillian Rubin's (1985: 63) 300 American male and female interviewees, one man says: 'I've tried reaching out to men from time to time, but they don't reciprocate ... Nobody likes to feel they've been made vulnerable to another man'. In Rubin's study, men tended to source intimacy elsewhere: 'I get along better with women because I can be more open with a woman' (1985: 63). Such findings have led some scholars to contend that men do not evaluate their same-sex friendships as highly as women. Studies indicate that women regard their friendships as a rich source of personal satisfaction (Bell 1981; Caldwell and Peplau 1982; Fischer and Narus 1981; Hacker 1981), whereas men appear to derive intimacy from other relationships including friendships with women, familial and matrimonial relationships (Komarovsky 1967; Lapota 1971). Taking all the evidence into account, psychologist Beverley Fehr declares: 'it appears that men are less intimate than women in their friendships because they may not particularly like it' (1996: 140–41). The sentiments behind Fehr's contention have gained currency in respect of many friendship researchers but crucially not all.

Certainly, there is good reason to be sceptical about the extent to which gender differences in men's and women's friendships can be characterised in this way. Duck and Wright (1993) argue that because men's and women's friendships have for so long been regarded as fundamentally different, psychology scholars have tended to regard the assumption of (non)disclosure in men's and women's friendships as 'safe' ground on which to explore gender relations within friendship. Striking, therefore, is that Duck and Wright position themselves in the cabal of scholars who have 'accepted this neat expressive-instrumental dichotomization without serious reservation' (1993: 710). One problem with this dichotomy is that it encourages generalisations about how men and women go about making and maintaining friendships. For example, Argyle and Henderson's (1985) study of human relationships supports an expressive-instrumental dichotomisation of women's and men's friendship. Regarding women in friendship, they state: 'women often act as mutual therapists, and there is evidence that some of them are just as successful as professional therapists' (1985: 75). This assertion is problematic not just because it leaves little or no room for considering how women's friendships may be instrumental or intimate in other ways, but also because women do not have a 'monopoly on closeness as a goal for intimacy' (Wood 1993: 43). Research also reveals that women are just as likely as men to provide practical assistance to their friends (Duck and Wright 1993).

Significantly, the dispositional approach towards conceptualising gender, adopted by Henderson and Argyle (1985), which is typical of the psychology research on gender and friendship, fails to recognise that self-disclosure has been coded as a 'feminine' style of relating (Cancian 1986; Jamieson 1998). As Wood (1993) and others (Swain 1989, 1992) point out, by failing to treat gender as fluid, dynamic, historically conditioned and socially constructed, researchers are at risk of falling into an essentialist trap of declaring certain styles of relating in friendship (for example, 'therapeutic') as 'masculine' or 'feminine' and, by implication, that some are more 'authentic' than others. On this point, some feminist theorists worry (with good reason) that the propensity to view disclosing intimacy as the quintessence of intimate friendship might inadvertently reinforce a sense of victimhood among women, who are constructed as only too willing to confide about personal, potentially damaging topics (O'Connor 1998; Raymond 1986). As I have previously suggested, it is misleading to think that certain intimacies are 'authentic'. From a poststructuralist perspective, intimacy can be regarded as a discursive construction that is understood and experienced through historically situated discourses. From this perspective, intimacy is constituted through text, ideas, images and actions that, together, enable the individual to construct the experience of 'intimacy'. Along these lines, intimacy has multiple meanings that are always culturally specific. This notion of intimacy discourages the study of 'natural' gender differences between men's and women's friendships because it refuses to see intimacy as an internal state, or as an essential property of the individual. Discourses on intimacy are shifting and changing, with some coming to the fore at specific historical moments.

While the argument that men's friendships lack intimacy has been, without doubt, a persuasive and widely accepted one, there are also signs of change that suggest this view is beginning to lose some of its cultural currency (Butera 2008; Walker 1994a, 1994b). For example, Walker (1994a, 1994b) argues that stereotypes of men's and women's friendships are symptomatic of cultural ideologies rather than, as Walker (1994a) puts it, 'observable gender differences in behaviour' (246). Walker's research reveals the contradictions in how men and women understand and experience friendship. For instance, one male interviewee is quoted as saying: 'Men keep more to themselves. They don't open up the way women do. Some women will spill their guts at the drop of a hat' (1994a: 251). Yet when asked to provide exact detail about the object of their friendships, incongruence emerged between what friends said and what they actually did in their friendships. For example, despite one male interviewee's vociferations to the contrary, he is reported to have regularly discussed sexual fertility problems with his male friends. As Walker writes elsewhere, gender differences in behaviour 'reinforce stereotypes about gendered forms of friendship, even if the differences differ substantively from the substance of ideology' (1994b: 390).

Striking, therefore, is the strong feeling among some scholars that neo-positivist perspectives on gender differences, which treat the dynamic between gender and friendship as a matter of interest in directional and causal relationships, are inadequate for exploring the gender complexity of men's friendships (Ueno and Adams 2007; Nardi 2007). Peter Nardi (1992b, 2007), noting the exhaustion in the scholarship on gender and friendship, argues that few researchers have taken as their starting point the idea that there may be greater variation within each gender than between genders. As should be clear by now, there is no inherent reason why men might be worse than women at intimate friendship, for example. It is for this reason and others that an understanding of how men's friendships have been variously represented and experienced is useful to include in an exploration of the variation within men's friendships.

Variation within men's friendships

Subscribing to a poststructuralist approach seems particularly appropriate for developing a nuanced and critical appreciation of the diversity within men's friendships. For we might, motivated by a poststructuralist impulse to denaturalise normative ideals of friendship, consider how men's friendships have been variously understood and experienced in certain contexts and at specific moments in time. Men, like women, draw upon a myriad of discourses to develop and interpret friendships, but the ways in which they do so are not uniform, consistent and coherent. In this section, then, I explore some historical accounts of men's friendships that demonstrate their fluidity and the contingent circumstances of choice under which they are formed.

Representations of male friendship

Easily construed as romantic and idealistic, classical representations of men in friendship paint a rather different picture of men's friendships to the one we are familiar with in the contemporary era. In *Just Friends: The Role of Friendship in Our Lives* (1985), Lillian Rubin argues that as we move closer to examine contemporary portraits and realities of men's friendships, past descriptions of 'romantic and impassioned' male friendship recede into obscurity. For Rubin, the 'lyrical tributes to the glory of male friendship' beautifully exemplified by Homer's *The Iliad* are now replaced by 'laments about men's problems with intimacy and vulnerability, about the impoverishment of their relations with each other – at least among heterosexual men' (1985: 60). For Nardi, this signals a quirk of fate:

How ironic, then, that some of the emotional and intimate descriptors of classic male friendship are the ones used today to extol friendship among women and to illustrate what's missing from the friendships of those who embrace hegemonic masculinity. (1999: 30)

Before examining the reasons as to why men's friendships seemed to have lost their place in the pantheon of human relationships, it is worth referring to Homer's *The Iliad*, in which heroism, unflagging loyalty and intimacy loom large in men's friendships.

Achilles' friendship with Patroclus plays a pivotal role in *The Iliad*. When the fabled warrior Achilles receives news that Patroclus has been slain in battle his sullen mood gives way to agonising grief:

… a black cloud of grief engulfed Achilles. He picked up the sooty dust in both his hands and poured it over his head. He begrimed his handsome features with it, and black ashes settled on his sweet-smelling tunic. Great Achilles lay spread out in the dust, a giant of a man, clawing at his own hair with his hands and mangling it … Achilles was sobbing out his noble heart. (17: 23–34)

Patroclus' death galvanises Achilles into a fatal course of action. Sharing her son's anguish over the murder of his friend, the goddess Thetis warns Achilles that if he avenges Patroclus's death he, too, will perish. Despite his mother's premonition, Achilles declares:

[Patroclus] was more to me than any other of my men, whom I loved as much as my own life … I have no wish to live and linger in the world of men, unless, before all else, Hector is hit by my spear and dies, paying the price for slaughtering Patroclus. (17: 81–93)

The mighty Achilles is inconsolable. The death of his friend sets into motion of chain of events that is now legendary in Greek mythology. Achilles weighs into the Trojan War, dispatches Hector and, as his mother augurs, is unable to escape his own death.

Homer's poetic representation of the friendship between Achilles and Patroclus has been greatly admired by countless readers who see in the bonds that unite the two warriors a friendship that is both virtuous and seemingly immortal (Konstan 1997). It is the steadfast loyalty, reciprocity, trust and love between the two men that many people marvel at. As Nardi (1999: 24) puts it: there 'is no more perfect depiction of heroic loyal friendship than that of Achilleus and Patroklos from Homer's *The Iliad*'. Yet Nardi's reference to Classical images of heroic male friendship sounds more than just a cursory note of appreciation. For Nardi and others (Halperin 1990; Hammond and Jablow 1987), the epic narrative of Achilles and Patroclus's friendship is understood as a potent cultural construction.

Halperin (1990: 76) elaborates this idea when he argues that *The Iliad*'s representation of male-to-male friendship is 'a historical artefact, the product of a particular turn of thought at a particular juncture in the artistic celebration of the traditional material'. Halperin goes on to say that Homeric and other classical portraits of heroic friendships between men, produced around the same time as *The Iliad*, drew upon earlier legends for inspiration such as the Babylonian tale of Gilgamesh and Enkidu, and David's friendship with Jonathan in the Old Testament. Collectively, these texts construct a model of friendship between warrior men that is characterised by unwavering loyalty, bravery and intimacy, all developed in adverse circumstances that often threaten the life of one or both friends. Further to this, Sherrod (1989) notes that classical representations of the intimate dimensions to male friendship are comparable to the images of intimacy associated with familial relations and romantic love. With this in mind, it is hardly surprising that in Ancient Greece the idea of male friendship finds a particularly high note (Konstan 1997). Of particular interest, then, is the net effect of these venerated fictions of men in friendship: namely, the cultivation of an idealised model of male friendship.

Feminist perspectives on men's friendships

More than most, feminist critics have been acute at problematising the cultural discourses on same-sex friendships between men. For example, Hammond and Jablow (1987) acknowledge the contribution of the Greek narratives on male friendship as well as earlier literary accounts that elevate the heroic feats of men united together in friendship:

> All make high drama of the relationship, endowing it with glamour and beauty. The friends are heroes: aristocratic, young, brave, and beautiful. In their free and wholehearted response to one another, they openly declare their affection and admiration. They engage in many adventures and battles, sharing danger, loyal to the death. Throughout life, they remain devoted and generous to each other. (1987: 241)

The context in which the 'high drama' of male friendship is played out is harsh and agonistic. Such landscapes, typically the battlefield, remind men they are subject to forces beyond their control, forces that are capable of rendering them vulnerable and expendable. The agonistic elements within these fictitious locales do much to accentuate the brave deeds of men. At the same time, these settings also provide the conditions for a particular discourse of masculinity to emerge, based on risk taking, adventure and danger. In the context of these homosocial settings, Hammond and Jablow point out that 'mundane affairs such as marriage, making a living, or having a family, which make up the lives of other men are of little or no concern to them' (1987: 256). In heroic male friendship discourse, men are led to believe they can find intimacy outside the family based on love and affection between equals, and thus a release from the tedious aspects of an 'ordinary' life.

Other representations of male friendship bear out Hammond and Jablow's argument. Turning briefly to the genre of war movies and literature, it is possible to find countless illustrations of male friendships that invoke classical forms of heroic friendship. Wolfgang Petersen's Hollywood version of the Trojan War, titled *Troy* (2004), valorises the friendship between Patroclus and Achilles while Oliver Stone's anti-war film *Platoon* (1986) also pays particular attention to the salience of male friendship as a source of emotional support. In similar fashion, US literature provides a rich seam in which to mine examples that celebrate male friendship. Ernest Hemmingway's *A Farewell to Arms* (1929) is centrally concerned with the friendship between two male US soldiers during World War I, and can be interpreted as a narrative that represents male friendship as stronger than men's relationships involving women (Armengol-Carrera 2009). Herman Melville's *Moby Dick* (1851) is also notable as a sympathetic text on male friendship, illustrated in this case by the loving and affectionate friendship between Ishmael and Queequeg. While some texts on male friendship project a fantasy of male friendship based on absolute equality between men (Hammond and Jablow 1987), other dramatists have focused on the challenges men face in developing friendships that can help them to develop mutual respect for human differences and for exploring the limits of the human condition. MacFaul (2007) develops this argument drawing upon the work of William Shakespeare. For example, friendship is a hoped-for cure for the anxiety and the alienation experienced by the ill-fated Prince of Denmark in *Hamlet* and, elsewhere, by Antonio in *The Merchant of Venice*. *Timon of Athens* promotes a nostalgic Aristotelian image of virtuous male friendship over friendships of utility. From this very short detour into film and literature, it is clear that the subject of male friendship continues to inspire writers and movie-makers alike, often with mixed results regarding the emphasis they place on the ideal rather than the actualities of men in friendship.

Despite differences in how male friendship is constructed in literature and film, feminist Lillian Rubin (1985) complains that classical representations of men's friendships have long been a template of what friendship is and how it ought to be. By comparison, women's friendships have been passed over. It is only relatively recently that feminist theorists have sought to refurbish the meaning and credibility to the friendships between women across different cultural contexts and in different historical moments (O'Connor 1992; Oliker 1989; Traub 2002; Vicinus 2004). Lillian Faderman's *Surpassing the Love of Men* (1981) was the one of the first and probably the most influential feminist historical analysis to act as a corrective against the iconography of male friendship. Exploring the romantic friendships of women from the eighteenth century onwards, Faderman highlights how women have been frequently cast as unsuitable for friendship, citing Michel de Montaigne's essay 'On Friendship' to illustrate her point. Quoting Montaigne myself:

... the normal capacity of women is, in fact, unequal to the demands of that communion and intercourse on which the sacred bond [of friendship] is fed; their souls do not seem firm enough to bear the strain of so hard and lasting a tie ... there has never yet been an example of a woman's attaining to this, and the ancient schools are at one in their belief that it is denied to the female sex. (1580/1993: 95)

Montaigne's notion of friendship, indebted to a classical ideal of friendship as the exclusive preserve of men, is narrow and uncharitable to women. As stated earlier, such perspectives are now at odds with contemporary discourses that suggest women are emotion 'experts' and thus better at 'doing' friendship than men (Bank 1995). Arguably the pendulum has swung too far in the opposite direction, as the qualities of friendship are heavily associated with normative constructions of femininity (Wood 1993). And it is feminist theorising, in part, which has turned Montaigne's assertion on its head.

Indeed, some feminist theorists have underscored the political dimension to notions of 'sisterhood' and female friendship for feminist politics (Friedman 1993; Raymond 1986), and denounced men's friendships as relationships that stunt individuality and intimacy (Daly 1978; Jeffreys 2003). This strand of feminist theorising has found more than a toehold in the minds of men and women alike. For many women, feminism's critique of women's relationships with men has spurred them on to forge close friendships with women and intimate relationships with men no longer based on dependence and subordination (Acker et al. 1981). Of course, the ebb and flow in the discourses that surround women's and men's friendships is not just influenced by feminist theorising and politics.

Feminist Stacey Oliker (1998: 18) argues that the construction of intimate friendship, based on a notion of self-disclosure, is a 'modern relationship'. As a form of friendship that has emerged over the last two centuries, intimate friendship requires individualism as a condition for its possibility: individualism is said to sanction the attention paid by individuals to their private life worlds. Oliker regards individualism as a dominant ideology that has particular consequences for men and women. Along these lines, discourses of individualism place emphasis on cultivating self-interest, observable in how individuals construct multiple selves. What is more, for men individualism is grounded in notions of autonomy and competition that are played out in the public realm, especially in the workplace. In contrast, individualism encouraged women to develop intimacy with each other in the private sphere of life, permitting the growth of intimate friendship in forms and ways not available to men.

Oliker goes on to note that women's domestic roles in the home became more pronounced. In contrast, men took up 'breadwinner' roles in the public sphere of work. As Wood (1993) points out, the industrial revolution gave rise to an ideology of separate (public-private) spheres. Men and women acquired new skills and the perspectives demanded of them in their respective domains. Arguably, the fiercely competitive nature of capitalist work organisations that generated rivalry and instrumentality in relations between men stymied opportunities for them to make friends, or at least the type of intimate friendships that are now commonly associated with the private domain. Building and maintaining intimate relationships, already linked with the private realm, became synonymous with 'women's work' and with cultural norms of femininity. Not surprisingly, cultural images of love and friendship shifted in accordance: from heroic forms of (male) friendship to expressive intimacy. This cultural shift, dubbed as the 'feminisation of love/friendship' by Cancian (1986), has privileged the expressive dimensions of personal relationships, obscuring other possibilities for considering how men and women may relate intimately in friendship among and between each other (Bank 1995).

But other changes have occurred, shaping how men's and women's friendships are understood and experienced. Continuing in a feminist vein of theorising, O'Connor (1998) suggests that the twentieth century has been witness to sweeping changes in education, work and marriage, all of which have influenced friendship development. For instance, the rise of expressive intimacy as the defining feature of contemporary forms of friendship is partly due to living against a cultural backdrop of a postmodern society. Arguing that the notion of a stable and unified self has been thrown into doubt, as traditional family and work structures have become increasingly insecure and fluid, constructing identities and selves is challenging. A notion of friendship that pivots on intimate confiding gains much currency here, since it is seen by O'Connor as a mechanism by which individuals can refer to others for assistance in fathoming out questions of identity and belonging. Popular culture grants legitimacy to this view, as television programmes and film (to mention only two examples) extol the virtues of expressive intimacy in women's and men's personal relationships (Plummer 2003).

Against this postmodern world, one still characterised by capitalistic and patriarchal values which inhibit an 'anything goes' approach towards forming identities and selves (Tyler 2009), commentators have explored who might be the 'experts' at developing intimacies within their personal relationships. Crucially, as I discuss in Chapter 2, some academics regard gay men as one group of pioneers in this field. However and returning to an earlier point, this does not mean to say that men have been uniformly inept at forming closeness in friendships with other men. In order to dig deeper into men's realities of friendship, it is to the research of friendship historians we must turn.

Historical accounts of men's friendships

Alan Bray's (1982, 1990, 2003) much cited research on friendship is highly illuminating of the historical changes in figurations of intimacies within men's friendship. Bray's work is primarily concerned with highlighting an array of non-sexual intimacies within men's friendships: for example, close physical contact, love, emotional and spiritual closeness. Friendship ties of this kind have sometimes been encompassed within what is known as 'romantic friendship': an intensely close but non-sexual friendship often involving physical intimacy (Nardi 1999). But sharp distinctions between romantic friendship and other relations such as those (homo)sexual in nature do not always hold up in practice. Nonetheless, Bray (2003) provides an eloquent account of the loving and non-sexual friendships (or 'sworn brotherhoods') between men from the eleventh to the nineteenth centuries.

One of the most compelling illustrations is the friendship between Sir John Finch and Sir Thomas Baines. From Bray's perspective, of particular interest is the tomb in the chapel of Christ's College, Cambridge, UK, in which the bodies of both Finch and Baines reside. Friendship is the key to unlocking some of the significance of Finch and Baines's shared funerary arrangements; in particular, the observation that the men's mutual affection appears to have been very strong. Based on archival evidence, it is reported that as Baines lay on his deathbed in September 1681, he received a last embrace from Finch, his life long friend. A year later, Finch died. The memorial erected to mark their burial, on which Finch had etched 'Animorum Connubium' (a marriage of souls), is regarded by Bray as an undeniable 'graphic expression of the nature of their friendship' (2003: 140–41).

Remarkably, Finch and Baines's shared grave is not the only example of this intimate union in death. Elsewhere, men had already used the same words to convey the height of their feeling for their male friends on similar burial memorials. Symbolic inscriptions and combined graves were not peculiar to men, as the shared graves occupied by women suggest, nor confined to the late seventeenth century. Bray describes the occupancy of the tombs holding two (in some cases three) male friends from the fifteenth to the nineteenth century, including one of the oldest examples: the Turkish grave of English knights Sir William Neville and Sir John Clanvowe, who died in 1391.

What motivated these men to intern their bodies alongside their closest male friends is not clear-cut. Modern interpretations of such friendships may speculate, as they tend to, about the presence of sexual intimacy. Yet Bray's archival evidence suggests the presence of a wider range of intimacies that entail the physical, emotional and spiritual. What is more, these remarkable graves and burial monuments at once commemorate the former pleasures of an array of intimacies in male friendship and emblemise these qualities as an ideal model of friendship. The tomb of Finch and Baines is a case in point. After all, it is possible to draw a parallel (as Bray also notes) with the Homeric rituals of male friendship. The requests made by one friend to another to share a single grave, as told in Bray's text, shadows the similar appeal made by Homer's Patroclus to his friend Achilles.

Documenting the intimate dimensions to men's friendship in the Renaissance period, Bray problematises the caricatured images of the Renaissance as a time that afforded men an unbridled rein in the articulation of emotional intimacy in same-sex friendship. Such versions of the Renaissance are nuanced by Bray's insights, lending much weight to the need to pay close attention to the context of men's friendships (see also DiGangi 2003). This can be illustrated by examining various social and cultural shifts taking place during the Renaissance that gave rise to new understandings of friendship. For instance, Renaissance Europe witnessed a renewed interest in classical discourses of friendship, incited by a sense of nostalgia for past ideals, as Renaissance scholars rediscovered the surviving fragments of classical texts. It cannot be denied that the Renaissance period was marked by some measure of sexual and artistic freedom. For example, Aristotelian notions of friendship, in which distinctions between love and friendship are blurred, served as a source of intellectual and personal stimulus for many men. Faderman (1981: 67) notes how Renaissance writers borrowed the ideals of classical friendship to depict the intimacy in men's same-sex friendship through intense 'sentiment and close proximity', even if genital contact was suppressed as an expression of same-sex intimacy. This is not to deny that the articulation of sexual intimacy into genital contact happened. Just as the Ancients often slurred the distinction between sex and friendship by engaging in sexual encounters with male friends, so some men in the Renaissance replicated these behaviours, as Rocke's (1996) study of Florentine males in Renaissance Italy shows.

However, Bray (2003) argues that the license the Renaissance period is said to have given men to express intimacy within male friendship was perhaps more evident in continental Europe than in England. Focusing on Renaissance England, Bray argues that from the second half of the seventeenth century, how friendship is understood changes significantly. To partly illustrate this point, Bray (2003) examines how the institution of the house and the daily household activities of entertaining, eating, sleeping, washing and dressing all contributed to the social dimension of friendship. For example, single occupancy of a bed was a luxury, and it was commonplace for people to share beds. Often men would sleep with other men (as 'bedfellows') and, together, enter into the business of discussing, among other more mundane matters, their commercial affairs. Indeed, profitable business deals could be struck up at such close quarters. As Bray and Rey (1999: 82) suggest, bodily intimacy (and the body itself) carried a wider currency as 'an instrument by which social relationships could be established'. However, the social dimensions to such forms of intimacy were to change dramatically.

For one, attitudes towards homosexuality stiffened. In the path breaking *Homosexuality in Renaissance England* (1982), Bray assembles ample documentary evidence of the horror with which homosexuality was regarded, as well as the cruelty in how it was penalised. In making such a move, Bray at once dispels the myth of the Renaissance as a period of unchecked sexual freedom. Renaissance England had inherited many of the cultural anxieties and fear of same-sex intimacies from the Middle Ages, which began to cast doubt on the idea of two (male) bodies lying in close proximity. Other changes would contribute to amplifying public suspicion about male same-sex friendship. For example, Bray (2003) convincingly argues that modifications made to the general layout of houses that annexed the daily routines of eating, sleeping and washing into separate quarters, meant that bodily intimacy no longer signified the public aspects of friendship in the way it once did. The notion of the house gradually becomes the home of the family rather than the arena of a wider set of public affairs. Spaces that were ambiguous in terms of their public and private dimensions slowly start to become segmented in ways that bear an increasing resemblance to how the public-private divide is understood in dichotomous terms.

According to MacFaul (2007), friendship in the Renaissance started to be understood as a private relationship that should not intrude into the public realm of work and politics. The Protestant Church in England also exerted influence here by espousing the ideals of the nuclear family as a keystone of society. As a consequence, family and friendship began to grow apart. While Bray (2003) rightly cautions against making sweeping generalisations in the history of men's friendships during this period, it is clear that changes were afoot in how the role and place of friendship were perceived within the fabric of Western societies. Men's friendships were being viewed with ever more suspicion. Nye (2000: 1663) explains: the perceived 'danger in men's intimate friendships was the fact of their privacy'. In other words, ties of friendship between men could no longer be apprehended in the public sphere, arousing uncertainty and speculation about their nature. One major concern related to the possible signs of homosexuality in male friendship. That closeness between men in friendship can be, and has often been, read as a sign of homosexuality has profoundly altered how men's friendships are understood and experienced (Bech 1997; Garlick 2002; Sedgwick 1985). Before discussing the dynamic between homosexuality and male friendship, I demonstrate here that while friendship was increasingly seen as a relationship of the private realm, ever more overshadowed by wider cultural concerns about the presence of homosexuality in society, evidence shows that many men continued to find opportunities to engage in intimate friendships with other men. Notably, some of these opportunities for friendship were shaped along the lines of class.

For example, Rutherford (1997) explores the connections between masculinity, whiteness and English ethnicity in men's lives against Britain's history of Empire, and comments that the gendered order of Victorian, middle-class life (re)produced the conditions for a passionate and homoerotic form of male friendship to emerge. The Victorian middle-class family was wrapped in a cultural ideology that encouraged fathers and sons to maintain emotional coolness and distance between each other. Deriving insights from psychoanalytic theory, Rutherford reasons that a 'cultural expression of manliness which had been intent on ironing out all the traces of feminine feelings had the converse effect; inscribing homoerotic desire into the psychic structure of masculinity' (1997: 22). At the same time, the Victorian fascination with medieval chivalry and the provision of a classical education within public schools 'fostered [a] culture of close male friendships and encouraged the worship of the young male body' (1997: 24). This is most clearly evidenced in Rutherford's description of published boarding school narratives about the 'romantic' friendships between adolescent boys. The sexual and chaste dynamics of these friendships were ambiguous and often replicated in the same-sex friendship ties between adult, middle-class men.

What emerges from Rutherford's analysis is the fragile and temporal quality of intimacy within Victorian middle-class friendships. Male friendship appears to be more easily formed and of particular meaning for men during transitional and sometimes stressful periods over the life course; most especially, the passage from boyhood to early manhood where claims to 'manliness' are negotiated. In this regard, male friendship is an important site for staking claims to identities of masculinity, as Seidler (1997) similarly notes.

Being on the threshold of manhood is not the only point at which men could exhibit intimacy with other men in friendship, as Hoffmann's (2001) commentary on Masonic lodges in nineteenth century Germany shows. The lodges afforded its members (men of 'wealth and education') private spaces to cultivate 'close emotional ties' (2001: 227). The lodges 'guarantee[d]' their male members intimacy by providing a highly coveted 'exclusiveness in regard to the profane – women, Catholics, the lower classes, and, in part, Jews as well' (2001: 228). The 'profane' were prohibited from entering the lodges. As such, once inside the walls of the Masonic lodges, men were insulated from those who might seek to challenge their authority and undermine their identity claims to normative masculinity.

Much the same argument is made by John Tosh (2005), whose work on English nineteenth century notions of manliness and masculinities notes the impact of male organisations on the promotion of male friendship. Fleeing from the stifling routine of domestic life, many young men of the affluent professional classes found sanctuary and emotional comfort in the all male clubs that proliferated at the time. Within these womanless boltholes, men could valorise same-sex relations including friendship. As the examples above show, married life could be a threat to the development of male friendship, requiring men to construct homosocial spaces in order to strike up and sustain bonds with other men. In other words, that men of the professional classes could enjoy intimate same-sex friendships was primarily due to the Masonic lodges and clubs that provided enclosed, exclusively male spaces. These settings allowed men to construct a sense of security grounded in terms of exclusivity and privacy, but not all men had equal access to these private spaces. The men who were most likely to gain entry into these bastions of masculinity were white, middle-class, well-educated, well-heeled and with leisure time to spare.

In contrast, Karen Hansen (1992) explores the intimacies in men's friendships but focuses on working-class men in Antebellum New England, America, as the object of her analysis. Hansen argues that parallels may be sketched out between working-class men involved in same-sex friendships and the intimate friendships documented among middle-class men and women. Hansen focuses on the friendship between teacher Brigham Nims and factory worker Jacob Foster Beal to support her case. Examining some of the letters Nims and Beal sent to each other over the course of their friendship, Hansen concludes that while the two men 'spoke a less eloquent language than their middle-class contemporaries: nevertheless, it was a language of caring and friendship' (1992: 52).

Interestingly, the Nims-Beal friendship did not require the enabling condition of an all male setting for the possibility of developing intimacy. Hansen speculates that working-class men like Nims and Beal may have enjoyed a wider scope for displaying intimacy in male friendship in the nineteenth century than their contemporary equivalents. Hansen suggests that US culture in the 1830s 'promoted an unprecedented expression of feelings, while not sanctioning individuals who professed their passion to those of the same gender' (1992: 52). However, this was about to change towards the end of the nineteenth century. The construction of homosexuality as a distinct sexual category (re)asserted an association between men's friendships and homosexuality, with devastating effect.

'Something wicked this way comes': Homosexuality and men's friendships

One crucial observation we may take from Foucault's first volume of *The History of Sexuality* (1979) is that the invention of the homosexual is bound up with the construction of sexual categories of knowledge. Foucault neatly sums up this point in the second volume of the history of sexuality titled *The Use of Pleasure* (1985). Here he conceives the discursive constitution of sexuality along three axes:

> (1) the formation of sciences *(savoirs)* that refer to it, (2) the systems of power that regulate its practice, (3) the forms within which individuals are able, are obliged, to recognize themselves as subjects of this sexuality. (1985: 4, italics in original)

In respect of the third axis, it is only comparatively recently that subjects of sexuality may understand themselves as 'homosexual' or 'heterosexual'. Foucault again: 'The nineteenth-century homosexual became a personage, a past, a case history and a childhood, a character, a form of life' (1979: 43). Sexuality not only begins to assume the categorical form that we are currently familiar with during this period, but also a high level of importance in how we define ourselves.

For my purposes here, Foucault's (1979, 1985, 1986) insights into the history of sexuality shows how the formation of homosexuality and heterosexuality as distinct sexual categories paves the way for sexuality to become 'individuated'. In other words, the introduction of 'heterosexuality' and 'homosexuality' heralds the arrival of the 'homosexual' and the 'heterosexual' as specific types of person/ identities with distinct sexual preferences. Significantly, different sexual activities become linked, inextricably so it seems, to different sexual identities. But, as historians of sexuality aver (Bristow 2007; Halperin 1990; Weeks 1977, 1995), there is no automatic, 'natural' bond between the people who muster around certain sexual identities and the sexual acts they might commit themselves to. Nor is it the case that anxieties and concerns about the relationship between specific sexual personages and sexual acts they commit are swept away – in fact, quite the reverse.

As has been suggested above, the rise of the 'homosexual' provided a discursive construction onto which people could affix their concerns and fears about the intimacies within male friendship. Foucault himself makes a similar observation in an interview he gave in 1984 to the news magazine *The Advocate*:

> One thing that interests me now is the problem of friendship. For centuries after antiquity, friendship was a very important kind of social relation: a social relation within which people had a certain freedom, certain kind of choice (limited of course), as well as very intense emotional relations ... I think that in the sixteenth and seventeenth centuries, we see these kinds of friendships disappearing, at least in male society. And these friendships begin to become something other than that. You can find, from the sixteenth century on, texts that explicitly criticize friendship as something dangerous ... the disappearance of friendship as a social relation and the declaration of homosexuality as a social/political/medical problem are the same process. (1984/1997: 170–71)

To develop Foucault's thoughts on the interconnections between a history of male friendship and a history of sexuality, I refer again to the work of Alan Bray. Bray (1982) is particularly good at showing how the homosexual subcultures that developed in the molly houses of eighteenth-century London brought forth renewed scrutiny of intimacy between men. The English molly houses, a name given to the taverns and rooms where men (often dressed as women and who often took women's names) could gather in order to dance, sing, drink and meet potential same-sex (sexual) partners, are regarded by Bray as 'a specifically homosexual world, a society within a society' (1982: 85). In other words, the molly houses represented a material manifestation of a gestating homosexual culture. At the same time, uncertainty about what characteristics signalled (un)acceptable male intimacy grew large in the public consciousness. Because the molly houses represented an 'extension of the area in which homosexuality could be expressed and therefore recognised', they 'gave hostility to homosexuality an object on which it could now fasten' (1982: 92). One consequence of this was that homosexuality could not be ignored in the way that it had been previously. The molly houses became targets of organised raids, which led to many of their patrons being prosecuted, even executed.

The notorious molly house trials gave voice to the cultural anxieties surrounding how to distinguish the bonds between men deemed to be 'acceptable' from those that were to be feared. The distinction between what Bray (1982) calls 'masculine friendship' and 'sodomy' was becoming ever more awry. Bray uses 'masculine friendship' to refer to an array of 'acceptable' relations between men that included formal displays of affection such as embracing and kissing, as well as ties based on patronage and commerce. But without a system of sexual categorisation, confusion and disorder sprung up because, as Garlick (2002: 561) writes, 'public signs of male friendship could, without undue difficulty, be read in a ... sodomitical light'. Indeed, the efforts to order and clarify relations of intimacy among men were both violent and bloody. As Bray (1982) and Garlick (2002) aver, the animating impulse of the brutal strategies to interrogate and regulate same-sex intimacies among men was the notion of sodomy. Previously associated with a wider range of social ills, sodomy (and buggery) became more closely aligned at the site of men's relations with other men.

Homophobia as an obstacle to men's friendships

While it seems clear, then, that in the advent of a system of sexual categorisation in the late nineteenth century men were afforded the convenience of a 'sexual minority [homosexuals] upon which to displace their fears' (Garlick 2002: 561), it is also the case that men's friendships were no less prone to suspicion than they had been, for example, in Elizabethan England. Rather, individuals (especially men) had been given a clear target on to which they could transfer their anxieties. However, the worry among men about being labelled 'homosexual' has become a significant obstacle in the formation of friendship between men.

This line of argument is supported by feminist/queer theorist Eve Kosofsky Sedgwick's conceptualisation of social and sexual desire between men. In *Between Men: English Literature and Male Homosocial Desire* (1985), Sedgwick draws upon eighteenth- and nineteenth-century English literature in order to outline and explore a continuum of social and sexual desire between men. Crucially, Sedgwick blurs the distinction between the concepts of homosexuality and homosociality, the latter term often used to refer to bonds between men that are non-sexual in nature. Sedgwick problematises the homosexuality–homosociality divide, by showing how homosocial friendships between men can contain elements of the homoerotic. For Sedgwick, the continuum between homosocial and homosexual is potentially unbroken, although to 'men in our society' the continuum is 'radically disrupted' (1985: 2), since many feel compelled to vitiate any sign of homosexuality in their relations with other men. Here, a sense is gained of the precariousness and of the tensions associated with and arising from how men position their desires at various points along the homosocial–homosexual continuum. Men are bound to the continuum since homosocial bonds can be a powerful form of perpetuating and sustaining male patriarchal interests and authority. At the same time, men experience a bind since homosocial bonds are often characterised by homophobia, and so they are vulnerable to what Sedgwick calls 'homosexual panic': the 'most private, psychologized form in which many twentieth-century western men experience their vulnerability to the social pressure of homophobic blackmail' (1985: 89). Powerful, if at times unstable, definitional leverage is gained through the activation of a vicious and psychologised homophobia. This serves to regulate relations between men, especially as they traverse the 'arbitrarily mapped, self-contradictory, and anathema-riddled quicksands of the middle distance' of the homosocial continuum.

Needless to say, anxieties about homosexuality have not left men's friendships unscathed. Men's friendships are rare, suggests sociologist Henning Bech (1997). From Bech's point of view, the emphasis friendship places on affinity and intimacy ushers in anxieties about whether signs of male intimacy will be read under the aegis of homosexuality. Although Bech does not dismiss other factors at play in rendering friendship between men problematic (for example, a perceived shortage of opportunities for friendship in the workplace and in the domestic realm), he is unequivocal about the impact of homosexuality in that respect. The alleged scarcity of men's friendship is seen to be an explicit indication of the presence of homosexuality as a force at work in the construction of male friendship. Thus, as Bech goes on to say, men must 'continually repudiate homosexuality' (1997: 73) in their same-sex friendships or avoid them altogether. Bech's prognosis of men's friendships is woefully bleak: 'the more one has to assure oneself that one's relationship is not homosexual, the more conscious one becomes to protect oneself against it. The result is that friendship gradually becomes impossible'.

However, as the empirical content of this study reveals, the influence of homophobia on men's friendships might not be as damaging as Bech avers. Nor is it the case that homophobia is an inevitable feature of men's friendships, mediating men's understandings and experiences of friendship involving other men. Following Sedgwick (1985), the historical continuity between homosexuality and homosociality is not coherent and fixed but shifting and contingent. Thus, while it seems that homophobia is a frequent element of men's friendships, this only has the appearance of being so due to the collision of discourses on homosexuality and homosociality in a particular historical moment. Crucially, the relationship between men and discourses is not a simple, predictable one. As I elaborate later, men's friendships may be understood as sites for questioning homophobia and normative discourses on gender and sexuality (Nardi 1999).

In saying as much I do not conveniently side step the literature that examines the gendered consequences of homophobia on men's friendships (Miller 1983; Messner 1992). For example, lamenting the absence of male friends in his life, heterosexual academic Stuart Miller embarks on a manhunt to find 'true male friendship'. A journey of several years, narrated over the course of several hundred pages in *Men and Friendship* (1983), Miller pinpoints homophobia as a potent barrier to the formation of close friendship between men. For Miller and the hundreds of men interviewed throughout his friendship quest, homophobia seems to keep men apart within friendship or at least exact a rather dulling effect on the development of intimacy. Indeed, Miller even goes as far as to record his 'fear of homosexuality' (1983: 133), anguishing over whether potential male friends might think he is 'homosexual'. Such speculations amount to a form of 'self-torture' in Miller's mind. The 'homosexual business' (1983: 138), as Miller later calls it, creeps into a conversation he shares with a male friend of whom he has sought advice about a work-related matter. Reflecting on the warmth he experiences from his friend, doubt enters into his mind as to whether the 'rosy good feeling doesn't have some erotic flavor to it. Something vague, general, *perhaps* sexual in some way' (1983: 139, italics in original). While Miller is correct to assert that rarely, if ever, is it possible to reduce the complex behaviours between men in friendship to the 'business of homosexuality', it is unquestionable that homophobia is a powerful current in carving out the contours of male friendship.

While Miller (1983) is a rare first hand account of the challenges some men face in friendship development with other men, he privileges a confessional style of discussion about his 'homosexual panic' at the expense of a critical interrogation of how homosexuality, homophobia and masculinity are embedded within gendered power relations (see Kimmel 1994). On that point, critical masculinity studies research has shown how the performance of masculinity within heterosexual men's friendships is an exercise in gendered power relations that often involves the subordination of gay men and women as the *Other* (Levy 2005; Messner 1992; Migliaccio 2009; Nardi 1992b; Seidler 1992, 1997, 2007).

The US male athletes Messner (1992) interviewed described their friendships with other male athletes as some of the most intimate relationships they had experienced, and often conveyed this sentiment using familial terminology. However, the men talked about the conflicts within their friendships that arose from competing within the hierarchical domain of athletics. Antagonisms in the men's friendships were revealing of the masculine identity construction work the men undertook which limited the range and displays of intimacies they experienced not only with their male friends, but also with women. The fear of becoming too close with other men, fuelled by misogynistic discourses of homophobia, denigrate the performance of femininity by men and, by implication, demean women by treating femininity as a sign of inferiority. Other studies of men's friendships within the field of sport (Harvey 1999) and in leisure sites (Gough and Edwards 1998; Blackshaw 2003) also incriminate homophobia as having a mediating effect on the expression of intimacies within men's friendships.

However, to repeat an earlier cautionary note, we must not blithely assume that homophobia is an inevitable feature of men's friendships, shaping relations between men based on sociability rather than intimacy. Given that dominant discourses on normative masculinity are open to alteration and, as I see it, increasing contestation within a postmodern world of sexualities and genders (Simon 1996; Weeks 2007), categorising men's friendships in this way is neither sustainable nor desirable. For one thing, much of the research on men's friendships cited above concerns heterosexual men's friendships, leaving unanswered questions about how gay men's perspectives might complicate existing stereotypes and traditional beliefs about how men understand and experience friendship with other men.

Summary

In this chapter I have sketched out some of the historical and cultural variation in how men's friendships have been represented, understood and experienced. One reason for so doing is to provide a rich backcloth against which to problematise the mainstay in thinking about men's friendships: women exceed men in achieving intimate friendship. This assertion is attracting more and more criticism from academics, who question whether the 'problem' with men's friendships is more a matter of narrowly defined gender norms (Nardi 2007). I am inclined to agree. How men engage in close dyadic friendship varies because, for example, constructions of gender and sexuality differ. Men's friendships are very sensitive to the influence of sexuality and gender, as historical evidence presented in this chapter demonstrates. However, it is clear that much of the literature reviewed above does not fully account for the different perspectives men hold on friendship. For one thing, friendship commentators generally have nothing to say on the issues that arise when gay sexualities are introduced into debates on gender and friendship. In the next chapter, I review the research that has addressed this gap in academic knowledge, suggesting that gay men have often been constructed as particularly good friendship makers.

Chapter 2
Gay Men and Friendship

Introduction

In the previous chapter I argued that men's friendships have been commonly understood within scholarly and populist writing as less intimate than women's friendships. Following other commentators who stress the danger of (re)producing dichotomous and universal discourse on men's friendships, I argue that it is important to explore the variation within men's friendships. In this chapter, I pursue this aim by examining gay men's friendships. This is a critical move because gay men have often been constructed as friendship 'experts' who are only too aware of the advantages associated with establishing friendships based on intimacy, trust, reciprocity and equality. This chapter will examine why friendship has played a crucial role in the lives of many gay men, with reference to a wider body of research on LGBT friendships. In discussing the role and salience of friendship in gay men's lives, I call attention to how gay men have been constructed as relationship 'experts'. This chapter draws on the work of Anthony Giddens to that end, but particularly on a rich body of research by sociologists, feminists and scholars sympathetic to Foucault, who argue also that gay men can forge friendships that depart from heteronormative discourses on adult relationships. I underscore the potential of a Foucauldian position in that respect, noting its emphasis on the situated and uneven quality of people's friendship choices. As a way of illustrating this, I review the scholarship on gay men's friendship patterns, with particular attention to how friendships are gendered, classed and racialised in ways that compromise and enhance the ability of gay men to transgress the limits to how the self can be constructed.

Gay men's friendships as 'safe havens'

As I suggested in Chapter 1, for many men the dread of being labelled homosexual has been a significant disincentive to making friends with other men. While anxieties about homosexuality still influence understandings of the intimate nature of the dyadic friendship bonds between men, some men's friendships flourished:

> For an emerging category of men who loved other men, friendship was one source of personal and social freedom. It was a search for other selves, and it led to the creation and social reproduction of community through a type of civic friendship. (1999: 33)

What Nardi's quote demonstrates is that the conditions under which friendship accrues significance for gay men may be quite specific, both culturally and historically. Following Nardi (1999) and others (Greenberg 1988; Weeks 1995; Seidman 1997), the invention of homosexuality and of the homosexual personage paved the way for the creation of a plethora of sexual identities and a diverse range of sexual minority cultures. The challenges to heteronormative culture in the West, principally from feminism and the gay liberation movement from the 1970s onwards, went hand-in-hand with an invigorated reliance on friendship to affirm newly forged identities and selves (Blasius 1994). Indeed, the role of friends in supporting LGBT persons in constructing and maintaining positive sexual and gender identities is not to be underestimated.

For example, research shows that friendships are pivotal in helping LGBT people to respond to the dilemmas and anxiety surrounding the development of meaningful identities (Weeks et al. 2001). Numerous studies have repeatedly demonstrated how LGBT persons can be particularly vulnerable to the inimical effects of homophobia in those moments when they disclose their sexual identity (D'Augelli 1998; Herek et al. 2002; Herek et al. 1997; Plummer 1999). Since disclosing a sexual identity is never a singular act, out of which crystallises a fully-fledged sexual identity, but a discursive process of becoming 'gay' that involves performing a continuous series of identity iterations (Butler 1990; Sedgwick 1990), gay men can be (re)exposed to forms of discrimination every time they 'come out' to another individual (Vargo 1998). In that respect, friendship can function to bolster gay men and others from external dangers such as homophobia. The friends of gay men provide protection, supportive intimacy and affirmation at various points in their lives (Grossman and Kerner 1998; Heaphy et al. 2004; Nardi 1992a, 1992b; Nardi and Sherrod 1994; Vincke and Bolton 1994).

Research on gay men's friendships in the context of HIV/AIDS is one of the most vivid illustrations of the power of friendship in protecting and supporting gay men. Drawing similarities with research that underscores the supportive role of friendship for helping individuals with serious illnesses to cope and recover (Mccorkle et al. 2009), first-hand accounts of living with HIV/AIDS show how friendships can help gay men to deal with death and disease within the confines of stereotyped perspectives about HIV/AIDS (Watney 2000; Sullivan 1998). From Watney's (2000) extensive fieldwork in this area, during the years when the virus made large dents in the gay male population, friends rallied to care for those buffeted by a deluge of HIV/AIDS fuelled homophobia that gushed out of the UK tabloid press (particularly at the time HIV/AIDS came to the public attention of the British public in the early 1980s). Friends also filled the gaps in the provision of care left by estranged family members, friends, work colleagues and prejudiced medical professionals. HIV/AIDS is a striking example of how serious illness can tear families apart and galvanise friends to provide an invaluable source of comfort and sustenance for those gay men living with the condition (Yoshikawa et al. 2004).

It is during these 'fateful moments' in people's lives – the 'times when events come together in such a way that an individual stands at a crossroads in their existence or where a person learns of information with fateful consequences' (Giddens 1991: 113) – that friends serve a far greater purpose than merely providing pleasant company. Weeks et al. (2001) agree. Friends can allow each other to be weak. Indeed, when acting as the main providers of care for gay men living with HIV/AIDS, friends frequently accept (and attend to) the weakness in another friend's body, as well as their mind. As such, they place themselves at great risk of experiencing the stress and victimisation associated with caring for and mourning the death of a friend who has succumbed to AIDS (D'Augelli 1998). Numerous studies (Hays et al. 1990; Hart et al. 1990; Johnston et al. 1995) bear out both Watney's (2000) reflections and Weeks et al.'s (2001) empirical-based observations on how friends rather than family members serve as 'life-lines' to gay men infected with HIV/AIDS. Indeed, as I explore in the next section, gay men may regard friends in familial terms, which suggests potential for subverting heteronormative discourses that distinguish friendship from kinship.

'We Are Family': Friends as family?

In 1979 the American all girl sibling group Sister Sledge said perhaps more than they knew in their massive UK and US top 10 hit single 'We Are Family'. In tune to a disco beat that was at its zenith in the 1970s, 'We Are Family' struck gold and a chord with countless gay men, among others, who crowded the dance floors of nightclubs on both sides of the Atlantic. The success and popularity of the song in 1979 was partly due to its potential for a 'queer' reading of the notion of 'family'; in other words, a concept of 'family' premised on individual choice as well as blood ties. From this perspective, the song delivered a message of hope to those who found little or no relevance (or pleasure) within heteronormative familial relationships. This unconventional and roomy notion of 'family' appeared to promise accommodation to a diverse array of sexual dissidents, allowing gay men (among others) to at once rejoice and shake their hips to an imaginary friendship-centred notion of family.

It is not altogether remarkable that the song's perspective on the idea of 'friends as family' has found empirical support in academic research. Kath Weston's (1991) US study of how gay men and lesbians construct notions of kinship has stood the test of time remarkably well in that respect. Weston's research remains one of the most cited and illuminating examples of how gay men and lesbians contest heteronormative concepts of family by creating 'families of choice', comprising of friends, lovers and kin. For instance, some of Weston's interviewees speak of the necessity of constructing families based on friendship when familial bonds based on blood ties had been lost through rejection. One gay man says: 'Tim and I fill for each other some of the emptiness of blood family that aren't there' (1991: 116). Examples of this kind reveal the motives behind friendship development. So much more than a matter of personal choice, these relationships are often created out of necessity, as Sullivan (1998) also notes.

This view is supported by research on ageing gay men and lesbians (de Vries and Hoctel 2007, 2009; Heaphy 2009). Studies show that the value gay men and lesbians attach to the supportive role of friendship can increase in later life not just for plugging gaps in ties of kinship, but also for combating loneliness, coping with the dehabilitating effects of poor health and dealing with parenting issues. But, as Heaphy (2009) is right to point out, the relational options available to some older gay men and lesbians are also restrained by how they can access economic, social and cultural resources. As such, the notion of 'friends as family' (or indeed, 'We Are Family') is not simply a case of accommodating anyone under the umbrella of 'family'. Understanding how friendship choices are situated is useful for exploring how terms such as 'friendship' and 'family' are given various meanings in different contexts and at specific moments in time.

Weston's (1991) study also reminds us that chosen families comprising of friends do not simply compensate for the absence of biological family ties. Other individuals Weston interviewed interpreted kinship as more an extension of friendship than seeing family and friends as mutually exclusive (even competitive) sets of relationships. Some gay men and lesbians referred to each other as 'friends' and as 'family'. In so doing, they generated senses of connectedness based on such things as intimacy, trust and love – characteristics of both familial and friendship bonds. Weston's study brilliantly portrays the fluid boundaries between kinship and friendship, and the different ways her interviewees went about building families of choice. This relationship building activity is not politically neutral. Following Nardi (1999) and others (Sullivan 1998; Vernon 2000; Weeks et al. 2001), these new relational forms help to destabilise heteronormative notions of family and friendship by exposing their limited capacity to accommodate LGBT people. Weston explains: 'what gay kinship ideologies challenge is not the concept of procreation that informs kinship in the United States, but the belief that procreation *alone* constitutes kinship' (1991: 34). Weston's study and those like it lend support to the idea that we should recognise and respect a growing number of ways in which the concept of 'family' can be understood and experienced. For some commentators, gay men might have a crucial role to play in helping to 'vent the family with the fresh air of friendship' (Sullivan 1998: 233). In the following section, I unpack this idea more broadly, exploring how certain commentators have positioned gay men as pioneers in forging other ways of relating intimately that appear loosened from the strictures of heteronormativity.

The significance of gay men in friendship

At this point it is useful to draw out, albeit loosely, a distinction in how the role of friendship in gay men's lives has been conceptualised thus far. From one perspective, it is within friendship that gay men may find the fortitude and courage to resist the threats (for example, from homophobia) to demolish and discredit sexual identities and subjectivities. This is seen most clearly in the research conducted on gay men and HIV/AIDS reviewed above. Here, friendship operates as a strategy for protection and preservation: a relationship that affords gay men the emotional and material support to carve out and defend ways of living and relating to others within heterosexist and homophobic societies. In this research the role of friendship in providing forms of social support is particularly strong.

From another perspective, friendship research on LGBT people in a post-AIDS era is focusing more and more on the creative possibilities that exist within friendship for constructing new senses of belonging and relating to others. For example, studies by Weston (1991) and others (Galupo et al. 2004; Nardi 1999; Weeks et al. 2001) illustrate the diversity in how LGBT people perform friendship, some forms of which are said to destabilise heteronormative discourses on romantic love, sexual relations and kinship.

Nardi's work (1992, 1999) explores the significance of gay men's friendships in that respect. Borrowing an Aristotelian notion of civic friendship, Nardi underscores the reproductive value of gay men's friendships in political terms: that is, generating another (gay) self for the overall 'good' of the community. Viewed as such, gay men's friendships act as politicised 'mechanisms of social reproduction in which gay masculinities, gay identities, gay cultures, and gay communities get created, transformed, maintained, and passed on' (1999: 7). Importantly, these identities, cultures, values can destabilise heteronormative cultural norms by denaturalising their taken-for-granted and normative status. Indeed, heteronormativity is often legitimised by reference to a 'natural' order and necessity, and gay men's friendships might provide a context for friends to question these kinds of assertions. For example, the intermingling of sexual relations and friendship is seen to challenge heteronormative discourses on friendship that suggest it is only 'authentic' when it is platonic. But more than this, Nardi hopes gay men's friendships might act as a site for the development of a modern form of heroic friendship in which 'valor, bravery, and devotion are inextricably linked to intimacy, sharing, personal disclosure, vulnerability, and emotional support' (1999: 206). This sentiment is echoed by Vernon (2000), who points towards the generative possibilities within gay cultures: it 'creates resources to deepen and extend other relational possibilities' (2000: 69). In this vein, gay men's friendships may function as an 'innovative challenge to transcend contemporary relational constraints in an embodiment of values and implications for action' (2000: 76).

These arguments are compelling. Why not understand gay men's friendships as a potential source of personal inspiration to others involved in overcoming relational constraints? A positive response to this question, of the type put forward by Nardi (1999) and Vernon (2000), might carry hope for others, especially those men who understand friendships with other men as emotionally tepid and instrumental. Yet, negatively, the revamped model of heroic friendship that Nardi (1999) proposes could be seen to represent another version of heroic male friendship that holds little appeal to women. Rather, I suggest that gay men's friendships might be a source of inspiration for helping others to develop new relationalities, but we have to examine the particular conditions required for this possibility to emerge. We also need to explore how gay men might characterise friendships differently to those who rely upon heteronormative models of friendship, especially among men. There is a further point here. Gay men's friendships are not unique in their capacity to pique the imaginations of others to challenge heteronormative discourses on adult relationships, as research on friendships involving women, lesbians and bisexuals indicates (Galupo 2007a; Raymond 1986; Weinstock 1998). If gay men's workplace friendships provide resources to think differently about friendships in more progressive directions, then such insights must be located against a rich backcloth of how friendship is variously understood and experienced by women, lesbians, bisexuals, transgender people and heterosexuals.

Recognising the innovation in how adult friendships are being (re)configured, not just by gay men but also by lesbians and bisexuals, Weeks et al. (2001) brand these people as pioneers of new relationalities forged on agency, creativity and choice. To propose that gay men (and some others) might somehow play a leading role in the process of reshaping intimate relations in people's everyday lives gives rise to a set of questions about why they might be accorded such a position of responsibility in the vanguard of relationship life. It also sparks debate about the conditions of possibility for such relationships to emerge and how the activities of gay men in that respect might be framed theoretically. In this section, then, it is my intention to substantiate and frame this argument; namely that gay men are key but not unique figures in using friendship to develop 'practices of freedom' that may help them and us to re-imagine the possibilities for developing relationalities that resist heteronormative discourses on adult relationships.

Gay men and lesbians as pioneers of egalitarian relationships

Beck (1992) and others (Beck and Beck-Gernsheim 1995) note various transformations underway in people's intimate lives, which they suggest signal a period of 'reflexive modernisation' within the development of Western societies. Marking out a new passage in social history in this way, these sociologists emphasise the erosion of traditional assumptions about how people's lives should be plotted, especially around the achievement of romantic love and the family. Precisely because normative social relations are no longer to be taken-for-granted, friendship is seen to accrue importance for 'increasingly reflexive people' in terms of continuity and identity making (Pahl 2000: 69). This theme of 'detraditionalisation' as it has come to be known in this segment of sociological literature, spotlights an apparent growth in reflexivity. In the face of uncertainty and irrelevance in regard to the traditional values and structures of the family, individuals are thrown back on themselves to fathom out new ways of relating to others. In other words, individuals are required to be critically reflexive about their actions and the choices they make in how their lives are constituted.

Crucially, academic opinion differs on the extent to which detraditionalisation offers new potentialities for a democratisation of intimate relationships. Anthony Giddens provides one of the most optimistic accounts in that respect, especially in regard to the role gay men and lesbians are said to play to that end. In the context of Giddens's work, the argument upon which claims of innovation in the ways LGBT people relate in friendship rest is that LGBT persons have often had little choice in the matter:

> Gay women and men have preceded most heterosexuals in developing relationships, in the sense that the term has come to assume today, when applied to personal life. For they have to 'get along' without traditionally established frameworks of marriage, in conditions of relative equality between partners. (1992: 15)

From the above quotation, gay and lesbian lifestyles are held up as exemplars of democratic relating. Crucial here is the concept of the 'pure relationship'. As an expression of the democratisation of intimate relationships, the 'pure relationship' is described as a social relation 'entered into for its own sake' (1992: 58). In other words, the pure relationship is sustained by the choices made by the individuals involved. Mutual disclosure, therefore, is critical, since it allows the pure relationship to continually (re)design its own frame of reference. Significantly, Giddens suggests that gay and lesbian relationships are more likely to approximate the notion of the pure relationship, not least because they are believed to be free from the constraining effects of relationship norms. Looked at in this way, the pure relationship concept is an upbeat reading of the consequences of detraditionalisation and the rise of reflexive individualisation. Against this backdrop, one characterised by the necessity for reinvention at the level of the self with limited recourse to traditional customs and values for guidance, Giddens highlights exciting possibilities for emotional democracy within relationship life.

Giddens's concept of the pure relationship has received mixed reviews from academics. It is certainly open to criticism about its inadequate account of power, deservedly so. For example, feminist theorists have chided Giddens for underestimating the influence of patriarchal ideologies, responsible for enduring gendered inequalities that structure heterosexual relationships (Jamieson 1998; Seymour and Bagguley 1999). In similar fashion, some commentators acknowledge that same-sex relationships are not free from the tensions and inequalities that arise from power relations that are gendered (Weeks et al. 2001), as well as those based on other differences such as class and ethnicity (Klesse 2005). Equally and relatedly, the principles of the pure relationship are in tension with sociological theories of friendship as relationships that do not run entirely on free choice (Allan 1989; Adams and Allan 1998). Friendships can be compromised by all manner of power relations, not the least of them being sexual and gendered in nature (Werking 1997). Significantly, these concerns are supported empirically, as research shows that gay and lesbian relationships are perhaps not as democratic and open as Giddens suggests, since they can (un)intentionally reinforce heteronormative relationship ideals (Worth et al. 2002).

Despite these shortcomings, Giddens's work has been warmly received by a number of scholars including Bech (1997), Weeks et al. (2001) and Roseneil (2000). While many of these commentators acknowledge the concerns expressed by some of Giddens's detractors, his positioning of gay men and lesbians in the vanguard of democratic relationship life has been applauded. Arguably, some studies appear to come close to evidencing what Giddens might have in mind on the matter of choice in forming and developing pure relationships. Weeks et al.'s (2001) study suggests that in the absence of 'legitimisation' from blood ties or from legal frameworks, LGBT people's friendships tend to display a strong emphasis on choice, love and trust that together, make 'egalitarian friendship' (2001: 70–71). However, it is important to reiterate that Weeks et al. remain critical of the pure relationship concept, treating it as an 'ideal' that might be worth aspiring to, while recognising that it does not have a universal and uniform bearing on the everyday lives of LGBT persons. I am broadly aligned with the position adopted by Weeks et al. (2001). But it is imperative to recognise that figuring out how to negotiate friendships that transcend relational norms and constraints is seldom an easy one. On this point, Foucault's writing might again remind us that people's choices in this matter are constrained, mediated, uneven and contingent.

Practices of freedom

Taking a cue from volumes two and three of Foucault's *The History of Sexuality* (1985, 1986), in which an 'aesthetics of existence' is outlined, Weeks et al. (2001) view the unconventional forms of kinship and friendship engineered by LGBT persons as explicit examples of 'practices that reject models of domination and subordination' (2001: 187). However, a Foucauldian perspective on the concept of 'freedom' does not view it in purely negative terms as, for example, a freedom from constraint. Rather, the notion of freedom involves more positive ideas of individual autonomy, such as the freedom of the individual to construct new modes of subjectivity. Here, then, Foucault's practices of freedom has a relationship with ethics or, to be more precise, an ethics of self-care. More specifically, ethics as practices of freedom invovles exploring new possibilities for developing identities, selves, subjectivities, relaitonships and ways of living. As Foucault himself remarked, practices of freedom are:

> an ascetic practice ... in other words, not in the sense of a morality of renunciation but as an exercise of the self on the self by which one attempts to develop and transform oneself, and to attain to a certain mode of being. (1984/1997: 282)

Thus practices of freedom are about the ethical choices individuals make as they attribute meaning to their own lives. For Weeks et al. (2001), practices of freedom permit individuals to explore the (re)formation of intimate relationships such as friendship. The variety of intimate relationships documented by Weeks et al. (2001) is used to evidence the argument that LGBT people are engaging in practices of freedom in their daily routines. But this is not to imply that gay men and lesbians are free from the normative discourses that come into play when developing new relationships. The subject cannot exist outside of discourse, which is not to suggest the subject is mired within a field of discursive relations, in the sense they lack any agency to identify and alter the limits of the construction of self. Rather, the subject can seek to modify and reverse normative discourses so as to transgress the limits to how the self can be discursively constructed. While discursive activities that may be described as practices of freedom might not trigger a seismic change in how, for example, discursive fields of relationships and identities are configured, they can generate tremors and localised disturbances that expose their incoherencies. As such, Weeks et al. (2001) propose, based on empirical insights into the inventiveness displayed by their study participants in how they relate intimately, that an 'informal revolution [is] taking place in everyday life' (2001: 187). In the following discussion I discuss the friendship patterns of gay men in order to gain further perspectives on how gay men's friendships might operate in that way.

Friendship patterns of adult gay men

Research on gay men's friendships is limited. Much of the published material in this area suggests that gay men select friends who are similar to themselves, often on the basis of sexual identity, age, ethnicity, and so on. As Nardi (1999: 106) writes: 'it should come as no surprise that gay men's close and best friends are other gay men who tend to be like themselves'. As I have suggested earlier in this chapter, there are substantial benefits for gay men who befriend other gay men. Gottlieb's (2008) edited collection of essays emphasises how friendships between gay men provide the support, acceptance and understanding not easily provided in other friendships where there are differences in sexual identities. Similarly, the majority of gay men who participated in Nardi's (1999) research felt closer to other gay men against the background of a heteronormative culture that often marginalised them. Likewise, one gay man in Weeks et al.'s (2001: 64) study comments: 'there's certain things I need to be able to talk to another [gay] man about, in terms of relationships, but also … it's things around sex and cottaging and all that kind of biz'. Taken together, these study findings indicate that gay men can come together in friendship, and in so doing come to understand and validate their perspectives and experiences of life as gay men.

Weinstock (1998) helps to shed light on why studies on the friendship patterns of LGBT people frequently report a high level of homophily. Apart from the long-documented proclivity people display for befriending individuals they perceive to be equal to and similar in terms of age, gender, class, and so on (Duck 1991), potential friends for LGBT people are often sourced through established but sometimes restrictive friendship networks. Weinstock says: 'it is no wonder that in a context of heterosexism … LGBT … persons tend to develop friendships within rather than across these boundaries' (1998: 144). Weeks et al. (2001) also support this view, noting that as people become more integrated into LGBT worlds so their friendships are more likely to become embedded there. Not surprising, then, is that research shows that lesbian women were more likely to strike up close friendships with other lesbians (Stanley 1996; Rust 1995). Notable, therefore, is that bisexual men and women are less likely to report friendships with those who identify as bisexual (Galupo 2007a, 2009). Interestingly, the majority of Galupo's (2007a) bisexual study participants experienced most of their friendships with heterosexuals, problematising the assertion that individuals choose friends who are similar to themselves. Research on bisexual men's and women's friendships although scare is extremely useful because it reminds us that sexuality influences friendship choices in a dynamic and sometimes unpredictable fashion.

At this stage, it is worth underlining a glaringly obvious point. Sharing the same or a similar sexual identity is no guaranteed access route into friendship, as many of the studies cited above point out. For instance, the gay men in Weeks et al.'s (2001: 64) study reported few friendships with lesbians and vice versa. As the authors remark, while there is a 'historical basis for this distinction, more often than not it comes from ignorance about each other's lifestyles'. Apart from some notable exceptions (Miles and Rofes 1998; Nestle and Preston 1994), research on the friendships between gay men and lesbians is noticeably underdeveloped. A similar story can be told in relation to the friendship patterns between gay men and bisexuals (Galupo 2009) and heterosexual men (Fee 2000; Price 1999). Besides sexuality, there are many other identity categories that can shape how friendship choices are made, such as class, age, race, ethnicity, disability, to mention but a few. Before discussing the influence of class and ethnicity on gay men's friendships in more detail, the following section examines the research on gay men's friendships that cross categories of sexual identity.

Cross-category friendships: Gay men's friendships with heterosexuals

In the *Friendship Chronicles: Letters Between a Gay and a Straight Man* (1994), Hassett and Owen-Towle present a first-hand account of their friendship through more than a decade's worth of correspondence. The two men call their friendship 'revolutionary' (1994: xiv) not just because friendships involving gay and heterosexual men are perceived to be rare, but also because of its depth and durability. The prolific letter writing between Hassett and Owen-Towle reveals much of the tenderness and heartache of wrestling with a friendship that straddles the heterosexual/homosexual binary, a theme dramatised in a small clutch of Hollywood films such as *Gods and Monsters* (1998) and *As Good As It Gets* (1997). These texts exemplify a general point I made in Chapter 1: that men have long had to negotiate the spectre of male homosexuality in how they conduct their relations with other men, especially in friendship. However, the letters exchanged between Hassett and Owen-Towle yield glimpses into an emotionally intimate friendship that shatters stereotypes about the emotionally lukewarm nature of friendships between men. Yet such insights into men's friendships are hard to come by within scholarly circles.

Research conducted in the US by Price (1999) and Fee (2000) demonstrates emotional intimacy is possible where both male friends are committed to negotiating issues of sexual and gender differences. Price's (1999) study on how gay and heterosexual male friends negotiate sexual and gender differences categorises friends into three types: those that embrace differences, ignore differences and struggle with differences. A number of the friendships Price analysed are classified as struggling to negotiate sexual differences. Here heterosexual men are positioned as reluctant or unable to accept or accommodate their friend's gay identity. However, it is important to note that heterosexual men can relate to gay men positively, as other friendship studies show.

Fee's (2000) research shows that some heterosexual men find gay men particularly appealing as friends. In the company of gay male friends, some heterosexual men were reported as saying they were more able to relax the display of normative heterosexual based masculinity, pursuing instead a schema of intimacy more typical of 'feminine' styles of relating in friendship. In similar fashion, some of the gay African American men in White's (2008) study offered their heterosexual male friends a safe relational context in which to develop alternative masculinities. Elsewhere, one of Walker's (1994a) heterosexual male study participants reported that he could shop for cosmetics with his gay but not his heterosexual male friends because he felt there was little risk of his 'masculinity' being called into question. As useful as these studies are for understanding the friendships between gay and heterosexual men, in order to better understand the capacity of these friendships to challenge heteronormative ways of relating in male friendships further empirical research is needed.

In contrast, research on gay men's friendships with heterosexual women is growing, with some striking scholarly and populist publications on the subject (de la Cruz and Dolby 2007; Grigoriou 2004; Hopcke and Rafaty 1999; Nahas and Turley 1979; Rauch and Fessler 1995; Shepperd et al. 2010; Tillmann-Healy 2001; Whitney 1990). Indeed, the last two decades have been witness to the emergence of the gay male-heterosexual female friendship dyad as a prominent cultural construction. While Richard Dyer (1979, 2002) maintains that the adoring affection shown by gay men towards heterosexual women (often iconic female stars in Hollywood films and within the music industry) has a long history, it is apparent that gay male and heterosexual female friendships have taken centre stage within contemporary popular culture. Over the last decade a series of Hollywood films have used this friendship dyad as a key narrative device (see *The Mexican* 2002; *The Next Best Thing* 2000; *The Object of My Affection* 1998; *My Best Friend's Wedding* 1997) for entertaining Western cinema audiences. Similarly, the stellar success of the NBC primetime hit television show *Will and Grace* (1998–2006) has been due in no small part to having caught the imagination of millions of viewers populating the suburban heartlands in both (though not limited to) the US and the UK. As Shepperd et al. (2010) note, this representation of gay male and heterosexual female friendship as 'normal' and mutually beneficial is 'new', in that heterosexual women have often been pejoratively labelled the 'fag hags' of their gay male friends (Moon 1995; Quimby 2005).

One recurrent view emerging from the majority of the literature on gay men's and heterosexual women's friendships is the heightened opportunity for developing affinity and various intimacies, when compared to gay men's friendships with heterosexual men. This outlook is partly rooted in the notion that gay men and heterosexual women may find mutuality in friendship because, while they have a shared sexual interest in men, they have both suffered at the hands of heterosexual men (Rubin 1985; Stuart 1995). While this argument has some validity, it has also rattled those feminists who argue that gay men are not exempt from holding misogynistic attitudes (Jeffreys 2003; Segal 1990; Stanley 1982). Gay men can partake in male privilege, which is seen by some feminists and queer studies scholars as reason enough to problematise facile representations of gay men as the 'natural' friends of heterosexual women (Maddison 2000; Ward 2000). As queer theorist Stephen Maddison avers, attention must be paid to the 'structural nature of affiliations between women and gay men so as to foreclose purely frivolous understandings of [their] relations and to validate the institutional difficulties such bonds endure, as well as the dissent potential they hold' (2000: 71). Yet insight into the gender complex dynamics of gay male and heterosexual female friendships is scarce.

One notable exception is Grigoriou's (2004) UK study. The gay men in this study struck up friendships with women because they saw them as occasioning the type of bonds that allowed them to understand themselves as 'normal' within a society that privileges heterosexuality (see also Maddison 2000). While the women Grigoriou interviewed said they valued their friendships with other women for the intimacy, fun and support they afforded, friendships with gay men provided additional pleasures. A male appreciation of personality without any sexual overtures was highly coveted. Furthermore, films such as *The Next Best Thing* (2000) and *My Best Friend's Wedding* (1997) show that women enjoy the flirtatious components to their friendships with gay men. Such forms of 'safe eroticism' appear to be more likely in friendships between gay men and heterosexual women than in friendships between heterosexual men and women, given that the risk of sexual attraction is thought to be greatly reduced or non-existent. As such, friendships with gay men may well provide women with a rewarding alternative to friendships with straight men that are largely shown to be troubled or ruined by the development of romance and sexual intimacies (Werking 1997; Monsour 2002; Rubin 1985).

Nonetheless, unlike O'Meara (1989) and Rauch and Fessler (1995), I argue that it is rash to assume that sexual attraction is nonexistent in friendships between gay men and women. For instance, Tillmann-Healy's (2001) narrative ethnography of her friendships with a small group of gay men in the US explores the possibilities these friendships generate for denaturalising differences in gender and sexuality. Scholarly and populist discourses that hold both sexual tension and sexual intimacy as missing dimensions in this friendship dyad gain little purchase against Tillmann-Healy's candid account of how she and one gay man experience mutual sexual attraction (2001: 168). Similar stories are told in the film *The Object of My Affection* (1998) and in the work of de la Cruz and Dolby (2007) and Whitney (1990).

On a different tack, Tillmann-Healy comments on how her gay male friends have provided the impetus to question her own homophobia and 'complicity in a system that suppresses and marginalizes gay and lesbian experience' (2001: 188). This appears to stimulate a shift in Tillmann-Healy's perspective on heteronormative discourses of gender and sexual difference:

> Becoming immersed in a gay male community has rendered [my] sexual and gender identities more queer ... I have developed strategies to resist binary constructions of sexuality and gender, freeing [me] to enact more fluid identities. (2001: 737)

Tillmann-Healy's ethnography is notable for revealing one woman's efforts to construct a 'queer' friendship. At the same time, Tillmann-Healy observes that some of her gay male friends withheld emotionally and appeared to display conventional woman-excluding behaviours redolent of normative modes of being heterosexual and masculine. Friendships with gay men may offer potential for resisting heteronormative discourses of gender and sexuality, but they may also bear the traces of earlier feminist complaints about gay men's sexist attitudes and heteronormative behaviours.

Lastly, gay men's friendships with transgender persons and with bisexual men and women are seemingly uncommon and under researched. For example, 2.1% and 1.4% of Nardi's (1999) gay male survey respondents identified bisexual men and women respectively as 'best friends'. There is no mention of gay men's friendships with transgender persons. Disappointing also is that Nardi does not analyse in detail his respondents' experiences of friendships involving bisexual men and women. By comparison, research on bisexuals' experiences of friendship is easier to find. Studies by Galupo (2007a, 2007b, 2009) on bisexual men's and women's friendships are notable for providing insights into cross-category friendships along the lines of sexuality and race. Galupo's (2009) analysis of the friendship patterns of bisexual men and women suggest they experience more cross-sexual identity category friendships than either heterosexual or lesbian and gay persons, yet qualitative insights into these friendship experiences are hard to come by. Galupo's research suggests that biphobia is a pivotal concern around which friendship choices of bisexual men and women are structured. Gay men, like lesbians and heterosexuals, can be the perpetrators of biphobia, limiting the available opportunities to befriend bisexual men and women. Yet, as Galupo (2009) and others (Weinstock 1998) aver, the complex dynamics of friendships between bisexuals and gay men, lesbians and transgender persons might yield fascinating insights into how friendships can serve as sites for resisting heteronormative discourses on gender and sexuality. In short, much remains empirically open.

Cross-category friendships: Class, race and ethnicity

While the foregoing discussion on gay men's friendship patterns has touched upon the dynamics of sexuality and gender, other identifications also influence gay men's friendship patterns. Class, race and ethnicity are discussed here as examples. The study of the dynamic between class and friendship has received sustained interest among scholars (Allan 1977; Harrison 1998; Paine 1969; Walker 1994a, 1994b). Providing an overview of the research in this area, Spencer and Pahl (2006) find that the general trend emerging from the bulk of studies is the middle classes are more likely to include friends and colleagues into their personal networks than the working classes. The latter, it is often argued, tend to incorporate and rely more heavily on family. However, Spencer and Pahl are correct to point out that, as with research on friendship and gender, it is crucial to examine the studies that buck the prevailing trend.

One pertinent argument that we can extract from much of the research on class and friendship is that issues concerning the material and economic circumstances of people's lives come to the fore. Harrison's (1998) UK study of the friendships of a small group of middle-class women emphasises the importance of having money and time for actively fostering their social lives. Similarities among the women in terms of incomes and available time to invest in their friendships enabled the women to develop meaningful friendships centred on pleasure, identity construction, intimacy and support. Although working-class women do not feature in Harrison's study, Spencer and Pahl (2006) argue that members of the working classes might not have access to the material resources required to develop friendships that cross different contexts, such as the domestic and work spheres of life. Historians have also shown how many working-class men lacked the education and money of their middle-class counterparts in order to gain entry to the most exclusive all-male clubs and lodges that provided a 'safe' context for the middle classes to develop male friendships during the nineteenth century, as discussed in Chapter 1. Thus the tendency for people to befriend others similar to them in terms of class may be one that is partly shaped by economics. However, it is important not to overstate the differences between the friendship patterns of the middle and working classes. Class is a slippery and contested term, meaning many different things to different people, raising thorny methodological issues about how it is deployed in studies on friendship (Spencer and Pahl 2006). As such, there might also be variations in how middle- and working-class individuals understand the term 'friendship'; conceptual similarities and differences noted by some but crucially not all friendship researchers (Walker 1994a, 1994b; Spencer and Pahl 2006).

With the above in mind, it is noticeable that there is very little in the way of scholarly material that explores how identities that relate to class can shape gay men's experiences of and perspectives on friendship. Yet class is a pressing issue in the everyday lives of many gay men, not least because representations of gay identities and lives in popular culture are typically portrayed as middle-class, white and affluent (Shugart 2003; Seidman 2002). For working-class gay men, including those who occupy 'middle-class' well paid occupations, representations of gay men as wealthy, middle-class urbanites can be alienating (Barrett and Pollack 2005). Remarkably, little is known about how this might affect the friendship patterns of working-class gay men. For a start, working-class gay men may seek out other working-class gay men as friends with whom they can validate identities that relate to class and sexuality. Cross-category friendships, such as those between working-class gay and heterosexual men, may be desirable for constructing a sense of self in terms of class, although might be problematic since working-class masculinities have been heavily associated with expressions of homophobia both in and outside of work (Embrick et al. 2007; Connell 1995; Willis 1977). The friendship choices of working-class gay men may be influenced by other sets of personal priorities determined by, among other things, lower incomes. Noting this, Sinfield (1998: 272) asserts: 'if you are lower-class, gay lobbying and lifestyle are less convenient and may seem alien'. This is not to propose that a defining characteristic of being 'working-class' is a low income, since class is a fluid, contingent and multifaceted term. Rather, it is to suggest that some gay men are only too aware of the material consequences of being working-class, signified in how they can(not) develop and maintain friendships of their choosing.

In similar fashion, sexuality, race and ethnicity can intersect in dynamic ways that are particularly complex and sometimes problematic. Green's (2007) US study shows how African American, gay, middle-class, urban men can experience a conflicted 'push' out of black communities and families and a 'pull' into predominately white urban communities. Many of Green's study participants found themselves caught on the 'horns of a dilemma', alienated from African American communities because of their sexuality and unevenly integrated into white urban gay communities because of their race. As a result, many of the men experienced struggles and dilemmas negotiating sexual and racial identities, and found it difficult to develop supportive networks of gay friends. These findings reinforce earlier studies that document the inimical effects on black gay men associated with constructing and maintaining identities that relate to race and sexuality (Boykin 1996; Siegel and Epstein 1996). While race and sexuality can clash in ways that have a limiting effect on the friendship patterns of black gay men, some studies suggest otherwise.

Research on race, ethnicity and gay men's friendships is scant, but insights can be gleaned from studies that explore the wider canvass of black men's friendships. White's (2008) study of African American men's feminist friendships is exceptional in that respect. Taking as a starting point the idea that friendships between men and women can potentially help men to develop alternative ways of performing gender, White analyses the capacity of African American men's cross-sex feminist friendships for challenging normative ideals about black masculinities. Notably, White's study participants variously identify as 'profeminist', 'feminist' and 'antisexist', and attached much value to friendships with feminist women. Donny is one such figure who describes how his feminist female friends have 'kept a check' on his sexism, wanting him to develop caring, sensitive and creative gender practices in his everyday life. Many also spoke about the merit of intimate friendships with other men. Donny again:

> I gather men together from time to time to have support groups to talk about their lives and what it means to be a man in this society. Most of the groups are with Black men, so we also talk about racism and sexism and the various ways we've been set up by these systems. (2008: 145)

White's research is captivating because it demonstrates how race, ethnicity and sexuality can intersect within friendship in transformative ways, showing how men can exercise reflexivity and agency in developing alternative masculinities. As White (2008: 146) argues, such examples demonstrate that men are 'open to being different kinds of men'. Female feminist friends can certainly have a profound effect in that respect, as well as the gay, bisexual and transgendered men in White's study, who 'seemed more adept at transforming their relationships with men than straight men' (2008: 146). There is no reason to doubt that similar agency and creativity cannot be found in gay men's friendships in the workplace.

Summary

In summarising this chapter, I wish to tease out several points. First, I have argued that gay men's friendships can perform a variety of roles, which can be broadly understood twofold: as sources of support and as relational contexts for constructing new senses of identity and relating to others. In discussing the roles played by friendships in LGBT people's lives, we need to be aware of the practicalities of why friendships are formed in particular contexts and at specific moments in time. In other words, friendships have often been developed out of necessity, for negotiating the heteronormativity of everyday life. Second, I have reviewed the work of Giddens and others who suggest that LGBT people have become exceptionally skilled in the art of forming intimate relationships based on equality, mutuality and acceptance. Earlier in this chapter, I cautioned against overstating this claim, pointing to research that indicates how gay men's friendships can (re)produce heteronormative forms of relating to others. A Foucauldian perspective is of use here because it reminds us that people's friendship choices are constrained, mediated, unpredictable and contingent. Saying as much is not to dispute the creativity and agency demonstrated by some

LGBT people in negotiating friendships and other relationships that undermine heteronormative discourses on adult relationships. Rather, these 'practices of freedom', as they might be called, are situated since it is clear there are very real obstacles and barriers to establishing friendships that permit gay men to transgress the limits to how the self can be constructed. Thus it is important to explore the conditions within friendships that permit individuals to (re)produce new subjectivities. As previous research on gay men's friendship patterns shows, negotiating friendships is clearly gendered, classed and racialised, which is particularly significant for discussing gay men's workplace friendships in that respect.

All of this leads me to raise a final, more general point. Despite the insights provided by research into LGBT friendships, little of it pays close attention to LGBT people's friendships in the workplace. This is vexing for a number of reasons, not the least of them being that many of us spend much of our waking day performing work-related tasks within organisational settings. In the next chapter I discuss why organisations are important sites for investigating gay men's friendships, and why there is a general tendency among organisation studies scholars to understand workplace friendships as a bottom-line concern. The limiting effect of this approach for exploring gay men's workplace friendships is outlined.

Chapter 3
Gay Men's Friendships in the Workplace

Introduction

It is no coincidence this study is rooted in contemporary organisational life. Organisations, it is robustly argued, often privilege heterosexuality as 'normal' and 'natural' (Skidmore 2004; Hearn et al. 1989; Hearn and Parkin 1987; Pringle 2008). The concept of heteronormativity has been a powerful analytical device for scholars concerned with exposing how heterosexuality achieves normative status in everyday life. For Skidmore (2004), heteronormative discourse exists in many organisational contexts, linking a binary opposition of gender with that of heterosexuality and homosexuality. As such, heteronormativity impacts on both heterosexual and homosexual people's lives, since all manner of individuals may struggle to conform to a particular construction of heteronormativity within their workplace. For gay men, discourses that have in specific historical moments variously framed homosexuality as a sin, disease and psychological disorder have negatively influenced how they develop and sustain sexualities, relationships and identities in the workplace. This chapter explores the implications for gay men's workplace friendships by drawing extensively on organisational research.

To begin, the wider organisational literature on LGBT sexualities is reviewed, establishing a backdrop for exploring the opportunities and challenges gay men might face developing and maintaining friendships. Noting the shortage of discussion on workplace friendships in this field of scholarship, the organisational literature on workplace friendships is then considered. Here the managerial bias towards understanding workplace friendship as an organisational resource is viewed as an impediment to advancing knowledge about how workplace friendships are important to friends themselves. The paucity of research in this area gives rise to unanswered questions about the role and meaning of gay men's workplace friendships, questions addressed in the empirical chapters that follow.

LGBT sexualities, work and organisation

Scholarly literature on the workplace experiences of LGBT employees spans just over three decades (Hall 1989; Levine 1979; Ragins et al. 2003). Although much of the scholarship in this area is rooted within psychology, sociology and cognate fields such as social work and counselling, scholars have approached the topic of LGBT people's work lives from various directions. Early research conducted from the 1970s onwards focused almost exclusively on gay men and lesbians, exposing the multifarious employment discrimination practices directed at these minority groups (Levine and Leonard 1984; Levine 1979). For example, UK surveys published in the 1980s (Beer et al. 1983; GLC 1985) showed that many gay and lesbian workers, after revealing their sexual identity to colleagues, had lost their jobs and become the targets of homophobia. These studies also highlighted how gay men and lesbians experienced violence, unequal treatment in decisions about recruitment, promotion, dismissal, compensation and benefits. Policies in these areas were exposed as heterosexist, denying gay and lesbian employees access to benefits and rewards afforded to their heterosexual colleagues.

Further research on employment discrimination carried out in the 1990s repeated the grim findings published in previous studies (Burke 1993; Hall 1995; Taylor and Raeburn 1995; Woods and Lucas 1993). Furthermore, certain occupational and professional work sites were found to be more hostile towards openly gay and lesbian employees. Studies on gay men in the police services and armed forces provide vivid accounts of the deleterious effects of workplace homophobia on LGB employees (Burke 1993; Hall 1995). At the same time, research conducted by Humphrey (1999) revealed that employees known to identify as LGB could find themselves being pursued by their employers for their 'insider knowledge' on sexual orientation, for developing equality work in this area. However, Humphrey argues that the path to becoming 'out and proud' is rocky, since LGB employees who are 'out' to colleagues and service users also risk persecution, not least because of popular discourse that links homosexuality with paedophilia.

As such, it is important to understand employment discrimination on the grounds of sexual orientation against a wider cultural backdrop of public attitudes towards LGBT people. A recent British Social Attitudes Survey suggests that attitudes towards homosexuality are increasingly liberal, with 36% of respondents regarding homosexual acts as 'always' or 'mostly' wrong, down from 62% when the British Social Attitudes survey was first carried out, in 1983. Overall, while public opinion appears to be generally favourable, homosexuality remains a moral issue that attracts controversy and divides public opinion, making attitudes towards homosexuality uneven within and across different contexts (Weeks 2007). Research conducted over the last decade indicates that while attitudes towards LGBT employees are gradually improving (Colgan et al. 2007; Williams et al. 2009), LGBT employees still face and/or fear discrimination in the workplace (Bowring and Brewis 2009; Ryniker 2008; Burnett 2010). Taking a different perspective on this matter, Embrick et al. (2007) argue to the contrary, contending that attitudes toward lesbian and gay rights are not becoming more progressive; instead various methods of covert discrimination are increasingly being used to exclude gay men and lesbians from the workplace.

What are the implications of this for LGBT workplace friendships? Important as research on employment discrimination has been for examining multifarious practices in this area, very few studies throw light on the dynamic effects of discrimination on LGBT workplace friendships. Yet it stands to reason that within work contexts characterised as hostile to the presence of LGBT employees, friendships are likely to be difficult to establish. For one thing, in such work environments, LGBT employees are apt to be very selective about those to whom they disclose information about their sexuality and gender. The potential for negative repercussions is a concern, potentially deterring LGBT employees from developing close friendships with colleagues. Under these circumstances friendly relations might be an easier option, since they do not require the intimacy that develops from sharing personal information. Be that as it may, friendships can take root within harsh environments, and it is plausible that LGBT employees can befriend colleagues who are similarly disadvantaged by the heteronormative elements of some workplaces. Indeed, as argued in Chapter 2, the opportunity to use friendship as a source of support and understanding is not to be underestimated in situations where identities and selves are negotiated under duress. Investigating the supportive functions of LGBT workplace friendships, when individuals feel at odds with dominant organisational expectations and norms, requires further consideration of how LGBT employees disclose and manage identities in the workplace.

Identity disclosure and management

Expanding earlier research on employment discrimination, scholars have examined the contrasting ways in which LGBT people have managed their sexual and gendered identities in the workplace (Button 2004; Creed and Scully 2000; Schilt and Connell 2007; Ward and Winstanley 2003, 2005, 2006a; Woods and Lucas 1993). For some individuals being in the 'closet' remains the only viable option to avoid discrimination. Woods and Lucas's (1993) US study of gay male professionals is well cited in that respect. They identified three main strategies for managing a gay male identity in the workplace: (1) counterfeiting; (2) avoidance; (3) and integration. Counterfeiting refers to efforts made by gay men to 'pass' as heterosexual in the workplace, thereby giving out the 'wrong' message about their gay identity, which remains concealed. Strategies of avoidance include attempts to disclose as little personal information as possible, deflecting attention away from private matters such as sexuality. In contrast, strategies of integration refer to 'coming out' as gay in the workplace. Crucially, Woods and Lucas show that being 'open' about a gay identity varies, as some participants tried to minimise the visibility of their sexual identity while others sought to normalise it, by conforming to prevailing expectations and cultural norms around sexuality and gender. Subsequent research supports many of the findings in Woods and Lucas's (1993) study, especially regarding the costs and benefits of deploying specific identity management strategies (Bowring and Brewis 2009; Burnett 2010; Trau and Härtel 2004; Ward 2008).

What does this mean for gay men's workplace friendships? Part of my response to this question is that remaining closeted can be a barrier to building friendships and other relationships with colleagues that allow gay men to feel included in organisational life. For example, a published Stonewall report, titled *Peak Performance: Gay People and Productivity* (2008), revealed that many gay and lesbian employees felt coming out strengthened existing workplace relationships based on trust and honesty. While coming out can hasten the development of trust and intimacy in LGBT friendships, it is not a prerequisite for experiencing closeness in friendship. For instance, gay men serving in the military have often concealed their sexuality but this does not prevent them from forming lasting and meaningful friendships in work contexts (Kaplan and Ben-Ari 2000). Other studies, however, underscore the disadvantages of establishing and maintaining friendships at the same as adopting strategies to avoid coming out.

For example, some of the gay men Woods and Lucas (1993) interviewed indicated how difficult it was to be friendly or develop close friendships with colleagues within heteronormative work environments, especially when preoccupied with concealing their gay identities from colleagues. For one closeted gay man, his strategy to avoid disclosing his sexual identity involved compartmentalising his life into public-private domains, revealing as little as possible about his personal life to colleagues. This also entailed partitioning work friends from his close gay friends outside work, thereby maintaining largely one-way friendly relations with colleagues in order to steer conversations away from personal issues. However, as another man pointed out, 'after a while, somebody's not your co-worker, they're your friend' (1993: 40). Crossing over from the identity category of 'co-worker' to 'friend' was experienced as a dilemma for some of Woods and Lucas's study participants. Rather than risk coming out to a friend only to be rejected, several men opted to end their workplace friendships to avoid this potential outcome altogether. Vignettes like these are undeniably useful for gaining traction on the topic of gay men's workplace friendships, but they are gleaned from studies that do not focus directly on workplace friendships. As such, they do not permit us to burrow deep into the friendship experiences of these men or lesbian, bisexual and transgendered employees. However, they do remind us that work contexts vary in their potential to facilitate and constrain opportunities for gay men's workplace friendships, a point that warrants further discussion.

'Gay-friendly' organisations

What emerges from the majority of studies cited above is that while many LGBT employees anticipate discrimination, the way in which they might actually experience it is enormously varied. In other words, organisations are not uniformly heteronormative, with a number of LGBT employees experiencing little if any overt discrimination in the workplace on the grounds of sexual orientation. With the advent of the Employment Equality (Sexual Orientation) Regulations in December 2003, banning employment discrimination on the grounds of sexual orientation, and the growth of diversity/equality policies and practices on sexual orientation in the workplace, many organisations have made progress in developing LGBT inclusive work environments (Colgan et al. 2007, 2008, 2009; Giuffre et al. 2008; Raeburn 2004; Williams et al. 2009). Research by Colgan et al. (2007, 2009) in the UK, suggests that many LGB employees felt their employers were making considerable effort to make them feel included, cultivating work cultures wherein they could be open about their sexuality. Although not yet enforced, additional protection is forthcoming in the UK Equality Act (2010), which is due to replace existing legal protections covering employment. As such, there is talk of 'gay-friendly' organisations. As Giuffre et al. (2008: 255) note, a 'new type of workplace has emerged, called "gay-friendly": an organization in which LGBT people feel accepted'. Notably, gay-friendly organisations do not, as Colgan et al. (2008: 65) correctly point out, 'guarantee a working environment which engages with and embraces "sexual minorities" or prevents homophobic attitudes and treatment across the board'.

For example, Williams et al. (2009) found there were costs associated with forms of visibility that sustain an openly LGB identity in 'gay-friendly' workplaces. Some LGB employees were expected to look and act according to stereotypes that make LGB identities intelligible to others, such as one lesbian employee who displayed 'visibly hairy legs and multiple piercings' (2009: 38). Some participants, however, reported that working in 'gay-friendly' organisations helped them to 'feel normal'. Here the performance of normality in the workplace was equated with conservative politics, being in a monogamous long-term relationship, dressing 'professionally' and having children. While Williams et al.'s (2009) study findings bear out Seidman's (2002: 9) assertion, that an increasing number of gay men and lesbians understand homosexuality as a 'natural, good part of themselves' and 'openly participate in mainstream social life', they suggest also that the normalisation of gay and lesbian identities in 'gay-friendly' organisations is not commensurate with a decrease in the salience of homosexuality in the workplace. Put differently, the normative status of heterosexuality remains largely intact as an arrangement of power relations through which gay and lesbian employees must still negotiate modes of invisibility and visibility in their work lives. Constructions of 'normal' gay and lesbian identities in 'gay-friendly' organisations can result in a state of invisibility because becoming 'normal' means embracing conservative politics, monogamy and being 'professional' (Seidman 2002; Rumens and Kerfoot 2009), thus appearing indistinguishable from heterosexual identities. In that regard, 'gay-friendly' organisations can (re)produce forms of organisational heteronormativity that permit the expression of gay and lesbian sexualities, so long as they conform to normative constructions about how these employees should look and behave.

With increasing visibility in scholarly research, the concept of 'gay-friendly' organisations is an important focal point of academic analysis. Not least because the initiatives undertaken by employers to project themselves as 'gay-friendly' might have a bearing on the choices made by some LGBT employees about how to establish friendships and other types of workplace relationships, and with whom. It might be easier to establish friendships with heterosexuals and other sexual minority employees as well as with a wider range of colleagues, clients and consumers. It might also be the case that within some 'gay-friendly' workplaces, friendships can help LGBT employees to normalise; blending into dominant organisational culture and groups. Exactly what the implications of a process of normalisation might be for LGBT employees are unclear, as are insights into how social differences might be understood and negotiated within workplace friendships in organisational settings more accepting of LGBT employees. All these issues merit empirical investigation.

In sum, the growing number of studies that continue to expose organisations as heteronormative arenas, with mixed consequences for LGBT employees, is of significant concern. The heteronormative dimensions of work life may influence the formation of gay men's friendships, with consequences for how these relationships are used as a source of pleasure, intimacy, identity building and as a form of organising that can challenge prevailing organisational expectations about sexual orientation and gender. Because of this, and as I have suggested in the Introduction, it is helpful to know more about friendships in the workplace. It is to this literature that I will now turn.

Friendships in the workplace: Theoretical background

Scholarly interest in workplace friendships has been intermittent, but an interest in understanding the importance of informal workplace relations can be traced back to the Human Relations school of thought. In the classic Hawthorne experiments (Roethlisberger and Dickson 1939; Homans 1951), Elto Mayo and his associates discovered, among other things, what most employees at the time already knew about the significance of informal workplace relationships. That is informal relationships with colleagues are an important source of pleasure, and that informal communication and interactions between peers influence employee behaviour and performance. The Hawthorne experiments paved the way for a new wave of management theories, but they also helped give rise to later research that shed light on the importance of informal workplace relations (Dalton 1950; Katz 1968; Kram and Isabella 1985; Lupton 1963; Roy 1959). For example, British anthropologist, Tom Lupton, examined the social factors influencing outputs in British factories with the intention of building upon the Hawthorne studies. Lupton's study, *On the Shop Floor* (1963), is celebrated for its account of how workers moderate and resist management practices, and its sensitivity to the study of human relations exposes the potency of the workers' informal workplace relationships as a barrier to the fulfilment of management objectives. Here Lupton develops a more nuanced appreciation of the informality of workplace relations, compared with the management-orientated view of human relations evident in the Hawthorne studies.

Studies incorporated within the sociology of work provide particular glimpses into informal workplace relationships. For example, Goldthorpe et al.'s (1968) 'Affluent Worker' studies are widely cited as a classic sociological analysis of class and work at the Luton Vauxhall factories. In this study, factory workers often made distinctions between 'friends' and 'mates', with the latter being indicative of working relationships structured by and largely confined to the workplace. One key study finding is that working class employees opted to select friends from outside the workplace, a point that Morgan (2009) suggests finds resonance with wider sociological arguments about the concept of the 'privatised worker', a figure whose approach to work is guided more by money than it is by job satisfaction. Looked at in this way, Morgan (2009) interprets Goldthorpe et al.'s (1968) observation, that making friends was not a typical feature of factory life for many working-class workers, has a moral dimension to it, one that is structured by a concern that mates should not be friends.

From another perspective, the documented paucity of friendship making in the Affluent Worker studies may be explained by sociological arguments, such as those grounded in Marxist theory, which suggest friendship struggles to find form within rational-bureaucratic societies. Alan Silver's essay (1990) is regarded by many as an eloquent rejoinder to the Marxist and conservative tradition of emphasising the inimical effects of commercial society and labour processes on the nature of personal relationships. Deriving theoretical insight from the Scottish Enlightenment thinkers David Hume, Adam Ferguson and Adam Smith, Silver suggests that the rise of commercial society in the eighteenth century provided the conditions for a new and 'morally superior form of friendship' to emerge (1990: 1481). In this way, friendship is not understood as a response to the instrumental bonds of a market-orientated way of organising, but as a key moral dimension to a new liberal society that was seen to be emerging at the time. Put differently, in the context of social shifts towards impersonalised modes of administration and organising, friendship relies more on intimacy for developing interpersonal trust. In Silver's analysis, an ideal notion of friendship is defined against an impersonal public sphere, but also dependent upon it for its emergence as a relationship to be enjoyed for its own sake.

In reality, how far an idealised distinction can be made between an impersonal public sphere and a private realm associated with emotional ties with friends and family is questionable. Friendship is intimately bound up with work and not easily annexed to a private-private divide, giving us grounds to reconsider how easy or desirable it is for many employees to confine friendship making activities outside the workplace. There is no reason to doubt that friendship making is a common and important feature of many organisational settings, as research dealt with later in this chapter reveals (Fine 1986; Kakabadse and Kakabadse 2004; Sias et al. 2003; Parris et al. 2008). But it is striking that recent research on workplace friendships tends to focus less on the idea that friendships are of considerable significance for those involved, and more on the potential workplace friendships hold for supporting the fulfilment of organisational objectives.

Explaining this, Sias (2009: 9) argues that the bulk of organisational research on friendship is theoretically grounded in postpositivism. Postpositivist science views workplace friendships as 'real' entities that exist beyond human perception but remain observable from indicators such as communication between friends and friends' attitudes and behaviours. Typical, then, is the tendency for postpositivist research on workplace friendships to concentrate on predicting relationship quality, and how quality and quantity of friendships are related to observable organisational outcomes such as reduced turnover (Feeley et al. 2008), enhanced job satisfaction and productivity (Berman et al. 2002; Shah and Jehn 1993; Song 2006; Song and Olshfski 2008). It also acknowledges the importance of the context of friendship by determining how factors within and outside organisations influence friendship development, noting the consequences for organisations (Mao 2006). Thus Sias (2009), for example, suggests that postpositivist research has made a significant contribution to furthering knowledge on workplace friendships.

I agree with Sias about the merit of this segment of the literature, but I am also concerned that studies grounded in managerially biased forms of postpositivism are maintaining a strong grip on the field of study. As Sias (2009) and others (Grey and Sturdy 2009) aver, much research on workplace friendships can be identified as epistemologically and ontologically grounded in managerialism, since it privileges the interests of organisations. In this vein, studies on workplace friendships are focused on determining how these relationships can contribute to organisational interests. This is particularly apparent in how workplace friendships have been subsumed under other topics such as social networks, relations of trust, informal organisational relations, social capital and relationship management (Buchanan and Badham 1999; Burt 1992; Ferrin et al. 2006; Granovetter 1973). In these strands of literature the concept of friendship is often incorporated into more organisationally palatable notions, such as 'social networks', 'social capital' and so on. Looked at in this way, friendship is in danger of being lost altogether from the lexicon of workplace relationships. For example, Ferris et al. (2009) review the literature on workplace relationships without any explicit mention of friendship, despite outlining dimensions of positive dyadic workplace relationships that may be understood in terms of friendship. In their effort to respond to Ragins and Dutton's (2007) plea to bring workplace relationships to the foreground of organisation studies, friendship seems to have been buried in what Grey and Sturdy (2007: 169) call 'a language of social capital, network ties, and similar terms'.

This has a seriously limiting effect on the capacity of organisation studies researchers to explore organisational life in its fullest sense. For example, it can marginalise and exclude the voices of others on the subject, most particularly those involved in workplace friendships. Marks's (1998) re-analysis of the Hawthorne experiments illustrates this nicely, because it is motivated by a desire to recover the forgotten voices of the female workers who worked in the Relay Assembly Test Room. The women's friendships, based on intimacy, developed through group gatherings and sharing personal information, were completely overlooked by Mayo and his colleagues as a serious topic of study. This is ironic given the value attached to the Hawthorne studies for showing how informal workplace relations can affect workplace behaviour. The informality of work life is viewed almost entirely from a position that is concerned with its compatibility with organisational objectives. By lifting the voices of those forgotten or marginalised but active in developing and maintaining friendships at work, we can avoid treating workplace friendship as a sanitised and homogenised construct that primarily appeals to organisations.

Understanding workplace friendships

In defining workplace friendship, organisation studies scholars have borrowed selectively from sociology, philosophy and psychology. For example, research by Sias (2005; Sias et al. 2004; Sias et al. 2003; Sias and Cahill 1998) suggests workplace friendships are unique from other types of relationship in two respects. First, workplace friendships are said to be voluntary, unlike some other types of organisational relations such as those between managers and subordinates, which are typically imposed and formalised. There is value in the emphasis Sias (2009) and others (Markiewicz et al. 2000; Parris et al. 2008; Song 2006; Winstead et al. 1995) place on the voluntary nature of workplace friendship, since it draws from a philosophical tradition of defining friendship primarily as a relationship formed and sustained by human agency. Similarly, the credence Sias (2009) attaches to the personalistic focus of workplace friendship as a second unique feature of these relationships is compelling. The idea that work friends relate to each other in terms of personhood and not just as the occupants of specific work roles is, as others have noted previously (Suttles 1970), a defining quality of friendship. As Sias (2009) points out, the personalistic aspect of workplace friendship is evident in what activities work friends do together and what they talk about. For example, they might share personal information and problems that do not have any origin in or bearing on their work lives. They may see each other outside of work, blurring artificially constructed boundaries between what is understood to be the 'public' and 'private' spheres of life.

However, organisational researchers do not always display sensitivity to the fluidity of workplace friendships not just in terms of how they might criss-cross the public-private divide, but also how they might interconnect with other human relations. For instance, in a study aimed at managers, Berman et al. (2002: 218) suggest: 'While workplace friendship is decidedly different from acquaintanceship, it is also different from romance in two important ways: Romance involves a relationship between two individuals from which others ordinarily are excluded, and romance is also more intense than friendship'. From one perspective, this definition and others like it are discursively imbued with assumptions of stability and simplicity, such that the way in which workplace friendship is conceptualised makes it difficult to imagine how they intersect with other human relations. As argued in Chapter 2, friendships have often defied simple categorisation in numerous ways, not the least of them being the potential for friendships to be sexualised, familial and romantic in nature. There is no reason to doubt that some workplace friendships can be experienced as such, complicating the ways workplace friendships are constructed and ascribed meaning in organisational discourse.

Part of the problem is that definitions of workplace friendship are not always empirically informed from first-hand accounts. Cognisant of this and the shortcomings of using *a priori* definitions, Andrew and Montague (1998), writing on their own workplace friendship in a feminist vein, take an alternative approach that understands workplace friendship as a vital source of meaning for those to whom it is a central part of organisational life. Here, then, workplace friendships are understood in terms of support and care giving, and for fashioning gendered identities and selves. By adopting a more fluid stance on the matter of definition, workplace friendships are not essentialised by reference to a list of specific features or distinct qualities. As such, Andrew and Montague account for the dynamic quality of workplace friendships, which grants more leeway for exploring how friendships vary in their meaning and how they are configured in terms of relationship attributes. This paves the way for theorising workplace friendship as a process of organising that is unfixed, dynamic and contingent.

Friendship as a process of organising

As I have hinted at already, one way of understanding friendship as a process of organising is to examine the experiences of friends themselves, with a view to exploring how work and friendship are interrelated. Grey and Sturdy (2007) are helpful to this end, since they conceptualise friendship as an organising principle and as an organising element of work life. For example, as an organising principle, friendships can be the crucible in which organisations are formed. To illustrate, the authors refer to the computer company Hewlett Packard, supposedly founded through two friends working together in a garage. As an organising element, friendship may be an important aspect of organisational life, especially from the perspectives of employees. Grey and Sturdy adopt this approach to provide a welcome steer on extending the range of organisational analyses to include the experiences of those involved in friendships at work. Thus a 'folk concept' of workplace friendship is propounded for understanding how friendships are worked at within organisational settings.

Indeed, by grasping the idea of friendship as a process of organising we are obliged to explore how friendships are shaped by the social and organisational contexts in which they are negotiated. Although the literature on workplace friendship development is small, scholars have approached the subject from a variety of theoretical positions (Gibbons and Olk 2003; Olk and Gibbons 2010; Neilsen et al. 2000; Sias and Cahill 1998; Sias et al. 2003; Sias and Gallagher 2009).

From the point of view of this book, research that regards friendships as socially constructed is notable for its capacity to delve more deeply than postpositivist studies on how friendships are developed and maintained (Sias and Cahill 1998; Sias et al. 2003; Sias and Gallagher 2009).

In an important article, Sias and Cahill (1998) show how workplace friendship development is fashioned by an array of individual factors such as sharing a similar personality or sense of humour. Similarity may be perceived (sense of humour, personality) or observable in personal demographics such gender, age and ethnicity (Sias and Gallagher 2009). Contextual factors in the workplace related to friendship development include close proximity, technology, culture, jobs and tasks. These factors, cited by Sias and Cahill (1998) and others (Jehn and Shah 1997; Sias and Gallagher 2009), are critical to aiding the transition from work colleague to friend, of which physical proximity is particularly influential since it allows employees to get to know one another at work. As Sias (2009) remarks also, this is related to the tasks performed by employees. Where employees perform interdependent tasks they are more likely to strike up friendships than those who work independently (Shah 1998). Some jobs may curtail the opportunities for interaction, such as call handling roles in call centres. Here friendships may struggle to develop where employee interaction is often subject to intense managerial scrutiny and surveillance. However, this is not to say call centre employees cannot transcend the restrictions of these jobs to form supportive friendships, as Korczynski's (2003) study demonstrates.

While physical proximity is a key element in how friendships are developed and organised, the emergence of sophisticated communication technologies complicates this assumption (Chan and Cheng 2004; Henderson and Gilding 2004; Green and Singleton 2009). For example, developing workplace friendships online can overcome issues of geography, especially where physical proximity is either impossible or restricted. Comparing offline and online non-work friendships, Chan and Cheng (2004) found that offline friendships involved more interdependence, breadth, depth, understanding and commitment than online friendships. Striking, then, is that the qualities of both online and offline friendships improved as the duration of the relationship increased, with the differences between the two types of friendships diminishing over time. Applying this into the workplace, there is no reason to doubt that developing friendships online, particularly in work contexts characterised by virtual organisational structures and geographically dispersed teams, may hasten the growth of friendly relations into friendship.

Elsewhere studies show how hierarchical work cultures can restrict the types of friendship between employees. Friendships between managers and subordinates may be discouraged or difficult to establish, not least because of the potential accusations of favouritism or preferential treatment from third parties (Morrison 2004; Zorn 1995). Mao's (2006) study on friendship development among employees at different hierarchical levels supports this observation, since managers reported greater difficulties and fewer opportunities for friendship making than employees positioned at lower hierarchical levels. But this does not mean that friendships cannot transcend workplace hierarchies. In fact, future research is merited here, not least for thinking how friendships formed across organisational hierarchies may have the capacity to generate ideas for new ways of organising that are less hidebound to schemas of organising grounded in bureaucratic hierarchy.

On a slightly different tack, Sias and Cahill (1998) also note that workplace friendship development is influenced by people, relationships and events that occur within contexts outside the workplace. For example, they suggest important life events can help work friends to become closer. The death of a close relative, a change in marital status, becoming a parent, changing jobs and illness are examples of life events that can draw friends closer together, particularly through the exchange of support and the provision of intimacy. Through increased closeness, work friends may engage in socialising outside of work, blurring artificial boundaries between work and home. For some individuals, the moment at which a friend enters their private sphere of life is a significant marker of the strength of a friendship. They may acquire privileged knowledge about each other's domestic and personal circumstances, knowledge reserved only for those who can be trusted (Spencer and Pahl 2006).

At the same time, contextual factors outside the workplace may also impinge negatively on friendship development. Workplace friendships must vie with other relationships outside work, sometimes putting a strain on how much energy and time friends can allocate to the development and maintenance of friendships at work. For example, Parris et al. (2008) found that Australian managers experienced anger and frustration at not being able to devote enough time to maintain friendships at work for a variety of reasons, not the least of them being trying to reconcile personal commitments to existing relationships in the private sphere of life and friendships at work. Clearly, keeping up with friends at work and in other contexts can take its toll, with some individuals missing out on the benefits of having work friends. Under such strained circumstances, workplace friendships can deteriorate and fail.

Indeed, acknowledging friendship as a process of organising is to recognise that friendships can deteriorate. Drawing upon in-depth qualitative interview data, Sias et al. (2004) was one of the first studies to examine friendship deterioration at work. They identified a number of principal factors influencing the decline of workplace friendships including negative personality traits, distracting life events, conflicting expectations about what is appropriate behaviour between friends, the promotion of one friend into a position of higher organisational seniority and betrayal. The consequences of friendship deterioration for individuals can be devastating, resulting in emotional stress for the friends concerned.

Gender, sexuality and the construction of workplace friendships

From the discussion above, it can readily be seen that there is a potentially extensive array of factors that can influence how friendships are organised. But, given that this chapter is being written in the context of gay men's friendships, what of the influence of gender and sexuality in the process of organising in friendship? The literature on gender and workplace friendships is an obvious source of insight. Recent organisational research replicates study findings reported several decades earlier in the wider literature on friendship and gender (Markiewicz et al. 2000; Elsesser and Peplau 2006; Fritz 1997; Morrison 2009a; Sias et al. 2003), reviewed in Chapter 1. As Sias (2009) notes of this research, the tendency is to treat gender and sex as fixed variables. There have been attempts to depart from this position, using feminism and other critical theories to examine gender as dynamic and culturally constructed, encouraging an analysis of the subtle variations in friendship development within and between genders (Sias et al. 2003). Here workplace friendships are not just understood as socially constructed but also as relationships embedded within gendered power relations.

From this perspective, one issue concerns how friendships between and among men and women can (re)produce gendered inequalities. Previous research demonstrates that women are often at a career disadvantage when they are unable to penetrate male dominated networks of friendship (Elsesser and Peplau 2006; Hultin and Sczulkin 2003; Ibarra 1993; Kanter 1977). These and other studies highlight the advantage men derive from supportive homosocial networks of male friends (Ibarra 1992, 1995). Within some heterosexual male dominated organisations, men exhibit a preference for the company of other men, organising in ways that establish their differences from women (Cockburn 1991; Wharton and Bird 1996; Kanter 1977). These friendship networks can have a strong glass-ceiling effect. For example, Elsesser and Peplau (2006) examine the obstacles to the formation of cross-sex friendships in the workplace. For female employees, the difficulties establishing friendships with men can diminish their ability to access material resources, people of influence and opportunities for being mentored, helping to reinforce a glass ceiling on women's career advancement. For men, normative barriers to cross-sex workplace friendships are limiting in other ways. Findings reveal that male participants often harboured reservations about befriending gestures being misinterpreted as sexual advances, making cross-sex workplace friendships difficult to develop. Thus men and women can miss out on gaining new understandings and perspectives of the opposite sex, noted in some cross-sex workplace friendships (Sapadin 1988).

However, there is little evidence here of how men may be connected and supported differently in workplace friendship, such as through sharing common life events rather than work related goals. In simple terms, it is not always the case that men draw on each other with the aim of furthering careers or their domination over others (Kaplan 2006; Martin 2001). Furthermore, studies in this area examine how men's informal friendship networks can help heterosexual men to construct masculine identities and selves, leaving unanswered questions about how gay men might use workplace friendships to similar ends. However, Ashcraft (2000) provides an illuminating analysis of how women can organise workplace relationships in ways that engender support, care giving and intimacy. Framed by feminist critiques of bureaucracy, Ashcraft's study reveals how the efforts of one feminist organisation to cultivate a 'feminine' mode of organising, where relating intimately and personally was encouraged, produced unexpected results. In seeking to encourage personal relationships as a corrective to traditional masculine modes of bureaucratic organising, Ashcraft found that while many female study participants reported the benefits of developing close workplace friendships, they also claimed their friendships were subject to accusations of favouritism, from colleagues who viewed them with suspicion and jealousy. Striking, therefore, is that the organisation adopted a bureaucratic response to this situation by introducing policies that discouraged employees from friendship making.

Feminist-inspired studies including Ashcraft's (2000) are particularly illuminating of the gendered power relations that undergird the formation and maintenance of informal workplace relations. As such, workplace friendships are placed in a new light, one that draws attention to how as a process of organising, workplace friendships are enmeshed within organisational power relations. Crucially, exercising power relations within the workplace can be productive, helping individuals to craft alternative ways of relating. Following Ashcraft, we may explore similar potentialities within organisational settings that support the development of gay men's workplace friendships. It is quite possible that, like some women's friendships, gay men's workplace friendships might help advance the study of workplace friendships as a gendered and sexual process of organising. In this vein, Ashcraft (2000) reminds us that the outcomes of experimenting with new forms of relating at work are unpredictable, giving us reason to examine further how employees and organisations benefit from the development of workplace friendships.

The benefits of workplace friendships

In this final section I examine the documented benefits of workplace friendships, arguing that more research is warranted on what friends themselves claim are the rewards of being in friendship. The first point to make is that the literature on the benefits of workplace friendships is slanted towards what is beneficial for organisations. Lincoln and Miller's (1979) study is often cited in that respect, demonstrating how workplace friendships can enhance organisational decision-making by increasing opportunities for collaborative working and easing the flow of information between employees. Following this, recent research has concentrated on the relationship between workplace friendships and organisational performance (Berman et al. 2002; Markiewicz et al. 2000; Morrison 2004; Riordan and Griffeth 1995; Song 2006; Song and Olshfski 2008; Francis and Sandberg 2000).

For example, Song's (2006) survey-based study of workplace friendships in Korea shows that workplace friendships can positively affect employees' attitudes towards work and job satisfaction, thereby increasing organisational productivity (see also Song and Olshfski 2008; Sias and Cahill 1998; Sias et al. 2003; Winstead et al. 1995). Similarly, Berman et al. (2002) surveyed managers and chief administrative officers in the US about the risks and advantages of workplace friendships, finding that while respondents expressed reservations about the potentially negative dimensions to workplace friendships, the majority felt they helped employees complete routine work tasks. Such positive outcomes were perceived to be associated with friendship rewards for organisations, observable in reduced levels of employee absence and turnover. Feeley et al. (2008) claim also that workplace friendships can help to reduce employee turnover. They found employees with large numbers of friends rather than those with few close work friends were more likely to stay with an organisation. Having large numbers of work friends meant greater availability of support and companionship at times of need, helping to make work life bearable for employees and reducing turnover for organisations.

In light of this body of evidence and from a managerial perspective, workplace friendships are constructed as organisational resources worth utilising. This is not the whole story, however. Workplace friendships have been incorporated within a small but important literature on 'problematic workplace relationships' (Fritz and Omdahl 2006; Morrison and Wright 2009). Here, then, workplace friendships are constructed as hotbeds of favouritism, making it difficult for friends to treat each other objectively (Morrison and Nolan 2007). Another concern is that employees might spend more time maintaining their friendships than toiling in their work roles. Workplace friendships require maintenance in order to survive and activities like chatting, exchanging information and socialising are vital to that end (Allan 1989). The fear for some employers is that work friends might prioritise their commitments to maintaining friendships over their obligations to their employer (Berman et al. 2002; Morrison and Nolan 2007; Nolan and Morrison 2009; Zaleznik 1997). Managerially biased perspectives in this segment of literature regard workplace friendships as having a distracting effect on employees' job performance, prompting some commentators to suggest that 'friendship' at work is a likely euphemism for fraternisation, and an idle form at that (Eisenberg 1994). Adopting a similarly managerialist tone, Morrison and Nolan (2007: 40) conjecture: 'just how much actual work is being done' when friends are getting 'too much of a good thing'?

Responding to organisational complaints about workplace friendships, academics and business press pundits have provided guidance to help employers 'manage' friendships in ways compatible with organisational performativity. For example, Berman et al. (2002) propose a number of 'workplace strategies' for managing the downsides of workplace friendships, such as ensuring managers avoid favouritism towards friends, alerting managers to the dangers of clique forming in the workplace and informing employees that loyalty to the organisation comes above friendship. But discussions on managing workplace friendships assume that the interests of friends and managers are compatible, giving rise to an important question: what are the benefits of workplace friendships for friends themselves?

Sias (2009) rightly points out that much of the literature on this matter still contains a managerial bias, since it articulates the benefits of workplace friendships for individuals in terms of 'social capital'; namely, the networks and memberships that individuals can use to advance their careers. Social capital is a concept of interest to organisations insomuch as the benefits individuals may derive from being in networks of informal ties can potentially advantage the organisation. Previous studies show how membership of organisational friendship networks can allow individuals to acquire material resources and cultivate influence from other organisational members, helping them to get ahead at work (Antcliff et al. 2007; Kennedy 2004; Podolny and Baron 1997; Seibert et al. 2001). The social support provided by work friends can also influence the formation of positive work-related attitudes and behaviours (Riordan and Griffeth 1995; McGuire 2007; Morrison 2009b). Taken together, these examples show how individuals benefit from workplace friendships in ways that are also helpful for improving organisational efficiency and productivity.

It is critically important to acknowledge that workplace friendships can produce benefits for individuals that do not directly advantage organisations. This aspect of workplace friendship is an equally important topic for analysis. The simple pleasure of being in friendship is a significant benefit, even if this is rarely examined by organisational scholars. Being connected to a friend can be a source of joy and fun, evident in the sociable interactions friends engage in and enjoy for no other reason than wanting to socialise at work (Pettinger 2005). While fun and humour at work are increasingly being colonised by managerialist perspectives and practices (Westwood and Rhodes 2007), the role of friendship for facilitating fun and humour between friends is vital to how friendships are sustained as life affirming relationships. Similarly, workplace friendships can be a source of intimacy, with some workplace friendships developing erotic and romantic elements. For example, some male soldiers in Kaplan's (2006) study of men's friendships in the Israeli army, experienced friendship as an intensely emotional and sometimes erotic relationship. These friendship ties could be more intimate than relationships with family and friends outside the workplace, helping some of the soldiers to not only cope working in an agonistic work context, but also to construct identities and selves that relate to work and personhood. These benefits of being in workplace friendships come to the fore when these relationships are understood as contexts for experiencing the extremes, both positive and negative, of what it is to be human.

However, organisational research on the identity building role of workplace friendships is rare. Returning to Andrew and Montague's (1998) personal account of their workplace friendship within a UK university is useful. They describe an academic work context in which men's identities and men's practices are privileged. As such, Andrew and Montague use friendship to organise consciously as 'women' and as 'feminists', in order to provide each other with the emotional and practical support required in sustaining organisational feminist and female identities. The process of identity development in friendship can be precarious, sometimes subject to tensions and antagonisms arising between friends and from people outside the friendship. For example, Andrew and Montague discuss how their friendship has come under fire from male colleagues, some of whom have found it threatening and exclusive. Yet their friendship provides opportunities to critically reflect on the objectionable criticism from onlookers, allowing them to sustain identities and workplace relationships that are at odds with prevailing gendered organisational expectations about women. In this study, workplace friendships are sites of sexual and gender politics insomuch as they can provide women with valuable opportunities to contest gender norms.

Summary

This chapter has drawn widely on organisational research in order to establish a context for examining gay men's workplace friendships. In the first part of this chapter, I have been at pains to convey how organisations can be understood as heteronormative, raising questions about how, why and with whom gay men might develop and maintain workplace friendships in these organisational settings. While the literature on sexual minority employees is short on insight into the role and place of friendship in LGBT people's work lives, I have delved into a parallel literature on workplace friendships. While the subject of workplace friendship now commands an engaging literature, it too contains next to nothing on the workplace friendships of LGBT employees. Moreover, research on workplace friendships tends to be framed by a broad set of rationalist and managerialist discourses, privileging organisational interests and understandings of the role placed by friendship in the workplace. A small number of researchers, typically those for whom workplace friendships are socially constructed and important in their own right, provide alternative perspectives on the role and meaning of workplace friendships (Ashcraft 2000; Andrew and Montague 1998; Kaplan 2006). Many studies in this strand of literature have yet to run more deeply into debates on LGBT sexualities, but they demonstrate that a critical focus on the topic is warranted, so we may view organisational life as encompassing the full gamut of human experience. As such, the empirical chapters that follow take an important step towards enriching existing research in that respect.

Chapter 4
Constructing Friendships in the Workplace

Introduction

For the gay men in this study, workplace friendships were often constructed as important sources of support, intimacy and pleasure. Without exception, study participants acknowledged the value of work friends as key providers in these areas, and for some participants workplace friendships had accrued significance as some of the most emotionally intense relationships in their lives. Indeed, what made friendship a 'special' relationship at and outside work for all study participants was that it had to be established. The familiar saying 'you can choose your friends but not your family' frequently cropped up in the interview transcripts as a way of representing friendship as the exemplary chosen relationship. Similarly, since the activity of paid work was an 'economic necessity' for almost all study participants, friendships were an important feature of gay men's workaday lives. For some participants, contact with work friends was more regular and frequent than contact with friends, family and partners outside work. That being said, it is crucial to state that this does not automatically make work friends important. Not all workplace friendships described to me were entered into for the same reasons or occupied a central place in participants' everyday lives. Analysis of the interview data shows that the place of workplace friendship in the lives of gay men varies, influenced by all manner of people, events and relationships as well as by the structure and nature of participants' jobs and workplaces.

As such, this chapter examines how participants organise ties of friendship made at work within the context of their everyday lives, revealing how these friendships are negotiated and embedded. Some interview accounts suggest that workplace friendship can be of central importance to some men while for others it occupies a secondary position behind relationships with partners and kin. Insights into the changing circumstances of participants' lives and their effects on workplace friendships are provided throughout the empirical content of this book, but they are given particular attention in the first part of this chapter. Following this, attention is paid to how the structure and nature of jobs and work environments can influence the development of gay men's friendships. Of interest, here, is how gay men develop friendships within organisational settings understood and experienced as heteronormative. Strategies to overcome obstacles to friendship making within these work contexts are examined before moving to address the issue of how gay men's friendships can (re)shape organisational relations. The last part of this chapter examines how gay men's friendships might perform such a role, noting the opportunities and limitations for (re)constructing 'gay friendly' work contexts.

Organising workplace friendships within everyday lives

Almost all study participants noted that work friends entered into and disappeared out of their lives as they changed jobs, places of work, following arguments or spells of little or no contact. At the same time, there were plenty of accounts of how work friends had become firmly established as significant others who could be relied upon for intimacy, fun and support. Examples of these friendships could be characterised by their capacity to endure, sometimes for years after one or both friends had moved into different jobs. Surviving the test of separation, which typically required friends to make an effort to stay in touch, some workplace friendships continue to grow and deepen, with many participants refusing to label them as 'workplace friendships', since they no longer depended on an organisational context to develop (Sias and Cahill 1998). Some participants reminisced fondly about friendships that had not survived, such as when one or both individuals had moved to another job. Equally, some casual workplace friendships were appraised positively as sources of fun and sociability, helping participants to improve the quality of their work lives. These variations notwithstanding, a strong impression running throughout all these accounts is that workplace friendships have to be established (Allan 1989). As argued in Chapter 3, when friendship is regarded as a process of organising (Grey and Sturdy 2007; Sias and Cahill 1998), attention is demanded to how events, contexts and circumstances at any given time in people's lives open and foreclose opportunities for friendship making. While it is self-evident to state that the work environment is the obvious setting for making workplace friendships, it is critical to acknowledge that individuals organise these relationships within a wider network of relationships (Spencer and Pahl 2006). Study findings revealed that friendships in the workplace may compete with commitments made to people in other relationships outside work.

For example, when jobs and careers are given primacy over friendship, work friends may be of little importance as intimates but extremely valuable as sources of support and influence for advancing careers. During the years directly after Grant graduated from university, making workplace friendships was the 'last thing on [his] mind'. As Grant explained, it was never his intention to stay with one employer for more than 'eighteen months', so there 'seemed little point' making the effort to form 'close friendships' with colleagues. Grant relied upon university friends and members of his family for intimacy and forms of emotional support, but established a network of informal and friendly ties at work that enabled him to facilitate mentoring arrangements and access sources of support to further his career.

Other participants found that when work commitments intensified, some workplace friendships suffered as a result of their inability to maintain regular contact (Parris et al. 2008). Working long hours, for example, was cited by Rupert as having a damaging effect on friendships at work, since time and energy to engage with work friends was in short supply. In these situations, some participants said they sought comfort and support from well-established friends outside work as well as family members and partners. These relationships seemed more likely to withstand periods of intermittent contact and neglect. Indeed, some but crucially not all participants suggested that workplace friendships were of secondary importance to relationships with kin or (civil) partners. For example, Denton commented that, unlike his long-term partner, his friends outside and at work did not occupy a central position in his life. That said, Denton had experienced emotionally close workplace friendships in the past but had ended them at his partner's behest. Jealousy can take its toll on friendship, especially when friendship vies with other intimate relationships. Denton was one of several gay men who confessed, with some apparent disappointment, that their partners had grown jealous of them spending 'too much time' socialising with work friends. On a slightly different tack, several participants described having been brought up to distrust friends in general. Finlay's account of his family and friendships exemplifies this point fully.

Finlay grew up in an environment where family members were regarded at once as kin and friends. In this context, where immediate family members are recognised as friends, friendships with non-family members tended to be bathed in a negative light. Finlay explains:

> My mother was suspicious of friends. She never had any herself because family always came first. She thought family was the first point of contact for intimacy … going outside of the family for that kind of thing was frowned upon because friends were seen as strangers … as outsiders that couldn't always be trusted. It was a case of blood being thicker than water.

As the interview extract suggests, to seek intimacy in friendship might be understood as a failure in the capacity of the family to deliver emotional support. Arguably, those who regard the family as an unparalleled source of intimacy, trust and love, fail to appreciate how friends can occupy a similar position to family along these lines (Spencer and Pahl 2006; Weeks et al. 2001). For some considerable time, Finlay admitted that friendships did not figure centrally in his life. However, leaving home, going to university and entering the world of paid work changed Finlay's perspective on the potential role and position friends at and outside work could perform and occupy. For Finlay, one effect of moving hundreds of miles away from home to work in an unfamiliar area quickly was to rethink how friends might be useful sources of support. Similarly, when Alex left behind his family and a well-formed network of friends to start work in a new job, he found himself 'alone' in a 'strange city'. Commencing work in an advertising firm that employed large numbers of graduates provided Alex with a 'golden opportunity', as he put it, to befriend people similar in age, outlook and education. As with Finlay, workplace friendships provided Alex with practical and emotional support, information about his new surroundings and opportunities to socialise.

For many participants the place of workplace friendships could be equal to or exceed that accorded to friends, partners and family outside work. In these examples, participants had actively negotiated the blending of work and personal relationships (Bridge and Baxter 1992), with some claiming that they could no longer distinguish work from friendship, and friendship from some other intimate personal relationships. In these accounts, workplace friendships appear to bleed into other relationships in ways understood and experienced by participants as something 'special', implying a strengthening of the ties that connect friends. In these examples, workplace friendships overlapped with sexual relations, exhibited family-like qualities and contained romantic elements. Detailed illustrations of some of these friendships are provided in Chapters 6 and 7. Of course, not all workplace friendships run into other types of relationships, as some participants tried to draw distinct positions for friends, family and colleagues to occupy.

One such participant is Gordon who, when he started work as a paramedic, tried to incorporate 'distance' in his interactions with colleagues as a way of 'making a good impression' to management by 'maintaining professional relationships at work'. This strategy did not preclude opportunities for being friendly, especially within a team-orientated work environment where trust and support from colleagues is pivotal to the success of paramedic interventions. Colleagues with whom Gordon is friendly are labelled 'mates'. Constructing a boundary between home and work is crucial here for being able to designate individuals as 'mates', since Gordon does not socialise with 'work mates' outside work and these friendly work based relationships appear to lack the intimacy that his friendships outside work seem to exhibit. Work mates are not people with whom Gordon discloses a great deal of personal information but, unlike 'colleagues', they are people with whom he can 'share a joke', 'have a laugh' and rely on for 'practical support' to get a job done. But they are not positioned as confidantes or providers of intimacy, as are some of his friends and family members outside work. Making these distinctions can become harder and harder as the circumstances of people's lives change (Spencer and Pahl 2006). While this might be a self-evident point to make, it supports the argument that there is no one immutable form of friendship. All I wish to suggest here is that workplace friendships are socially constructed, as Gordon's account indicates, evident in how friendship norms are used to notionally separate friends, colleagues and family, and the roles assigned to them in specific contexts. In this example, friendship is discursively constructed as a private pleasure, perpetuating a stereotype about friendship as a relationship of the private sphere of life.

Finally, study findings showed that initial impressions of the friendship potential of the workplace are also coloured by participants' friendship preferences. The loneliness some participants said they experienced after moving from one city, town or village to another was due, in large part, to feeling unconnected with other LGBT people. When Kris moved from Liverpool to the south of England to start work as an administrator at a university, his workplace did not seem a likely source of gay friendships. Regardless of how accepting many heterosexual colleagues were about his sexuality, Kris wanted to make friends with other gay men with whom he could establish a broad sense of common identity. While heterosexuals can provide gay men with rewarding friendship experiences (Fee 2000; Tillmann-Healy 2001), there is ample evidence to show that gay men appear most at ease in friendships with other gay men (Nardi 1999; Weeks et al. 2001; Sullivan 1998). While Kris went on to make some important friends out of several female colleagues, discussed in Chapter 6, workplace friendships with other gay men remained elusive, reminding us that some work settings contain particular obstacles and barriers to gay men's friendships.

In summary, the discussion so far has started to highlight the variation in how gay men organise their workplace friendships. Significantly, intimate, trusting and loving relationships can take place at work and are not just confined to biological kin or friends outside work. However, what emerges from the analysis above is a sense of how workplace friendships, although established through choice, are influenced by the contexts in which they are embedded. Here, then, it is critical to examine the opportunities and obstacles to gay men's friendships in the workplace.

Opportunities and obstacles to gay men's workplace friendships

Interview accounts provided numerous insights into how organisational settings influenced the formation of gay men's friendships. As suggested in Chapter 3, the heteronormative features of many organisational contexts shape the circumstances under which gay men can develop friendships, and this was borne out in the study data. Before commenting on this, it is important to acknowledge that all manner of things such as patterns of work, the duties associated with performing specific jobs, proximity and organisational architecture affected the availability of opportunities for friendship making at work. Some of these examples warrant illustration not least because gay men's workplace friendships are not uniformly influenced by organisational heteronormativity. Indeed and at the risk of stating the obvious, gay men's workplace friendships are no different to other people's workplace friendships in that respect. Accordingly and in the interest of not channelling the empirical analysis always to issues of sexuality and gender, it is wise to adopt a wider perspective, for a more rounded picture of the opportunities and obstacles to gay men's workplace friendships.

For example, consistent with previous scholarly research (Kakabadse and Kakabadse 2004; Rawlins 1992; Sias and Cahill 1998), interviewees who experienced shift work instead of 'normal office hours' reported finding it particularly hard to strike up workplace friendships. One explanation provided by Douglas, a paramedic, was that it could be difficult getting to know colleagues when face-to-face contact was irregular. As Sias and Cahill (1998) argue, a key transition phase in the development of workplace friendship involves moving from friendly relations to friendship. Crucial at this stage of development is proximity and the disclosure of personal information. Variable shift patterns can make it hard for people to get to see each other at and outside work, impairing the growth of workplace friendship in the early stages. However, some workplace friendships, typically those already established, are able to weather periods of neglect. These workplace friendships are able to 'tick over', as Douglas put it, because a lot of the building work has already taken place. But this is not always the case. Prolonged periods of neglect can cause work friends to drift apart, as Gordon, another paramedic working shifts, pointed out.

In contrast, Ciaran recalled a former period of employment as a call centre supervisor. In that role, Ciaran worked 'very unsociable hours' but it was during the night shifts when informality presided. At these times, Ciaran made friends with the 'night people', as he called them, those individuals who regularly worked night shifts. During the 'small hours', when call volumes were at their lowest and fewer supervisors present, Ciaran found there was plenty of time to converse with friends, a 'luxury' unavailable to 'day shift' workers. With regular opportunities to spend time together in the workplace, Ciaran found that informal relations with some colleagues, characterised as 'light-hearted friendliness', developed into relationships described in terms of trust and intimacy. Yet Ciaran, like Douglas, acknowledged the problems trying to socialise outside of work. Ciaran's call centre friendships were tightly framed by the nocturnal work context in which they were initiated, since Ciaran and his friends were often 'too tired' to socialise (especially through shared activities) during the day.

Organisational hierarchy appeared also to influence opportunities for friendship making. Some participants expressed reservations about workplace friendships crossing organisational hierarchies, especially by participants employed in managerial roles (Morrison and Nolan 2007). For instance, Steve, employed as head of department within a university, felt uneasy about a friendship he developed with one of his female subordinates. Aware of his growing 'fondness' for this particular friend, Steve began to wonder if he could remain 'impartial' and 'objective', qualities he said were expected of him as a manager (Morrison 2009b; Mao 2006). Blending the duties of friendship with those of work in that respect can be challenging (Bridge and Baxter 1992), particularly as friends often expect to be given preferential treatment. Steve was acutely aware of the potential for onlookers to accuse him of favouring his friend over his other subordinates, but he admitted he was unsure as to how to 'manage this risk'. Other participants, who sensed their loyalties being torn, opted to 'cool down' their friendships by reducing the time they spent with friends outside and at work, focusing more on work-related issues or, in some cases, letting the friendship fade through lack of maintenance. However, it is important to state there was a general consensus among participants that friendships could transcend the problems associated with organisational hierarchy, but it would require constant vigilance and negotiation on the part of friends themselves.

Within organisational settings where hierarchies between employees were much flatter and less rigidly demarcated, participants described informal work cultures that appeared conducive to friendship making. Some organisations appeared keen to develop informal relations between employees, with several investing resources in order to help employees get to know each other through team away days, providing leisure facilities, funding gym membership and encouraging employees to socialise outside work, as illustrated by Grant's employer, a media company in London. Endorsing his employer's efforts to cultivate a 'climate of friendliness in the office', Grant felt there were benefits to being able to befriend at work:

> There is an efficiency in getting on with people at work because you automatically become better at your job if you have good friends ... because you can ask people and they will help you out, it's something dramatically overlooked by a lot of people.

For Grant it pays to have 'good friends' at work, but the organisation also benefits. Grant notices that job performance is enhanced by using work friends as sources of support. Other participants provided extreme examples to illustrate this observation.

For example, Finlay recalled working at a small record label in the music industry, an experience which he affectionately described as 'a non-stop party'. Employed in an office characterised by a 'work hard play hard culture', with music constantly playing in the background and drugs and alcohol freely available, Finlay felt the 'office was a party' for most of the time. From one perspective, this exerted a positive influence on being able to construct workplace friendships. Finlay comments: 'if you get drunk and take drugs with your colleagues, you get to know people very well because it's quite intimate'. For Finlay, the shared risk taking of drug use and the subsequent partying brought people together, with a 'real blurring of what was business and what was social, which felt really good'. The blurring of the public-private spheres of life seemed to open up opportunities for friendship making, since many employees frequently worked late, treating the office as an extension of their home for socialising, eating, drinking and entertaining. Working in close proximity and for prolonged periods of time can help employees to develop friendships (Sias and Cahill 1998). Still, in an office environment described by Finlay as a 'pressure cooker of emotional highs and lows', many workplace friendships did not endure since people often left the organisation, struggling to 'cope with the come downs from drug taking and the non-stop partying'. Despite or because of the constant revelry the record label was successful, producing a number of hit records.

Lastly, organisational architecture merits discussion as an illustration of how workplaces open and foreclose opportunities for befriending. For example, many participants had experience of working in open plan offices, with several finding it difficult to informally socialise with colleagues when they were sat near to their managers and colleagues who might criticise them for spending too much time away from their desks. Be that as it may, corridors, canteens, toilets, offices, kitchens and social areas were often mentioned as important meeting places for people to gather and socialise, exchange news and gossip. Impromptu or planned encounters in these areas helped participants to strike up friendly relations and friendships with colleagues. Those participants for whom the amenity of a single occupancy office afforded them privacy to get on with work or catching up with friends undisturbed, sometimes found these offices hindered friendship making. For instance, Michael works in a university where academic staff from different subject groups are scattered across three floors in single occupancy offices, with few communal areas for socialising. Michael experienced this as a barrier to friendship making, since the 'monastic' feature of the building's architecture coupled with a 'work at home culture', meant meeting colleagues on a regular basis was often difficult.

Notably, electronic forms of communication were frequently cited by participants as solutions to overcoming some of the drawbacks of working in open plan or single occupancy offices, remote organisational outposts and at home. For example, email was considered an effective way of interacting with people in other parts of office buildings as well as in other geographical areas in the UK and other countries. Some participants reported finding it easier to enter into dialogue with colleagues online since they could take time to edit and rephrase emails before sending them. Other participants preferred emailing and chatting online to face-to-face conversations, feeling it occasioned opportunities to be more confident, humorous and even flirtatious, potentially hastening the development of closeness with another individual. In these interview accounts, the necessity of physical proximity for friendship development was removed or reduced. Indeed, many participants suggested that communication technologies had enlarged rather than restricted the scope for making workplace friends (Sias and Cahill 1998), with some participants developing virtual workplace friendships with individuals geographically located in other parts of the UK and abroad. Similarly, several participants used internet applications on their mobile phones to establish contact with other gay men in the workplace with mixed results in terms of friendship, discussed later in this chapter.

In summary, the discussion above shows how the nature of different organisational settings can influence the development of gay men's friendships. As suggested previously, gay men's workplace friendships are not unique in their susceptibility to the influence of things like job tasks, physical proximity, communication technology, and so on. While further insights into these issues are possible, I shall develop the point that gay men experience certain barriers to workplace friendship development in particular ways.

Constructing friendships within heteronormative work environments

As argued in Chapter 3, organisations are places in which the assumption of heterosexuality tends to loom large. Oddly the idea that work organisations are, in differing ways, heteronormative is rarely if ever mentioned in the literature on workplace friendship. Heteronormativity can affect friendship development between and within men and women (Elsesser and Peplau 2006), and it is not something that has a unique effect on gay men's friendships. Yet, as the study data reveals, the influence of organisational heteronormativity on gay men's workplace friendships can be profound and complex.

The first point worth making is that sexuality is not an easily observable category of individual difference. One implication of the 'invisibility' of sexuality is that, against the assumption of heterosexuality in many organisations, it can be hard for LGBT employees to connect with each other. Put differently, gay men might not be any better placed than their heterosexual colleagues in being able to identify LGBT colleagues. It is not always straightforward to interpret correctly the signs and clues that some LGBT workers provide about their sexuality (Skidmore 2004). Far from being uniform, the way in which some gay men choose to openly participate in work life varies widely. Indeed, while all study participants were open about their sexuality at work, they were not 'out' to all colleagues and friends at all times in every situation. Most were very selective about how and to whom they disclosed their sexual identity, often making 'coming out' decisions based on an assessment of which individuals they felt ought to be privy to such information (Ward and Winstanley 2003; Woods and Lucas 1993). As indicated by the interview data, it was uncommon to find decisions about non(disclosure) being motivated by self-loathing, a sense of shame or a fear of discrimination. Rather, opting to 'come out' was often stimulated by a desire for closeness or by a wish to acknowledge the strength of an existing bond of friendship. These are personal issues, requiring different approaches in work contexts experienced as heteronormative.

For instance, James began his career in the caravanning industry working in a small caravan showroom. His boss was described as 'homophobic', a man who would 'think nothing' of telling 'homophobic jokes' to staff', making James feel 'nervous' and 'vulnerable' about disclosing his sexuality to colleagues. Whilst working for this company, James developed a close friendship with a colleague, called Lester. James was not out to Lester but suspected he might also be gay, admitting he was at the time 'too afraid' to ask, in case Lester reacted negatively. This situation carried on for nearly two years, during which time James found out that Lester had a long-term male partner:

> Lester hadn't come out to me, but I found out that Lynton was his partner ... Lynton used to ring up the office to speak to Lester, using different names so no one would suspect he was seeing Lester. Then one time he rang every day, for like three weeks, each time giving a different name ... it was crazy. And then

he rang and, without thinking, I just said: 'I know who you are, don't worry about it'. Shortly after this we came out to each other. Once we both knew that the other one was gay, it was like something else to keep us together as friends.

James and Lester have remained 'close friends', despite leaving the company to work in different organisations. While this friendship has what James described as a 'happy ending', his experience of befriending in a homophobic work culture is telling of how challenging it can be for gay men to connect with each other in the workplace. In this example, the homophobic dimension to James's work environment shapes how James and Lester manage their sexual identities, opting to avoid coming out to each other for some considerable time. Yet in difficult work contexts, strong friendships can emerge when employees turn to each other for support and sense making (Sias and Cahill 1998; Korczynski 2003). In contrast to James, other participants told stories of how the process of coming out and friendship development had been hastened in workplaces hostile towards gay employees.

Michael recalled a recent period of employment as a manager within a social services department. During this time he was bullied by a group of female colleagues. Michael told me how his female peers regularly made jokes and insults about gay men, and often asked him if he was 'queer', usually within earshot of clients and other staff employed in the office. The relentless taunting undermined his confidence and, like a few other interviewees who told similar stories, became so unbearable that Michael quit his job before being able to secure another form of employment. In these work contexts, where management turned a 'blind eye' to workplace homophobia, the chance of being able to establish friendships might be negligible. Michael's account begs to differ:

> The only friendship I ever developed was with my line manager. As it happens she was being bullied by the same staff that were bullying me, but for different reasons. Strange really, because Maud was not the sort of person I'd say was ideal friendship material. She was old enough to be my mum and I didn't think we had anything in common. But we were in this shitty situation together at work ... literally thrown together and we were drowning in all the crap. We'd meet up for supervision and just talk about it rather than work itself ... I quickly came out to her because it just felt right to do so, because she had revealed a lot of personal information about herself, and I felt entirely comfortable telling her. We became close very quickly. We looked for any opportunity to meet up for coffee, lunch, whatever really. We needed each other for support.

Like those workers who develop friendship ties with colleagues that help them to improve the insufferable nature of their work lives (Westwood 1984; Pollert 1981), so Michael and Maud forge a friendship to the same end. As Michael's interview extract reveals, the simple pleasures that workplace friends may enjoy together, like meeting up for coffee and lunch, hold additional significance as occasions to off-load negative emotions and confide in each other about their worries and fears. Accounts of workplace friendships in homophobic work environments were rare, but there was a general consensus among participants that spotting potential friends who share a common but 'invisible' sexual identity is often challenging. While some participants felt they were 'drawn' to gay men in the course of their workaday lives, others adopted a less passive approach to friendship making.

For example, some gay men claimed to rely upon a finely tuned sense of intuition. Tom called his intuitive ability 'gaydar'; a term used to describe, among other things, listening for 'messages about people's sexuality'. Tom recalled experiences of conversing with colleagues whom he suspected of being gay, listening out for indicators of sexual identity by, for example, noting how personal pronouns were used to refer to a partner or whether the names of gay bars and clubs were mentioned in conversation. Other participants said they dropped hints into conversations with colleagues they suspected of being gay, like referring to their male partners by name or talking sympathetically about gay characters on television. Some men searched for other clues such as whether colleagues presumed to be gay had photographs of their partners on their desks, while some felt they could identify gay men in the office by the labels and details of their clothing. Chic designer brands were considered by several participants to be the wardrobe staples of gay rather than heterosexual men. Clearly, some of this perceptual detective work mobilises gay and heterosexual stereotypes about how gay men should look and behave to categorise colleagues in terms of sexual orientation (Williams et al. 2009), but it was surprising how many participants felt their intuitive ability was highly developed, with an apparent positive effect on finding like-minded peers and potential friends at work.

Some participants found social networking sites useful for connecting with LGBT people employed in the same organisation. For example, Conor, a university lecturer, uses 'Grindr', an iPhone application that allows gay men to locate and communicate with each other instantly. The application, which identifies the user's GPS position to explain where they are in distance from the next gay man, enabled Conor to establish contact with a number of gay men in other parts of the university. After time spent chatting online to one particular man, who was not out to his colleagues in another university department, Conor and he agreed to meet face-to-face, and have formed a 'friendly' workplace relationship. Although 'grinding at work' has not given Conor a 'best pal to hang out with', it has helped him to overcome the problem of connecting with other gay men who might not be open about their sexuality to colleagues in person. At the same time, switching on the application at work did give rise to potentially awkward situations, since some gay students were also using Grindr to the same end. Feeling uncomfortable about inadvertently outing himself online to students, Conor was at the time of interview considering whether to stop using the application.

Constructing 'gay friendly' work contexts

From the examples above, it is clear that organisational contexts can influence how gay men are able to develop friendships. In some interview extracts we can catch glimpses of the creativity in how gay men can surmount particular organisational barriers to friendship, giving rise to questions about how friendships might shape the corporate landscapes in which they are negotiated. One theme to emerge from the interview data was the role of gay men's workplace friendships in helping to construct 'gay friendly' work environments.

Most of the men I interviewed worked in organisations they variously described as either 'tolerant' of LGBT people or 'gay friendly'. I identified three characteristics from the interview data about 'gay friendly' places of work: (1) the presence and commitment from management to the implementation of policies and work practices that included LGBT people; (2) feeling able to come out to colleagues; (3) the existence of support networks for LGBT workers. Other features included workplace demographics such as the visibility of LGBT employees and organisational contexts in which women outnumber men. In work contexts characterised by some or all of these features, gay men tended to ascribe more positive meanings to their work lives. While Day and Schoenrade's (1997, 2000) research highlights the crucial role played by employers in fashioning work environments understood and experienced as 'gay friendly', they underplay the agency of LGBT employees in performing a similar role.

In line with White (2008), university settings occasioned opportunities for gay men to forge cross-sex friendships with feminists, lesbians and heterosexual men and women sensitive toward LGBT people. These friendships flourished in university work contexts constructed by participants as 'liberal' and, thus, conducive to being openly gay. University work contexts also furnished participants with other preconditions for friendship making such as proximity, time for interaction and opportunities for collaborative working. For those employed in academic roles that involved multi-disciplinary working, opportunities arose for connecting with people in different disciplines and in other universities, giving them options to experience different kinds of friendships. Some participants, who had only experienced friendships with women and gay men, encountered heterosexual men at work who were committed to developing 'queer positive' values and behaviour, giving rise to possibilities of friendship. Of the few workplace friendships participants formed with lesbians, most were developed in academic work contexts. Notably, examples of cross-sexuality friendships were particularly prominent in those interview accounts of academic work life. Forming ties of friendship with men and women in other academic disciplines was valuable for those participants employed in domains not well-known for engaging with issues of gender and sexuality, such as the mainstream branch of organisation and management studies.

For Michael, currently a lecturer in the field of management, connecting with sociologists, feminists and queer studies scholars on research projects and at conferences has led to the formation of friendships that offer a practicing ground for developing alternative ways of doing gender and sexuality at work:

> I work with women and men who identify as feminist or profeminist and it's an invigorating environment in which to learn about your own shortcomings as a man, feminist, queer, however you wish to identify. I've come to understand, largely through these friendships, that it's one thing to say you're profeminist and another to actually act on it. It's given me a lot to think about, especially in terms of how I perform my own masculinity at work. I try to be supportive and self-reflexive as a man, not to rely on male privilege which I can exercise as a gay man.

As I argue in Chapter 7, these types of workplace friendships can expand and enrich each friend's understanding of how gender and sexuality can be performed at work. More than this, however, is the potential for these friendships to (re)shape forms of organisation and organising. In Michael's case, the development of workplace friendships with feminists has touched the work lives of other men and women in the department:

> My feminist friends have infiltrated the business school (laughs) ... and because we socialise with other members of the group they have become more exposed to different points of view. It's not been a case of ramming feminism or queer theory down everyone's throats, it's more restrained. Like setting up a research seminar programme on gender and work, it's brought a lot of the subject group together, particularly the women who have been sexually harassed by senior managers. It's given us a forum to share our experiences of gendered work life in the university. It's even affected some of the men, who I noticed had started to reflect on some of this. Several have even spoken up at meetings when people have been sexist or homophobic. None of us expected that to happen.

Workplace friendships can play a potentially powerful role in helping to alter the gendered dynamics of organisations, as Michael's interview extract illustrates. These friendships can set new norms for relating and becoming, as well as providing support and acceptance to men who wish to challenge heteronormative constructions of masculinity, men, women and gender relations. Notably, feminist friends can be powerful allies in that respect (White 2008). In contrast, accounts of private sector organisations contained few if any friendships involving feminist identified women or men, but this did not prevent some gay men from organising politically.

Some participants employed in the private sector were heavily involved in organisational LGBT support networks and groups, regarded by some as an important source of friendship and an opportunity to further equality work on sexual orientation in the workplace. In these examples, organisational LGBT support networks were also open to LGBT supporters, or 'straight allies' as several participants labelled them. Heterosexual allies were constructed as people who are supportive of LGBT persons and are informed about and accepting of LGBT people. Not surprisingly, friendships between gay men and straight allies were found to be particularly rewarding. In the example below, we can see how one friendship involving a straight ally affirms the experience and rights of one participant (Damien):

> Daisy and I share the same political beliefs in equality, especially in terms of how they translate into a workplace that celebrates equality and diversity. It's what we both strive for, challenging the views of others who infringe that sense of equality. It's brought us together in a powerful way because we connect with each other at a fundamental level … it's enabled us to get to know each other as people. I never feel like an outsider in Daisy's company, I feel completely valued for being gay.

It is apparent in these accounts that workplace friendships can be constructed as relationships that are politically-edged. This theme, revisited in Chapter 8, emerges here as an organising principle in Damien's friendship with Daisy. One effect of the intermingling of friendship, politics and forms of LGBT organising is that the promotion of equality and justice in the workplace can slowly transform the sexual and gendered landscapes of some corporate environments (Raeburn 2004). Workplace friendships can perform a key role in that respect, providing the social glue that unites members of disenfranchised social groups who share common political goals and values (Rawlins 2008). Equally important is the capacity for workplace friendships to connect marginalised organisational members with those who occupy positions of privilege and influence, some of whom we might call 'straight allies'. In Damien's case, Daisy is an example of someone who affirms his sense of self as gay and chooses to confront the homophobic and heterosexist values of others. Of course politically motivated alliances and friendships can be riven by tensions and antagonisms (Ward 2000), putting a strain on the efforts of individuals to build cooperative and egalitarian workplace environments and relationships (Raeburn 2004). Other concerns relate to the transformative effect of these friendships, especially as some forms of LGBT organising can become too closely aligned with managerial agendas that seek to cultivate a more productive workforce through diversity initiatives (Colgan et al. 2009). One risk here is that workplace friendships might help to accommodate marginalised organisational members, rather than challenging normative beliefs about the value of particular identities in the workplace. These reservations notwithstanding, it is noteworthy that work environments characterised by the mingling of friendships and modes of LGBT organising can be beneficial for gay men.

Working within one such context, Lee felt energised to seek out other gay men as potential friends. Lee, who is a single parent, recently came out to his teenage sons and to members of his existing circle of friends, after the collapse of his marriage. Some of Lee's friends have struggled to adjust to his new identity, and at the time of interview Lee was keen to establish new friends. Framed in this way, coming out is more than an identity declaration: it is an opportunity to establish friendships (Blasius 1994). Befriending other men who share a similar sexual identity, currently absent from his repertoire of friends, was regarded as being particularly desirable, for gaining legitimacy and acceptance as a gay man during this initial post-coming out period (Weeks et al. 2001; Nardi 1999; Burnett 2010). Lee's workplace is constructed as offering new friendship possibilities, not least because a number of Lee's work friends have encouraged him to participate in the organisation's LGBT support group. Lee told me he was 'nervous' about attending his first meeting, but had turned to his female work friends for emotional support and was, therefore, feeling hopeful that he could meet other companionable gay men.

Other participants in 'gay friendly' organisations provided contrasting perspectives. While none of the study participants were employed in organisations run by LGBT people or devoted to providing services and goods to LGBT consumers, a small number had experience of working in occupations with longstanding reputations for being 'gay friendly'. For example, some participants had worked front and back stage in theatres and other domains within the performing arts. In these work locales, characterised by higher concentrations of LGBT employees, participants seemed to enjoy numerous opportunities to strike up friendly relations and friendships characterised as sociable, supportive and fun, with some friends participating in good-natured flirting. These friendships appeared to help (re)produce work environments and relationships where informality and collegiality presided. Yet it did not automatically follow that friendship making with other gay men was always easy.

Theo, a general manager employed in a small family-owned theatre company, said he often struggled to make friends out of other male colleagues:

> There's this thing in the industry that everyone assumes men are gay … probably because a lot of theatre directors and agents and actors are gay. What happens though is that a lot of men tend to camp it up, including straight [male] actors. It's so bizarre. When we go out for a social after work they dance to all the gay disco music, talk about gay stuff, some even wear T-shirts with gay slogans on them … some try to mince when they walk, so as to give you the impression they're gay (laughs). Then they tell you, when you least expect it, they've got a girlfriend or they're married … they will do it because it's seen that they will get on in the industry … like getting work, or getting along with a certain director, or because it's seen as a hip thing to do … it's just bizarre. Lots of people have asked me why I struggle to make gay friends and it's because it's so difficult to tell who is really gay. I've made a fool out of myself so many times because I've got it wrong … you just wish sometimes they'd wear a badge saying so.

Theo describes a number of stereotypical expectations that his workplace requires of male performers. Responding to these expectations heterosexual male actors appear to work at being 'gay' in a performative manner (Butler 1990), wearing clothes emblazoned with gay slogans, discussing gay issues and posturing the body in exaggerated ways. Interesting is the possibility that some heterosexual actors might regard this as respite from conforming to heterosexual norms, developing workplace relationships that permit them to perform a visible gay identity in a fun and sociable manner. At the same time, the stereotypical expectations Theo's workplace requires of male performers applies to gay and heterosexual men, with both groups of men subjected to and judged by stereotypes that some might find uncomfortable. As noted by Williams et al. (2009), livelihoods might be at stake if individuals do not conform to organisational expectations about how gay men should look and behave. Theo admitted he felt frustrated by the male actors who perform as visible gay men in stereotypical ways, feeling he had little in common with many of them. Theo commented that he struggled to befriend other men at work, particularly gay men: 'the only way I can describe it is to say it's like the saying: water, water everywhere and not a drop to drink'. For Theo, the risk attached to reading the performance of (homo)sexuality incorrectly is a disincentive to making friends with other men. But, more than this, the performance of being gay at work is off putting, since Theo appears to have no truck with conforming to gay stereotypes. However, unlike many of the male actors within his workplace, Theo's livelihood is not contingent on conforming to the same stereotypes in the same way, giving him greater licence to explore his sense of self.

Summary

This chapter has aimed to paint a detailed picture of how workplace friendships are dynamic, particularly the way they are ascribed importance and centrality in gay men's lives. Here, then, we can frame workplace friendships as a process of organising, since their possibility, place and role is shaped by the influence exerted by different people, other relationships and life events at particular points in time. Looked at in this way, this chapter has shed light on how friendship is an important part of how gay men organise in the workplace. Emphasis in the foregoing analysis is weighted towards examining how organisations influence individual choices and social interactions in the workplace, opening up and foreclosing opportunities for befriending. Study findings reveal that gay men's workplace friendships are no different to other people's workplace friendships, in that the conditions of their possibility are susceptible to the commitments and pressures of holding down jobs and building work careers. The structure of jobs and workplaces are also influential in that respect. Yet for gay men, the heteronormative dimensions of work life may be experienced in particular but not necessarily unique ways, making some friendships especially hard to establish.

As argued in Chapter 3, research shows how organisations can be difficult for LGBT employees to openly participate in work life. The friendship potential of work settings characterised as heteronormative can be impaired, insofar as they might inhibit the full range of possibilities for participants (and others) to connect with and benefit from workplace friendships with LGBT employees. At the same time, it is important to acknowledge the agency displayed by many participants in surmounting the barriers to friendship described above. Be that as it may, organisational efforts to create environments conducive to the development of workplace friendships are welcome. As shown in this chapter, 'gay friendly' work cultures are at least a step in the right direction as far as gay men's workplace friendships are concerned. However, the study data gives us reason to contemplate how gay men's friendships might help construct work environments that are sensitive toward and informed of the needs and interests of LGBT employees. This issue continues to be of interest and relevance in the next two chapters, not least because sexual and gender identities can shape the path gay men's friendships take in the workplace, and the meanings they hold for those who participate in them. The next chapter pursues this issue by examining gay men's workplace friendships with other men.

Chapter 5
Gay Men's Workplace Friendships with Men

Introduction

The majority of study participants described close dyadic workplace friendships with women. However, participants were also fully capable of experiencing intimate workplace friendships with men. The interview data revealed some striking examples of these friendships, characterised by mutual disclosure of personal information, vulnerability, physical closeness and commitment. These friendships problematise stereotypes of men's friendships as emotionally tepid and more likely than women's friendships to be based on sociability rather than disclosing intimacy. Furthermore, this chapter complicates existing research on men's workplace friendships as largely instrumental and motivated by self-interest. The exploration of gay men's perspectives and experiences of male friendship in the workplace helps to show that men's friendships are far from unified.

To begin, the first part of this chapter focuses on workplace friendships between gay men, revealing the supportive functions of these friendship ties. However, the analysis also shows how divided participants are in their friendship preferences, with the majority of men indicating they would not intentionally seek out other gay men as work friends. This contests a currently widely held view among scholars that gay men are more likely to formulate close friendships with other gay men. This assertion tends to be predicated on the assumption that sexual identity can be an important point of similarity that may draw gay men together in friendship. This chapter argues that sharing a sexual identity is not always an obvious or meaningful point of reference between gay men. Here work and organisation are influential in structuring the friendship preferences of participants in that and other respects. Many participants expressed a preference for befriending heterosexuals, so the second part of this chapter explores workplace friendships between gay and heterosexual men. This section of analysis focuses on gay men's experiences of negotiating issues of sexuality and gender in ways that limit and open up the opportunities available to them for establishing friendships with heterosexual men.

Workplace friendships between gay men

As Chapter 2 established, research shows that a gay man's closest friend is most likely to be another gay man (Nardi 1999; Weeks et al. 2001). It is striking, then, only a small number of participants said they had experienced workplace friendships with other gay men. From one perspective, this finding is not altogether remarkable since many work environments privilege idealised norms of heterosexuality (Skidmore 2004), with the effect of marginalising LGB sexualities (Ward and Winstanley 2003). As Chapter 4 revealed, these organisational settings can obstruct friendship making processes between gay men, yet prior research has often neglected to take full account of the workplace as a context for gay men's friendships.

From another perspective, the small number of workplace friendships between gay men merits further analysis because many participants expressed a preference for befriending heterosexual men and women. An obvious but pertinent point is that a shared sexual identity is by no means singularly sufficient to bring gay men together in friendship. Many participants articulated this view, suggesting that personality, sharing the same sense of humour, pastimes and professional values were more influential in shaping the path to friendship (Spencer and Pahl 2006). As sections of analysis below demonstrate, some participants actively resist a discourse of similarity among gay men, constructing them as workplace rivals and competitors. Others point to the complications of sexual attraction in workplace friendships involving other gay men. Before exploring these issues, it is significant that a number of participants drew upon a discourse of similarity and allegiance among gay men to emphasise shared interests and experiences of living openly gay lives, that would help to establish relations of friendliness, possibly leading to friendship.

For example, Hugo, an academic, was typical of those participants who felt experiences of discrimination based on sexual orientation provided important common ground among gay men. He explains referring to a work friend he made some years ago:

> One of the reasons we were friends was because we were gay. We had this shared understanding of what it was like to be a minority, to be gay in the workplace. This was a time when homophobia was more blatant ... gay men who were out often got bullied. Mind you, I still think it's like that for some gay men today. But my point is that gay men have lived in fear and on their wits for years ... so there's a shared understanding between us ... not all the time you understand, but I'd say it's there in the background, binding us together.

In this interview excerpt, Hugo builds an argument that connects gay male identities through a shared sense of oppression and discrimination. This is seen to be viable basis for friendship in the workplace, particularly as organisations are viewed as difficult places for gay men to be open about their sexuality (Woods and Lucas 1993; Ward and Winstanley 2003). Rupert, another academic, echoes Hugo's comments: 'when all's said and done, gay men share the same history of sexual oppression as a minority group ... we have that much in common'. From one perspective, it might be little coincidence that Hugo and Rupert, both in their fifties with experience of living openly gay lives during the 1970s and 1980s, when workplace homophobia was often overt (Levine 1979; Beer et al. 1983; GLC 1985), ascribe gay men a minority group status. Positioning gay men in this way stands in stark contrast to the stance adopted by many other participants, particularly the younger men in the study sample, who felt homosexuality is a 'normal' feature of society (Seidman 2002). As such, they rarely if ever articulated the idea of developing affinity with other gay men based on a shared sense of being *Other*. Yet, from Hugo's and Rupert's interview excerpts, a desire to connect around shared understandings of living as a minority opens up possibilities of gay male friendship based on care giving and support. Indeed, the impact of gay men supporting each other in friendship could be profound.

When Hugo's late partner was diagnosed as HIV positive, he was careful about which people he confided in. Concerned colleagues might assume that he was also HIV positive, and that his domestic situation might be the subject of 'idle gossip', Hugo turned to a trusted gay male work friend. One advantage noted by Hugo was their mutual understanding of caring for a loved one with HIV:

> Conrad was the obvious person to talk to. He knew what it's like to care for someone who's slowly dying in front of your very eyes. He knew what that meant for a gay man having to hold down a job and be a carer and deal with the shit about queers getting what they deserve if they contract HIV ... I eventually told other people at work, who were all very supportive, but no one except Conrad could really relate to what I was going through ... his love and support kept my head above water.

At crisis points in people's lives, friendships based on similarity can have a positive effect, providing the emotional support needed to enable individuals to carry on with their everyday routines (Weeks et al. 2001). In this case we see how work friends can display a strong sense of responsibility towards each other, which far exceeds any sense of obligation they might have to each other as colleagues (McGuire 2007). Indeed, this is a particularly heart-warming illustration in that respect, one that reminds us that the supportive functions of workplace friendships are not restricted to helping friends to advance careers. Indeed, outwardly supportive workplace friendships between gay men may hold the potential to establish friendship norms that can transfer to friendships between and among gay and non-gay individuals.

Hugo's friendship with Fraser, another gay academic, undermines the normative construction of depersonalised professional workplace relations between men:

> Our warmth and affection for each other spills over into our work life...quite spontaneously. Other people in the department are aware of it. In fact one [heterosexual] male colleague came up to me some time ago and said how refreshing it was to see two gay guys being openly demonstrative ... which I think he felt was unexpected in an environment where people are generally a bit cagey about getting personal.

It is suggested that gay male friendship can be understood not just in terms of support, warmth and affection, but also as a relationship that has the capacity to rupture organisational discourses on how men (and women) ought to relate professionally to one another. Despite the risk of being (re)positioned as 'unprofessional' by his colleagues, Hugo had little to say about any openly negative responses from onlookers. On the contrary, Hugo felt that colleagues seemed more than 'intrigued' by his friendship with Fraser. Several heterosexual male colleagues admitted to Hugo they 'admired' the two men's 'public displays of affection', with one suggesting to Hugo that he was thinking about how he could make some of his heterosexual male workplace friendships more 'emotionally open'. It might be that gay male friendships can be drawn on as a source of inspiration for designing alternative discursive schemas of closeness that are less hidebound to heteronormative forms of masculinity (Foucault 1982/1997; Fee 2000). With all this in mind, this gives rise to a question seldom asked about how discourses on gay sexualities might influence how friendship is understood and experienced within an organisational network of gay men.

Illustrating how discourses on gay sexualities can be positive and empowering, Stafford recalls his experience of being part of a gay male friendship network within a local government housing department:

> There was a powerful little hub of people in the department. All the senior managers were gay ... I've never come across it since ... we were all supporting each other because we were all gay ... it was well known that we did this. Eventually it got to the stage where we had taken over the department ... that's what we planned [laughs] ... that we'd have the management of half the city's housing to ourselves.

From this interview extract we can appreciate how discourses of gay sexualities can inform the construction of an empowering gay male subject position. Indeed, Stafford described this professional work site not merely as a 'gay-friendly' workplace but as one that 'promoted gay sexuality as a force to be reckoned with'. Despite perceived anxieties of how homosexuality can threaten how the self is understood as 'professional' (Rumens and Kerfoot 2009; Woods and Lucas 1993), Stafford did not appear to be circumspect in the workplace about acknowledging his desire for other men. He reflected on this: 'in the beginning it was harder to talk openly about gay things because there weren't many of us, but as more joined the department chatting about boyfriends and other gay stuff became something we all did openly, like it was no big deal'. Notable here is that topics of conversation which develop privately between men at a dyadic level gradually permeate the dialogue between men at a collective level, enabling Stafford and other gay men to be 'out and proud' about their sexuality. This has a positive effect on the quality of Stafford's work life. As Wharton and Bird point out, one benefit of homosocial relations at work is that they enhance the self-esteem of those involved in such networks, because the 'preference for similar others implies a preference for self' (1996: 100). Reflecting on how his 'confidence' levels soared as a result of belonging to this network, Stafford described it as a critical moment in his life for affirming his identity as a young gay man.

From one angle, we can observe how gay male friendship is understood to be a productive form of organising within the workplace, which stands in stark contrast to the literature that examines how organisational gay sexualities are often marginalised and discredited (Ward and Winstanley 2003; Humphrey 1999). Furthermore, unlike research that reveals how gay men's friendships are typically understood as sources of emotional and practical support to help gay men navigate the obstacles of heteronormative life, this example also points to the normalising effect these friendships can generate. Stafford remarked: 'my time in the department helped me to feel that my sexuality was a normal part of me, like it is for straight people'. By this reading, gay male workplace friendship is understood less as a relational site for coping with the inimical effects of being *Othered*, as Hugo exemplifies, and more as an arena for constructing a form of homonormativity that privileges gay male sexuality. As such, the possibility for demonstrating how gay men can contribute positively to organisational operations is conditioned within a homosocial context.

On that point, the homosocial gay male friendships described by Stafford approximates those male friendships criticised by feminist researchers for (re)producing masculine values of domination, exclusion and control (Elsesser and Peplau 2006; Wharton and Bird 1996; Kanter 1977). The negative effects of these friendships is illustrated nicely by Stafford's account. During our interview conversations Stafford was strangely silent on the exclusive nature of these friendship ties, from which other men and women are seemingly barred. When pressed on this issue, Stafford seemed to become uncomfortable, conceding that this web of gay friendships prevented many non-gay employees from advancing their careers in the department. At the same time, networked friendship ties among gay men can offer these men positions to critique heteronormative definitions of themselves as the *Other*, but at the cost of homogenising gay men's needs and interests. Most striking is how gay men's workplace friendships can re(produce) gendered modes of organising based on domination and exclusion. On this matter, while giving the appearance of friendship, most notably in how gay men give one another preferential treatment, the nature of these relationships are less suggestive of notions of idealised friendship at a dyadic level, where individuals typically have moral obligations to ensure relations of friendships are marked by trust, reciprocity and equality (Pahl 2000).

Gay men as workplace rivals

Research and popular discourse has tended to represent men's interactions with each other as aggressive, competitive and concerned with the exchange of external information such as that pertaining to work (Rubin 1985; Sapadin 1988; Seidler

1992). Study data provided some evidence of how workplace relations between men can be competitive but, unlike prior research, this study reveals how gay men may view each other as competitors within work cultures that understand gay men to be naturally more creative than their heterosexual colleagues. Another overlooked dimension to competitive relations between men at work is the possibility that gay men may view each other as rivals in the art of friendship making.

To begin exploring these issues it is worth mentioning that some participants expressed reservations about befriending other men at work due to the competitive relations fostered in some organisational settings. For example, when James spoke about his close friendship with Lester, introduced in Chapter 4, one reason they found they could blend responsibilities towards each in other in friendship and in terms of work was because they were employed in different roles:

> It [the friendship] wouldn't have worked if I had been a salesman like Lester. Lester was too bloody-minded and highly ambitious. And he wanted to be top salesman. I would have wanted to be top salesman … it just wouldn't have worked out. We would have hated each other.

As with a number of studies that have shown how men jockey with each other at work for recognition, one consequence is that friendships between men are emotionally tepid (Rubin 1985; Wellman 1992). For several participants, cultivating instrumental relations with other men (and women) was pivotal to success in the workplace. For instance, Michael, felt there were times when he pretended to like people he really disliked. This strategy, which required participants to suppress their emotions towards people they did not like, was adopted in order to maintain the appearance of a professional self, for the sake of workplace harmony and getting particular jobs done. In these examples, the idea of acquiring men as work friends is not regarded by James and Michael as being disagreeable. Rather, the story that might have been told if, say, James and Lester had been career rivals suggests that competition is regarded by some gay men as a challenge to forming close workplace friendships.

Yet the sense in which men may view each other as workplace competitors is more complex than much current research gives credit for. As stated in Chapter 3, studies on men's workplace relationships largely focus on heterosexual men. We have remarkably little to go on for understanding how gay men might complicate what we know generally about the competitive nature of some workplace relations between men. For example, interview accounts revealed how several participants were positioned within organisational discourse as 'experts' in particular areas of work, creating workplace rivalries. This is illustrated well by Alex. Employed in high profile media company, Alex said he felt gay men had 'a lot to live up to' in matching the stereotypes of gay men as the 'natural' experts in 'creativity'. As Levin (1999) found in her study of gay and lesbian owned businesses, clients often thought they were getting more creative advertising if a gay man was working the account; likewise, Alex's senior managers ('gay and straight') leverage the stereotype in order to 'curry favour' with clients. Alex found himself being represented to clients in a particularly positive light, offering him opportunities to lead on exciting advertising projects, sometimes at the expense of his heterosexual peers. This had caused some 'bad feeling' in the office among his heterosexual colleagues. It had a similarly negative influence on his decisions to befriend others at work.

To illustrate, Alex referred to 'friendship' with one of his peers:

> I have a cautious approach to my friendship with Russell, even though he's one of the most acceptable gay men you could possibly imagine ... we work in the same department and, because the gay men who work here have to maintain reputations as exemplary artists, it's a bit dog-eat-dog in the office.

Alex is 'guarded' in what he discloses to Russell about his private life and work-related matters. Alex says: 'it pays to be a bit circumspect about what I disclose to Russell ... I'm never too sure if he would use any of my ideas to his advantage'. Such disclosures might render Alex vulnerable to the political manoeuvring of gay men, like Russell, who are equally committed in getting to the top of his profession. As a young gay man, career hungry and in the ascendancy within a company that has appropriated modish notions of gay men for commercial gain, Russell is understood as a 'friend' and as a 'competitor'. As such, it is not altogether surprising that I could detect doubt and ambiguity in how Alex understood his relationship with Russell as 'friendship'. During our interview conversations, Alex appeared to question the level of 'trust' between them, and wondered if they were more 'friendly rivals' than 'friends'. Interesting, then, is that in this example gay sexuality is imbued with the meanings of superiority, offering the potential for gay men to gain acceptance and privilege in the workplace. From one perspective, this might condition the possibility for developing ways of relating at work in unselfish modes of relating at work, given that gay men have often been positioned closer to women in their capacity to develop caring and emotional relationships (Shepperd et al. 2010). But here it appears to have the opposite effect, intensifying competition between those gay men for whom career advancement is a primary goal.

While some participants positioned other gay men as career rivals, far more constructed them as friendship rivals. For these participants, gay men were constructed as having a more highly developed capacity than heterosexual men for emotional sensitivity and building friendships. Rupert, for instance, suggested: 'from my experience straight men are emotionally constipated ... gay men are far better at cutting through all that macho crap and being emotionally available'. Despite the gendered binary division this construction (re)produces, the positioning of gay men in this way was generally seen to be positive, particularly for friendship making involving heterosexual men and women, explored later in this and the next chapter. However, the construction of gay men as friendship 'experts' also gave rise to rivalries that limited the types of relations developed between gay men in the workplace.

Austin, employed as an occupational therapist, exemplifies this point beautifully:

> If a gay man came into the team I would find that a huge threat. It would be the hardest thing of all, because he would then be someone I would have to compete with because of his gayness. I see that as a threat to my own existence, to what I am at work. I would be afraid that I would lose the admiration and likeness of my colleagues. They might go over to that person because they might find that gay man funnier and more endearing ... and then I'd be left on the shelf. However, if the gay man were more masculine than me, it would be easier because his masculine side would fill a gap in the team, which is all female.

What we can draw from the quotation above is the narrow way in which Austin positions himself in a discourse of gay sexuality that equates 'gayness' with a natural capacity to be witty and charming. As such, if wit and charm are all Austin thinks he has to offer his work friends, the hypothetical scenario of another gay man entering the office environment is bathed in a negative light. Austin, like a number of study participants, commented they had invested considerable time and effort in gaining acceptance in the workplace as gay men, allowing them to develop close friends out of colleagues. Some of these men were quite possessive of their closest work friends, constructing them as though they were their exclusive property. It was fascinating to listen to some gay men as they spoke of their anxiety about being marginalised, through losing their place in established friendship networks. Work friends were constructed as being passive in that respect, easily won over by the 'natural charm and charisma' some gay men were said to exude.

Still there is good reason to question Austin's assumption that his closest work friends are so fickle as to transfer their affections from one gay man to another, on the basis of being able to get a better friendship deal elsewhere. While Aristotle certainly thought friendships based on pleasure were prone to this, the types of friendship Austin went on to describe were longstanding, intimate and supportive. On my reading, it seems more plausible that Austin sells himself short as a friend. In this vein, the quotation above hints at the importance of work friends for sustaining a sense of self that is secure. In reality, the construction of the self is an insecure project (Foucault 1986), signalled here by Austin's fear that other gay men might threaten his 'existence', undermining his sense of identity in the workplace. This is particularly apparent in Austin's crude construction of gay men along the lines of gender into two categories. On the one hand, Austin draws on a discourse of gay men which links them with effeminacy insofar as effeminate gay men are naturally witty and charming. These men are represented as the most dangerous friendship rivals. On the other hand, some gay men are positioned within discourses of masculinity, and presumably less likely to enjoy a surfeit of emotional skill and expertise in friendship making. Alternatively, they are able to plug a hole, as Austin puts it, in the gendered dynamics of the team by providing a welcome injection of masculinity. Whichever way you look at it, the construction of gay men in this dualistic fashion severely limits the opportunities available to Austin for developing different types of workplace friendships with other gay men.

Sex, work and friendship between gay men

Another reason why participants felt workplace friendships with gay men were complicated was the potential for unwanted sexual attraction. This finding is not entirely surprising given the tendency for friendship to be discursively constructed as a non-sexual relationship (Werking 1997). Also, the workplace has long been constructed as an inappropriate site for conducting sexual relations, although scholars have rightly challenged this view of organisation (Hearn et al. 1989; Brewis and Linstead 2000). Nevertheless, as Chapter 2 suggested, studies have shown how gay men can use friends as sexual partners, blurring boundaries between friendship and sexual relations (Nardi 1999; Weeks et al. 2001). These studies, however, overlook the workplace as a context for examining the relationship between friendship and sexual relations. Some of the interview accounts help to shed light on intermingling sex and friendship in the workplace.

In many interview conversations, sexuality tended to be telescoped to sexual attraction or a sexual encounter based on genital contact. In these examples, participants voiced a number of concerns about not only the negative outcomes of workplace friendships incorporating a sexual dimension, but also the difficulty in distinguishing behaviours motivated by friendship from those stirred by sexual attraction. As Chapter 4 established, while the majority of participants felt very comfortable with striking up friendships in the public arena of work, many of the same men felt that workplace friendships ought to be differentiated from sexual relations. This point of view was not directed at preserving the uniqueness of sexual relations against all other relationships, but aimed at keeping sex out of the workplace. For these men, sex/uality was constructed as 'dangerous' in two respects.

First, some participants suggested that mixing casual sex with friendship would lead to the ruination of friendship, resulting in the loss of a good friend (O'Meara 1989; Werking 1997). It was noticeable in these interview accounts how participants mobilised normative discourses on friendship to give voice to their concerns. Gordon provides a typical example in that regard:

> I find it difficult to see how you can have a friendship with a gay man and have sex at the same time. For me they're two different things. Friendship is platonic … throwing in a bit of sex turns it into something complicated, usually at the expense of friendship.

The term 'friendship' normatively means a non-sexual relationship, although changing social mores indicate that the borderlines between friendship, sex and love can be crossed (Pahl 2000; Nardi 1999). Whether friends can be lovers and vice versa is a heated topic of debate with a long philosophical pedigree (Rawlins 2008). It often comes down to friends themselves to negotiate the enabling and limiting discourses that shape the experience of friendship. For example, from the interview quote above, Gordon relies on an idealised notion of friendship to support a moral dimension to the argument that gay men *should* not be at one and the same time friends and lovers. This does not imply that friendship and sexual relations cannot interpenetrate, but it reveals how individuals like Gordon choose to build friendships that do not contain sexual relations. Gordon's reservation about treating gay men as both lovers and friends is structured by a concern that sex introduces into friendship complicated issues about possession. As Gordon went on to say, 'lovers are possessive' whereas 'friends have more freedom' to explore who they are with each other. The challenge of combining sex and friendship confronted a small number of participants, discussed later in this and the next chapter. But participants also highlighted particular concerns about the workplace as a potential site for friendship and sex to coalesce.

Men like Douglas relied on another set of norms to justify why sexual workplace friendships with other gay men are not desirable. Drawing on localised understandings of what counts as 'professional' workplace relations, participants often pointed out that sexual relations had little or no place at work. Again, such an argument is located within a normative discourse on professionalism that treats sex and work as polar opposites, despite evidence that suggests the boundaries between the two can be blurred (Deverell 2001). Framed in this way, Douglas was able to articulate specific concerns about putting gay work friends to use as lovers. The horror of 'screwing your best friend, things going tits up and then having to face up to it in the office the next day' seemed unimaginable to Douglas. Far easier, Douglas argued, to take that 'kind of risk' in a friendship outside work. Even those participants who had engaged in sex with gay men in the early stages of friendship formation appeared to be influenced by norms about keeping workplace relations immune from sex.

For example, Tony and Edmund both work in the National Health Service and met for the first time at a work conference. After a 'few beers', they retired to their hotel room for some 'hanky-panky' and parted company on glowing terms the next morning. Several months later, Tony went to work at the same hospital as Edmund and they soon 'bumped into each other'. This change in circumstance provided an opportunity to develop a friendship in a work setting. Indeed, already being acquainted with other sexually helped the two men to get to know each other as friends, but Tony was unequivocal about not rekindling any sexual activity. Reincorporating a sexual element into their friendship was not seen as being 'professional' in a work context where the two men have regular contact with each other in a clinical capacity. Although particular knowledge of each other's bodies in a sexual encounter is used to develop further opportunities for relating as friends, it precludes sexual intimacy. Here, then, Tony fashions not only an ideal-typical model of workplace friendship that allays organisational concerns about the disruptiveness of sexual relations at work, but also a normative construction of what it is to be professional, in which professionalism and sexuality are mutually exclusive.

Second, some participants constructed gay sexuality as 'dangerous' in the workplace by linking it with lust and excessive sexual desire. This enabled participants to highlight the risks associated with having gay friends who might use friendship as an access route to sex. This was generally regarded as being problematic for the upset that could arise from being deceived about the sexual intentions of another friend. Denton explains:

> I once struck up a close friendship with a gay guy at work. It happened one time in an email conversation at work. It started from a flirty email he sent me one day, then we got friendly, we'd go and have lunch, have coffee, that kind of thing. Then we got closer, starting confiding in one another, that sort of thing ... looking back, I now know what his motives were. He wanted something more than friendship, whereas I just wanted friendship. It actually became a problem in my home life. My partner found out and became suspicious. I then started to hide conversations that we'd had because it had come up as a topic of doubt for my partner. It didn't help because he was working in Exeter. I was working in London ... he didn't know what was going on. It all got too much for me, so one day I just ended the friendship, really abruptly. I'm not proud of that. But it wasn't worth ruining my relationship with Ray for that kind of thing.

Denton's interview excerpt highlights the confusion and anxiety that can occur when workplace friendships develop in unexpected ways. Part of the problem is that close friendships between gay men are vulnerable to being read as a dry run of romantic coupledom or involving some sexual component, as have friendships between heterosexual men and women (Monsour 2002; Werking 1997). In Denton's account, workplace friendship is increasingly subject to internal and external scrutiny over its nature, a process that culminates in its termination. Realising that his friend might have other intentions, suggesting something premeditated and planned in how one friend shapes the future path of friendship, Denton appears to be left with an overly cynical view of the friendship potential of gay men. They are represented as devious sexual predators: 'I have this thing now that a lot of gay men try and break up people because they're jealous or that kind of thing'. Positioning gay men in this crude manner, Denton forecloses the opportunities for imagining how friendships between gay men at and outside work might operate otherwise. For Denton and other participants with a similar outlook, friendships with other gay men are a fraught enterprise. In contrast, friendships with heterosexual women were deemed to be a 'safer bet' for experiencing closeness, without falling foul of sexual attraction, explored in Chapter 6.

Gay men's workplace friendships with heterosexual men

Nardi (1992a: 2) argues that a contradictory message is broadcast to men: 'strive for healthy, emotionally intimate friendships, but be careful – if you appear too intimate with another man you might be negatively labeled homosexual'. Acknowledging this, some commentators have promulgated discourse on men's friendships as being in a state of disrepair (Bech 1997). Yet this gloomy picture of men's friendship might well be a lot brighter. Times are changing and attitudes towards LGB people appear to have softened (Weeks 2007), and heterosexual men are now encouraged to express emotions and build intimate relationships with others (Lupton 1998). While progress in both these areas is uneven, it is plausible to suggest that these social conditions have helped to bring some gay and heterosexual men together in friendship. Indeed, a number of participants described such friendships, often enthusiastically and affectionately.

The remaining discussion is structured into four parts. The first part examines how participants construct heterosexual men as potential friends. In the second part, I examine various accounts of intimacy within these friendships. The third part builds on the second, by analysing how some participants and their male friends negotiate differences in how they identify sexually. The fourth part explores the comments of some participants that friendships with heterosexual men can have an energising effect on everyday work-based interactions. Attention is drawn also to the pressure levied on men to manage the expression of intimacy in ways that evade the finger-pointing and the tongue-wagging gay-heterosexual male friendships can attract.

Constructing heterosexual men as friends

As might be expected, not all participants said they had close workplace friendships with heterosexual men. Still, accounts of friendships with heterosexual men outnumbered those involving other gay men. This finding problematises an observation made by Peter Nardi (1999) that very few gay men (less than 5% in his study) designated a heterosexual man as a 'best friend'. Indeed, participants often credited their male friends for challenging their stereotyped views about heterosexual men, helping them to feel comfortable with developing different sorts of male friendship. Before I present examples of these friendships, many of which problematise the starkest cultural stereotypes about male friendship, it is worth mentioning the apprehensions that some gay men expressed about the friendship potential of heterosexual men.

Sam and Denton vocalise a perspective on the eligibility of heterosexual men as friends that is in tune with a pessimistic note sounded by some friendship commentators on the prohibitive effect of homophobia on the formation of intimate male friendship (Bech 1997; Miller 1983; Lehne 1989). For example, Denton suggested: 'I don't regard straight men as potential friends … straight men have always been figures of homophobia throughout my life'. Not surprisingly, those participants who recounted unfavourable experiences of interacting with heterosexual men in their lives, whether at school, within their families, in leisure contexts or in other work environments, felt the friendship potential of heterosexual men was poor. This knowledge of heterosexual men is built up through routine encounters over the life course. The accumulation of knowledge of other men was revealed in the way some participants spoke about heterosexual men, especially in the stories they told about workplace homophobia, which were more likely to figure heterosexual men as the primary perpetrators of bullying and harassment towards gay men. Cast in this way, heterosexual men evoke discomfort in the minds of some gay men, even those with little or no prior experience of befriending heterosexual men. Sam is one such example, feeling 'wary' of heterosexual men at work, unsure if they are open to the invitation of friendship from a gay man. While it is understandable that gay men like Sam express doubt here, some of the more extreme statements made by gay men involved spurious moral evaluations of heterosexual men as 'insensitive', 'aggressive' and 'emotionally stunted'. Constructing heterosexual men in this way, which confined them to stereotypes, participants limited the range of interactive possibilities available with these men. As such, uncertainty surfaced in some interview conversations about the likely return on any investment made in befriending heterosexual men. A very small number of participants perceived the dividend to be so small as not to warrant the effort.

However, one pattern to emerge from the study data was the significance of the workplace as a context for encouraging gay men to re-evaluate whether their attitudes towards heterosexual men were reasonable. Michael is an example of someone who has challenged his own prejudice towards heterosexual men, with friendship playing a pivotal role in that respect. Michael has negative experiences of heterosexual men growing up, particularly when he was at school. Bullied by men throughout much of his schooling, Michael entered the world of work with fixed views about heterosexual men as the obvious foes of gay men. This point of view went unchanged for over a decade until, shortly after taking up an academic post in a university, he met Ian:

> To be honest I have struggled throughout my life to trust or get close to straight men … I guess that all changed when I started work at [X] university … it was there I met Ian … but when we were first introduced I really didn't think we'd become friends. For one thing he's straight. For another, he's is working-class and from up north, so he's … and he won't mind me saying this … got quite a gritty personality that some people find aggressive. He also drinks way too much. So, I just assumed he'd be your typical northerner. It turns out that he's one of the closest friends I have.

As in other studies that examine men's friendships (White 2008; Kaplan 2006), opening up emotionally to another man requires trust, especially if the friendship cuts across sexual identity categories. This can affect men's ability to form close relationships with other men, as Michael's quote reveals. But it is clear that friendships between gay and heterosexual men are not only possible but they can exhibit warmth, affection and intimacy. The important point here is that such friendships are negotiated, sometimes under tough circumstances, rather than given. In Michael's example, his university work context is crucial for providing the preconditions for friendship such as proximity and an intellectual environment wherein academics are paid to scrutinise and analyse. Michael credits the activity of academic debate with helping him to get to know Ian beyond a set of stereotypes about his sexuality and class. For example, Ian is initially constructed as a stereotype of the working-class heterosexual man, with the associated cultural freight this carries about how working-class heterosexual masculinities are linked to homophobia (Embrick et al. 2007). However, it was not long before Michael and Ian found they had much more in common with each other than Michael, at least, anticipated.

Indeed, although Michael and Ian appear to come from different backgrounds they share the 'same professional values'. The similarity they share in work values, exemplified in their shared 'passion for teaching', acts as a bridging mechanism allowing each friend to view facets of the other's life world. Equally important for Michael is that Ian expresses masculinity in less conventional ways. Despite his initial 'pigeonholing' of Ian as a 'gruff working class northerner', Ian is a man who is sensitive and understanding. He is also interested in 'cosmetics', 'fine dining' and 'shopping', pastimes not typically associated with the performance of normative forms of working class masculinity (Walker 1994a; Connell 1995). In Michael, Ian finds someone he can confide in and with whom he can indulge his non-traditional interests and tastes.

Michael's gay identity appears crucial here, opening up opportunities for Ian to perform gender in ways that are less likely to come under criticism for being 'soft' or 'feminine' (Fee 2000). Conversely, in Ian, Michael finds another man who has exposed and shattered his own prejudices, altering his view of heterosexual men. Indeed, Michael spoke enthusiastically about the importance of forming friendships outside and at work with men from all walks of life. The transformative effect of this workplace friendship has been an incentive for Michael to establish sociable and supportive relations with other heterosexual men elsewhere in his life.

Other participants also spoke about the friendship potential of heterosexual men in positive terms, often referring to the supportive functions of these friendships. Ciaran's remarks were typical of those participants who voiced the benefits of having supportive heterosexual male work friends:

> I'm much happier for having these guys as friends ... they're great, always there for me, like when my father died ... they just wanted to listen, to lend an ear ... because you don't expect straight men to open up and be supportive that makes it such a great thing when it happens ... it's heart-warming stuff ... being gay

probably helps because it gives them permission to be that way, without fear of getting the piss taken out of them for being soft.

As demonstrated in Ciaran's interview quotation, gay and heterosexual men stand to gain from forming friendships, despite the unwelcome attention these friendships can draw from others who struggle to make sense of them (Fee 2000; Walker 1994a; Nardi 1999). In particular, it is suggested that men can use workplace friendships to demonstrate and share feelings and emotions, a dimension to men's workplace friendships often ignored by organisational scholars. On this point, Ciaran's interview extract warns us about how limiting it is to understand men's emotional concern for each other at work in terms of self-interest. Of course the capacity of men's workplace friendships to operate in this way is often, but not solely, dependent on the degree to which men are prepared to be open to a deeper level of disclosure and relating. Scholars have argued that men's workplace friendships are particularly vulnerable to the threat of competition, which can have a stultifying effect on the ability of men to trust and relate emotionally with each other (Bird 1996; Seidler 1992). However, it is critical to acknowledge that not all men are in competition with each other, which is to recognise that some men do not experience the distrust and cautiousness around each other that both popular and academic discourse suggests is commonplace. There are plenty of reasons for men to relate to each other at work that engender letting down their defences to disclose deeper aspects of the self.

Indeed, Ciaran's example is not unusual in that respect. Study findings revealed how gay and heterosexual men could rely on each other emotionally at times of personal crisis such as when one friend lost their job, experienced a family bereavement, discovered their partner was having an affair or had filed for divorce, and so on. Equally and relatedly, emotional and material support was also forthcoming at times when friends encountered some of life's routine challenges such as dealing with a demanding line manager, trying to diet in order to lose weight, moving house, needing a lift into work, and so on. In accounts of supportive friendships with heterosexual men, it was noticeable that participants often said they learned a lot about themselves and their male friends, particularly how to dismantle their own prejudices and challenge cultural expectations about how these friendships should be organised. There is a sense in these accounts about how men have to work at developing close dyadic friendships in order to experience the associated benefits.

Working at intimacy

What should be clear by now is that gay men's friendships with heterosexual men are both a very real possibility and, as I explore below, can be secure from anxiety about the display of tender emotion being misread as a sign of homosexuality. As the discussion above suggests, a number of participants deemed their friendships with heterosexual men to be significant, by virtue of the deep disclosing intimacies these friendships appeared to occasion. Not surprisingly, this form of intimacy appeared to be spoken about in auspicious terms because it was often said by participants to be atypical of the gendered stereotype of the emotionally feeble heterosexual male. As such, disclosing intimacy was singled out as a quality that marked some of these friendship ties as 'special'.

Intimacy does not always spring forth spontaneously. Disclosing intimacy, as it is broadly understood in Western societies, involves 'close association, privileged knowledge, deep knowing and understanding and some form of love' (Jamieson 1998: 13). Disclosing intimacy may take time to develop because in order to find expression, trust and reciprocity are usually required. One theme explored here is that disclosing intimacy in workplace friendships between gay and heterosexual men is subject to negotiation, not least because of the risk associated with tenderness in men's friendships being read as an indicator of homosexuality (Bech 1997; Nardi 1992). Additionally, heteronormative discourse that suggests gay men may use friendship to induct heterosexual men into homosexuality, or to elicit sex from a (un)willing heterosexual male friend, must be seen as complex narratives that are told and granted legitimacy in specific cultural and historical moments, as Chapters 1 and 2 suggest. In these narratives gay men are constructed as sexual predators chasing sex not intimacy. But alternative scenarios emerged from the interview findings. To illustrate, however, I shall examine one workplace friendship at length, involving two healthcare managers.

Morgan first met John one evening in a local gay nightclub. Presuming John to be gay, on the basis that John did not disclose otherwise, Morgan proceeded to 'flirt' with John over the course of the evening. The culmination of Morgan's efforts was a 'night of passion', after which they parted company. Morgan did not expect to see John again but later noticed him in the hospital staff canteen:

> After someone told me where he worked in the hospital, I approached John to say that I'd seen him in the canteen. He was pleased to see me but I think he felt caught out slightly, because he'd never mentioned his job or wife or kids to me. Funnily enough it didn't bother me really … and I wasn't expecting anything to happen, but he suggested we go for a coffee and, over a long conversation in the canteen, he told me that he had always fancied exploring his sexuality. I found John interesting because he didn't strike me as being the typical straight man trapped in the closet kind of person … thinking about it … if we hadn't slept together, I doubt whether we'd be friends today.

In order to make sense of Morgan's interview excerpt, it is worth referring to Price's research on friendships between gay and heterosexual men. Price (1999: 46) argues that while it is not unusual for gay men to have sexual relations with heterosexual men, it is 'rare for them to become or stay friends afterward'. In Price's study, participants provide two explanations: first, the heterosexual men makes sexual advances to his gay friend, resulting in awkwardness and tension;

second, the gay man, not yet out, makes sexual advances to another man whom he suspects is gay. In this scenario, the closeted gay man comes to terms with his sexuality and wishes to engage in further sexual contact but is rebuked by the other man, who professes his sexual curiosity. In this case, the heterosexual man forgoes the option of friendship, not wishing to be reminded of his sexual experimentation. Both explanations are bleak not just in how they anticipate the demise of friendship before it has even started, but also in how gay and heterosexual men are represented as frustrated, closeted and in denial. As with a small number of Price's study participants, my study findings offer alternative possibilities.

One reason a friendship develops between Morgan's and John is because they enter into dialogue about their sexual experience. Crucially, they talk about it at work during lunchtimes and coffee breaks. Since the time they spend together at work is spent largely talking, Morgan and John's friendship veers away from normative constructions of men's friendships as predominately activity based (Caldwell and Peplau 1982; Fehr 1996; Rubin 1985). What is more, the conversations Morgan and John enter into are wide ranging and personal, including topical issues at work, family matters and leisure activities as well as the more delicate issues surrounding sexuality. As such, they complicate research that suggests men tend towards conversations about activities and are less personal than the topics discussed between female friends (Markiewicz et al. 2000; Elsesser and Peplau 2006; Sias et al. 2003).

Striking is that sexuality is not regarded as a barrier to intimacy. As Morgan said, 'if it wasn't for John wanting to explore a side of his sexuality we'd never have become friends'. That John is ready to acknowledge the fluidity of his own sexuality, giving rise to questions about whether he is 'bisexual', has been crucial to the development of their friendship. Morgan again: 'I think I've helped John to affirm something he has long known, that men are either one hundred percent straight or gay is something of a myth'. Both men acknowledge that sexual identity is more changeable than normative discourses of sexuality suggest. Workplace friendship not only provides a relational context for such conversations to take place, but it allows the perspectives of each friend to be validated. As Morgan pointed out, even talking about sexuality can be 'risky'. In other words, in the company of 'less well informed men', as Morgan said, individuals might quickly find themselves navigating 'deep water' about what behaviours are deemed to be homosocial and homosexual (Sedgwick 1985). For Morgan at least, this is an important benefit of a friendship that crosses boundaries of sexuality.

In friendship the two men can aerate their views, ventilating fresh air into stale stereotypes about, for example, heterosexual men who sleep with other men as demonstrating idle sexual curiosity. Although the two men have already made 'real' a sexual desire for other each, it does not mean that the issue of desire has been put to bed (sic) for good. From the interview data it was clear that Morgan and John still talk about their one-night stand, sometimes as a joke, sometimes in tender terms and, at other times, in expressions of indifference. In so doing, the men continuously erase, defer and signify its potential re-articulation.

However, one major problem is that John's wife does not know about their friendship, or her husband's infidelity. Looked at in this way, the friendship is maintained on a form of deception, lest John risk losing his wife's trust and his marriage. Pressure is brought to bear on the two men to 'keep quiet' about their friendship outside work. Further questioning in the interview revealed how the two men rarely talk about the emotional undercurrents of being committed to preserving a secretive friendship. Morgan suspects that John periodically feels guilty about this, citing it as the likely motivation behind some of the longer intervals between their regular 'catch ups' in the hospital canteen. Notably, the workplace is the only arena in which the friendship is developed and sustained. In not a distinct way to how some gay men maintain separate groups of (non) work friends as a way of avoiding coming out as gay to colleagues (Woods and Lucas 1993), so Morgan and John establish unambiguous boundaries between the public and private realms that enable friendship and family life to co-exist peacefully. This gives rise to speculation about what might happen if either friend left the organisation.

Morgan and John's friendship reminds us that healthy workplace friendships with other men require them to negotiate the cultural taboo of tenderness in male friendship. As indicated above, this might be felt keenly at the start of a friendship. One option available to friends is to talk about sexuality, in order to challenge normative constructions of masculinity that demand men put distance between themselves and other men. This can lead to the development of empathy in friendship, where friends try to understand what it is like to be in each other's shoes. As noted in research that touches on friendships between gay and heterosexual men (White 2008), empathy appears to be a crucial component in friendships where both men can call on each other for acceptance rather than tolerance of alternative gender and sexual identities. Here, then, there is greater likelihood for heterosexual and gay men to question the assumptions both types of men make about each other and the types of friendships possible between them. However, the interview data revealed the normative pressure brought to bear on men's workplace friendships from outsiders can be a significant barrier to the construction of intimacy.

Outside perspectives

Audience evaluations of the outward face of friendship can bring pressures to bear on men (and others) to choreograph their behaviours in ways that legitimise or conceal closeness in workplace friendship. Not surprisingly, gay men's friendships with heterosexual men are particularly susceptible to conjecture about the non-(sexual) nature of these friendship bonds (Bech 1997). Indeed, of all the friendship dyads explored in this book, those involving gay and heterosexual men seemed to draw the most pointed speculation from outsiders.

As Kaplan (2005) argues, men's activities often take place in the 'public' sphere and thus have a public focus, which presents a number of challenges for men seeking to incorporate intimate emotions into male workplace friendships. Participants involved in friendship with heterosexual men were all too aware of this. Austin, for instance, was concerned how some colleagues read the closeness between himself and one of his heterosexual male work friends as a sign of 'homosexuality' or 'bisexuality'. Regardless of whether a man identifies as heterosexual, other people's homophobia can still have a negative effect if he is perceived to be gay. In the context of friendship, it can be a case of 'guilt by association', where assumptions of homosexuality are made based on the company men keep (White 2008). Austin expressed concern for his friend, who was apparently 'indifferent' about this office tittle-tattle. Austin, however, was angered by the gossip and decided to exercise caution in how he displayed affection towards his friend at work. This often meant refraining from displays of physical intimacy, but other participants in similar situations found this strategy hard to maintain.

For instance, Jack is in his early fifties and is a director within an environmental consultancy firm. In one of our interviews Jack described a friendship with a younger heterosexual man called Martin, who is in his mid twenties. According to Jack, they are both 'terrible flirts'. But their flirting is, due to the 'conservative' office work culture in which it takes place, carefully stage-managed. For example, when Martin approaches Jack's desk he 'deliberately sits more closely' to Jack 'than anyone else does'. He also 'undoes the top button of his shirt' every time he sees Jack, exposing some of his chest hair. Jack is acutely aware of the flirtatious nature of Martin's actions, admitting that he enjoyed the titillation of male bodies being as physically close to each other as possible, without breaking the 'office taboo' of 'touching'. These subtle gestures, designed for the specular consumption of friends in certain ways, may go unnoticed by onlookers in the swirl of everyday work life (Kaplan 2006). As such, male workplace friendships can operate as important and pleasurable circuits of homosocial desire, where actions and gestures may contain an erotic subtext (Roper 1996). As in Roper (1996), homoerotically charged feelings pep up the dynamics of how friends work with each other. For Jack the 'buzz' that such sexualised interactions generate help the pair to work together more 'intuitively': they are in synch with each other's thoughts and body language during meetings with clients. Jack's clients have also picked up on this, one remarking positively on the 'dynamism' between Jack and Martin in skilfully handling complex negotiations.

Still, it was no bombshell to hear Jack talk of tongue-wagging and finger-pointing from colleagues. In these moments friendships can become 'lightning rods', attracting 'normative pressure' to define them (Reid and Fine 1992: 149). The intimacy that Jack and Martin enjoy together at work has caught the attention of his colleagues. In similar fashion to Austin, Jack was anxious and concerned for his friend because he had recently become aware of 'rumours' circulating in the office about Martin's 'sexuality'. It irked Jack considerably: 'it angers me that just because I'm gay that other people should think Martin is when he isn't'.

Responding to normative pressure brought to bear on the friendships from outsiders, Jack indicated he planned to speak to Martin about 'drawing back from the friendship at work', in order to 'cool down' its closeness. However, in our second interview, three months later, I asked whether the friendship had developed along the lines Jack had proposed. He replied: 'I think we managed it just for one day. After that we went back to normal. It was a case of why give up something that feels so right?' The friendship clearly carries the risk of being seen by colleagues as exclusionary, and the men themselves being labelled as the office 'odd couple'. But putting distance between each other seems to a pointless exercise for Jack and Martin when the ambiguity of their friendship is exciting and fulfilling. Here the two men are drawn into and sustain interactions that are both pleasurable and titillating, giving little away about the future path their friendship will take.

Summary

This chapter has shed light on the diversity in how gay men develop and benefit from workplace friendships with other men. The empirical data bucks the trend of constructing men's workplace friendships as instrumental and focused on promoting self-interest. While men's workplace friendships can be established along these lines, this chapter expands the horizon of possibilities for understanding how men can relate as friends in the context of work. Gay men's experiences and perspectives on workplace friendships with other men challenge taken-for-granted assumptions including: that a shared sexual identity provides common ground for gay men to establish friendships with each other; that gay men are more likely to experience close friendships with other gay men; and that heterosexual and gay men do not find it easy to build intimate friendships together. This chapter does not dismiss outright any of these assumptions but instead problematises them. In so doing, this chapter lifts the voices of those men who have acknowledged the importance of forming friendships with men from a variety of backgrounds. What is suggested from the foregoing analysis is that men who appear comfortable with acknowledging sexuality as fluid and diverse are more likely to experience a richer array of supportive and intimate friendships. Striking is the creative agency exercised by some participants in negotiating friendships with other men, despite being subject to scrutiny and normative pressure to organise them in particular ways. This raises questions about how these friendships can act as relational contexts for performing gender and sexuality in different ways. This chapter hints at the possibilities here, especially as they relate to the construction of all male intimacies. Before I pursue this theme in Chapter 7, the next chapter examines the types of workplace friendships most commonly reported by participants: namely those friendships involving women.

Chapter 6
Gay Men's
Workplace Friendships with Women

Introduction

As established in Chapter 2, gay men's friendships with women have long been a fixture on the radar of popular culture. In particular, gay men's friendships with heterosexual women are increasingly represented as the ideal cross-sex friendship, since both women and gay men involved in these friendships are said to be secure from the threat of sexual attraction. What is more, the tendency to be constructed as 'friendship experts', both gay men and women appear to make 'perfect' friends. It is not surprising that study participants found it easier to establish close workplace friendships with women rather than men in general, and with heterosexual women in particular. Few participants had experienced workplace friendships with lesbian women and no illustrations were provided of friendships involving bisexual women. Despite the disappointing paucity of these types of workplace friendships, the study data revealed that gay men's workplace friendships with women are diverse, sometimes ambiguous in meaning and shaped by the influence of gender and sexual norms. To begin exploring the richness of these friendships, the first section of this chapter focuses on gay men's workplace friendships with lesbian women. Primacy is given to a small number of participant accounts of these friendships, which demonstrate how gay men construct the value and meaning of these friendships. The second part of the chapter presents examples of participants' workplace friendships with heterosexual women, organised and analysed thematically: how gay men use gender norms to construct women as potential work friends; how a shared sense of *Otherness* can be a basis for friendship in the workplace; the ways in which issues of sexual desire and attraction are negotiated; and the importance of constructing emotionally intimate and supportive friendships with women.

Gay men's workplace friendships with lesbians

It is not altogether remarkable that very few of the men I interviewed reported having little or no experience of friendship with lesbians, both at and outside work. As noted in Chapter 2, divisions between gay men and lesbians stem back many years. Segal (1990) and other feminist theorists (Jeffreys 2003; Stanley 1982; Ward 2000) point to the early days of the Gay Liberation Front for evidence of the problems lesbians encountered working alongside and relating to gay men. Many lesbian women rightly complained that gay men often appeared reluctant to confront their own sexism, or critique the super-macho forms of gay masculinities that helped to reinforce sexist attitudes. For instance, feminist Cynthia Cockburn (1991) notes, in her often cited study of men's resistance to sex equality in UK organisations, gay men can be complicit in homosocial male bonding, especially when they wish to advance their careers. Although this might mean remaining tight-lipped about their own sexuality to ensure smooth passage through the organisation, in so doing they maintain a male hierarchical work culture predicated on misogyny. This has angered feminists, claiming that many gay men do not have a stake in feminist politics, having more in common with heterosexual men than with women (Stanley 1982; Jeffreys 2003). From these feminist points of view, gay men and women are not positioned as 'natural' allies, complicating media constructions of friendships between heterosexual women and gay men that suggest otherwise (Shepperd et al. 2010).

As with Weeks et al. (2001) and Nardi (1999), who conclude from their empirical research that gay men and lesbians tend to hold strong, sometimes stereotyped, opinions about each other's lives, my study data revealed a similar model of understanding. That is to say, participants relaxed into stereotyping lesbians in a number of ways, not the least of them being as follows: 'lesbians are way too aggressive'; 'lesbians seem to think all gay men are out to screw any man they can find'; and 'lesbians don't seem to be approachable'. Even Philippe, one of few participants to have experienced friendships with lesbians at work, commented in a negative fashion: 'based on those I have met and befriended, I tend to find them terribly thuggish, not the type of people I'd have as friends'. In these cases, participants resisted a discourse of allegiance between gay men and lesbians as members of marginalised sexual minority groups, with some promoting negative representations of lesbian women which had a detrimental effect on how they appeared to relate to lesbians at and outside work.

However, several participants spoke differently about lesbian women, noting the dangers of constructing lesbians out of tired sexual stereotypes. Callum exemplifies this point:

> I like the access to lesbian lifestyles because I never had any lesbian friends in the past. The more I know about it, the more I realise how different they are to gay men's lives. Much more different than I expected ... not just about the basic stuff like finding out who they fancy on the TV, but challenging the whole myth of lesbians being gruff people that fight with each other ... and seeing that actually this is not the case ... so you learn all these things, and other stuff like a lot of gay scene spaces are not for them because a lot of scene spaces are for gay boys of a particular sort. And it's like, I never really thought about that.

As Callum's interview extract demonstrates, discourses on lesbian women can have a huge effect on the people gay men choose as friends. When gay men, like

Callum, challenge sexist and heteronormative discourse, opportunities emerge for understanding and learning (White 2008). Indeed, Callum's commentary touches on the benefits of befriending lesbian women in the workplace: the potential to question sexual stereotypes; gain insights into how women can be positioned differently to gay men; and valuing lesbian perspectives on living a lesbian identity at and outside work. Of course experiencing these benefits requires a supportive lesbian friend, and it was striking that the workplace emerged as a key location for some gay men to meet lesbian women. As I have mentioned previously, the workplace was considered by many participants to be populated with individuals whom one might not expect to come into contact with outside work. For example, Callum indicated that the likelihood of befriending lesbians in his leisure life was small, since much of his spare time is spent at home in front of a computer writing research papers, or used to maintain a small network of close friendship ties. In similar fashion, Danny is someone who primarily socialises within an already established circle of gay male friends, leaving him little opportunity to come into contact with lesbians. However, Danny's public sector work environment appeared to be a more promising context in that respect.

In his current healthcare setting, Danny has struck up a friendship with Leah, a hospital Ward Sister. He described a friendship in which mutual respect and understanding were pivotal to developing a sense of affinity and trust. This friendship is a significant aspect of Danny's work experience, enabling him to explore the complexities of gay–lesbian relations. Comparable to how some participants valued workplace friendships with other gay men for the occasions to discuss 'gay issues', Danny similarly attaches value to his friendship with Leah for conversing about issues associated with sharing a similar sexual identity. Here, then, is a sense of how workplace friendships can be developed and sustained on a basis of how each friend is *Othered*. Of course, feminist theorists have highlighted how gay men and lesbians are not symmetrically positioned in that respect (Jeffreys 2003), but this does not mean to say they cannot help each other to develop sensitive perspectives on each other's sense of marginality. In the 'quiet' periods on the hospital ward, especially when working the nightshift together, Danny and Leah find time to retreat to Leah's office in order to 'chat' undisturbed. These opportunities to converse involved talking about and exchanging views on 'coming out' to family and colleagues, 'relationships', 'homophobic doctors and consultants', the 'gay scene' and 'gay sex'. In this way, the conversations friends have together can shed light on issues that one or both friends were previously unaware of. These moments of discovery between friends do not just relate to issues connected to sexuality.

For instance, in the early stages of getting to know each other, Leah assumed Danny had a privileged upbringing. After being enlightened otherwise, Leah took an interest in Danny's family background and experiences as a working-class child growing up on a council house estate. Learning about each other as sexual and classed *Others* can help friends, like Danny and Leah, to see each other less in terms of being 'gay' and 'lesbian' or 'Registrar' and 'Ward Sister', and more in terms of 'fully rounded individuals'. The type of friendship that can emerge as a result is powerful for its capacity to blend friendship with work-based obligations and responsibilities (Bridge and Baxter 1992). Danny explains:

> We both know how to suddenly click into a professional way of relating to each other. We can be having a gossip together and then, in a matter of seconds, flip into our work roles when a patient's life is at risk. I think it takes a lot to be able to do that ... to flip in and out of these roles as friends and something more professional. You have to know the person intimately because when we're professional we're not cold and detached. We're constantly reading each other's minds, and because we're good friends we can pick up on non-verbal signals very quickly.

Danny and Leah's friendship is a positive account about how gay men and lesbian women can potentially relate in ways that mingle friendship and work, remaining sensitive toward the particular circumstances of each other's lives. While there is evidence of how friendship has been personally and professionally transformative, it is wise not to stretch the point in feminist terms. Unlike the feminist work-based friendships between men and women in White's (2008) study, this friendship does not empower Danny to sustain a feminist commitment to performing gender and sexuality differently, or challenge patriarchal discourse and practice in the workplace. But there is no reason to discount the possibility that gay men's lesbian workplace friendships might enable gay men to reflect on their gender privilege. Sadly, the paucity of interview data on this matter prevents further exploration, but the potential to grapple issues of sexuality and gender featured in many participants' accounts of workplace friendships with heterosexual women.

Constructing workplace friendships with heterosexual women

The friendships most frequently talked about by participants were those involving heterosexual women. Yet these friendships remain understudied within academic circles (Nardi 1992a, 1999; Tillmann-Healy 2001; Shepperd et al. 2010; Stuart 1995; Whitney 1990). As such, this section builds on existing research along a number of themes. The first theme concerns how gay men construct women as eligible friends and vice versa, noting the propensity to rely on gender dualisms to do so. Second, attention is paid to how a sense of shared *Otherness* between gay men and women can be used as a basis for friendship in the workplace. The third theme is focused on issues relating to sexual attraction and desire, noting how sexual identities may be used by participants as discursive resources to legitimise these friendships as non-sexual. Lastly, the final part of this section examines the importance of befriending women for developing emotionally intimate and supportive friendships at work. These friendships may draw criticism from onlookers for being exclusive, but they are more likely than gay men's male workplace friendships to be appraised in positive terms, helping to render these friendships visible and acceptable in the workplace.

Constructing gender differences

In speaking about heterosexual women as work friends, many participants drew upon discourse that links femininity with emotionality. Stafford illustrates this point well:

> Women are more emotional than men ... much better at expressing emotions and talking about emotional issues ... it's so much easier to get to know women because they tend to be more sensitive, more communicative.

From the quotation above, women are constructed as emotion experts and men are positioned as emotionally incompetent. This gendered dualism emerged in numerous interview conversations, with few participants questioning the idea that emotional competence is the province of women. Indeed, while it is important to reiterate the idea that gay men are able to form emotionally close friendships with other men in the workplace, as Chapter 5 shows, some participants voiced their frustrations at trying to get some of their male friends to 'open up' emotionally. Hugo put it thus: 'it's like trying to crack a nut without a nutcracker, just not worth the effort'. For participants like Hugo, the perceived ease with which women initiate and sustain emotionally close friendships, especially with other women, heightened their magnetism as eligible friends. Hugo went on to say: 'I just want to befriend those kinds of strong, gutsy women'. Although some commentators might argue there is something in men's and women's behaviour that corresponds to Hugo's understanding of gender differences in friendship (Rubin 1985), the realities of men's and women's workplace friendships are more complex than gendered dualisms can account for. Yet, the dichotomous thinking that establishes dualistic stereotypes of men as suffering an emotional deficit, whereas women enjoy a surfeit of emotional skill and expertise, appeared to open an aperture for many participants to construct friendships with women in favourable terms.

Intriguing, then, is that while some participants relied upon powerful, although stereotypical, discourses of masculinity and femininity to valorise women as experts in friendship and emotion, they sometimes complained about how their female friends acted similarly. Lee explains:

> Some of my female friends at work think that, because I'm gay, I'm therefore interested in clothes, male grooming, having a clean and tidy house and all these things. It's a complete stereotype ... my house is not a show home, I've got two teenage sons and it's a mess most of the time.

Damien comments in the same vein:

> I first met Laura at work around Christmas time. We met for coffee one day
> in the canteen and she said: 'Oh, I'm so excited, I have never had a gay friend
> before, let's get a pink Christmas tree with pink tinsel'. She then said, 'we can
> go shopping together' … it got my back up a little. So I just put my hand on hers
> and said: 'We need to have a little chat'.

In making sense of differences between gay men and themselves, participants like
Lee and Damien were put out by how their female friends relied on gay stereotypes
to construct them as eligible friends. As other participants suggested, on the basis
of these and other stereotypes about gay men, they felt they were fashioned by
their female friends as a 'safe bet' for friendship. Discursively constructed as being
closer to normative discourses of femininity than heterosexual masculinity, gay
men might be cherished as 'male' friends who are more emotionally expressive
than heterosexual men (Grigoriou 2004). For example, Hugo described his appeal
as a friend to Esther, a heterosexual woman in his workplace: 'the reason we
get on like a house on fire is because I'm gay, and a lot of gay men are, by
nature, more sensitive, expressive and witty, and infinitely more appealing to
women'. Unlike Lee and Damien, Hugo is an example of someone who draws
upon a discourse of gay men as sensitive to suggest that gay men are intrinsically
preferable friends for heterosexual women. Viewed in this way, gay men are seen
to offer women a source of male sensitivity, an offering that is supposedly valued
by women, as demonstrated in media constructions of friendships between gay
men and heterosexual women (*My Best Friend's Wedding* 1997; *The Object of
My Affection* 1998). Yet the positioning of gay men (and women) in discourses on
femininity and masculinity is complex, not least because gay men are constructed
to be able to speak to women in ways heterosexual men cannot (Shepperd et al.
2010). In such instances, gay men are assumed to be proficient at performing
expressive forms of intimacy, encoded in normative femininity, while at the same
time maintaining a link to masculinity. Here, then, potential exists for gay men to
be excluded and included within discourses on men and masculinity, depending
on how women and gay men speak about themselves and their friendships with
each other.

For example, it was suggested by some participants that their female friends
expected them to be, as Damien put it, 'more like men than women'. Damien
went on to say that one reason his female work friends have found him appealing
as a gay man is because he is perceived to display masculinity in a similar way
to heterosexual men. His distaste for 'gossip' and 'bitchiness' is a quality that
some of his female friends value, which brings him closer to normative ideals of
heterosexual masculinity than discursive constructions of femininity and bitchy
forms of gay masculinity. Damien feels his female friends regard him as 'more
dependable than a woman for being able to keep a friend's confidence'. At the
same time, one important reason why women develop workplace friendships with

gay men like Damien is because they are seen to offer a 'male perspective' in a way heterosexual men cannot (Shepperd et al. 2010). As Damien suggested, referring to his friendship with Laura (introduced above), 'I give Laura a male angle on things, like her relationships with boyfriends … without a hidden sexual agenda'. That a gay identity is taken to denote an absence of sexual interest is crucial in the construction of many friendships between gay men and heterosexual women, as I shall explore later in this chapter. Here gay men are positioned as sexually neutral observers and gender representatives speaking for and of the category of 'men', a position that is deeply problematic. As noted in Shepperd et al. (2010), such an assumption implies uniformity and stability in the world of men and men's perspectives, a world marked and fractured by difference (Nardi 1992b, 2007). Damien did not seem conscious of the flaws in this line of thought, feeling capable of obliging Laura in that regard. In this respect, a positive, albeit stereotypical, discourse of masculinity is used to construct the value of having a gay man as a friend (Grigoriou 2004). Despite the opportunities this presents for befriending, it remains an area of human activity that is prescribed through prevailing gender norms. This raises the question: what are the implications for organising and getting work done?

From some interview accounts, it was clear that these friendships facilitated productive workplace interactions between gay men and women at work. Sam explains:

> Being a gay man, I've always been more drawn to relationships with women. There's less competition going on … men are always looking to climb the corporate ladder … whereas with women, the whole sort of work thing is a bit more fluffy and open. So, Morag and I talk about things a lot more openly, which helps you to get to be where you want to be much quicker than being very business-like about things … and so much more masculine about things in that respect.

From Sam's perspective, at least, normative masculine values that permeate 'business-like' modes of interacting in their place of work are perceived to have a limiting effect on 'getting things done efficiently'. Such a viewpoint rails against the positive appraisals of organisational forms of masculinity. For example, Alvesson and Billing (1997: 202) suggest that masculine orientations and ideals (such as being 'objective', 'explicit', 'action-orientated') are necessary for getting things done in the workplace. But for others, organisational feminists in general and Sam in particular, masculinity can also be problematic in the workplace when it is synonymous with hyper-competitiveness, hierarchy and career advancement (Cockburn 1991; Kerfoot and Knights 1993, 1998). Seen from this angle, there is a valid concern over men's inclination for instrumental engagement with others at work, which privileges a masculine logic and set of values that often excludes women and gay men. Striking, then, is that Sam suggests relations of friendship can bypass organisational processes that are heavily freighted with normative masculine values. Friendships between gay men and heterosexual women are represented as having an important role to play here, not least because they are seen to be relational contexts for practicing femininity in ways that can speed up decision making and getting jobs completed. That workplace friendships between gay men and heterosexual women might help to legitimise 'feminine' ways of organising is an attractive proposition, but it is also problematic. Constructing heterosexual men as being 'more business like', and women as 'fluffy', reinforces an essentialist view of gender differences. In an attempt to celebrate the place of femininity in workplace relations, Sam at least locks men and women into a gender dichotomy.

Friendship making on the basis of shared oppression

To recap an earlier point, scholarly research suggests that friendship tends to come about because two individuals have something, or a number of things, in common with each other (Allan 1989; Fehr 1986; Spencer and Pahl 2006). Of course, the qualities that friends find mutually attractive vary enormously, but some may be considered particularly pertinent to specific friendships. For example, describing her friendship with Tom, Helen Fielding's celebrated female diarist and singleton Bridget Jones writes: 'Tom has a theory that homosexuals and single women in their thirties have natural bonding: both being accustomed to disappointing their parents and being treated as freaks by society' (Fielding 1996: 27). Despite its comedy value, the observation of Bridget Jones's best gay friend strikes a chord with some academic perspectives that suggest gay men and heterosexual women may find mutuality in friendship for the very reasons Tom suggests.

Elizabeth Stuart reasons that in friendship gay men and women experience 'mutuality', since both have been 'deprived of a sense of self and who have been taught to despise themselves' (1995: 44). Stuart's contention echoes earlier debates regarding mutuality in gay men's and women's experience of oppression (Jay and Young 1972). The idea that women and gay men may share common experiences of being oppressed does not hold universal value for explaining why gay men and heterosexual women are often constructed as compatible friends. As I mentioned earlier, gay men may be implicated in women's oppression – feminist theorising tells us that much at least (Jeffreys 2003; Segal 1990). But as an instance of 'having something in common', as one participant put it, a shared experience of being *Othered* can bring individuals closer together in the early stages of establishing friendship ties (Christian 1994). Several participants regarded this as not only an important basis for establishing friendships with women at work, but also a significant reason for why they were valued.

Describing his experiences as a 'thirty-something', openly gay man holding a senior academic job within a prestigious school of acting, Rupert narrated a moving account of the hardships of having to endure a homophobic work culture. Despite working within the field of performing arts, a sector of employment often thought to be accepting of gay men (Levine 1989), Rupert describes his youth but particularly his sexuality as the targets of attack from junior heterosexual male colleagues. Soon after his appointment as the principal, their 'initial friendliness' curdled into bitter, homophobic hostility. One of Rupert's appointees, Blanca, recognised the damaging effect this was having on Rupert's work life:

> The turning point that made us friends rather than colleagues was the day I remember Blanca coming into my office, seeing that I was at breaking point, and she said: 'Are you alright?' ... I said: 'No! No!' I absolutely broke down and sobbed for an hour and she just came and put her arms around me. And after I tried to pull myself together, she said to me: 'I think you're absolutely fantastic because you are just so determined to be who you are, despite the reactions you get from the men here. I know what it feels to be on the receiving end of that here ... to be an outsider. I've got such respect for you'. When she said that, I thought there is someone else who understands what I'm about.

From this account we observe the genesis of a friendship that is forged out of a sense of being *Othered*. It is a touching testimony to Blanca's capacity and desire to empathise with Rupert, a figure who appears marginalised and clearly exhibiting the signs of human frailty. Connecting with individuals who are openly vulnerable and weak in positions of authority might be considered politically unwise for those who wish to get ahead at work. As Rupert said, one of his tormenters had told him to his face that he had 'cajoled' other staff not to 'support' any of his decisions as a departmental head. This blunt remark confirmed what Rupert had already suspected about his increasing isolation within the department. The deplorable actions of some of his colleagues seemed to engineer a tactical distancing that showed up Rupert's apparent 'incompetence' to keep the lecturing staff motivated and united. Such political machinations are undoubtedly gendered. The attempts of Rupert's oppressors to sabotage his career signify how normative forms of aggressive heterosexual masculinity can marginalise gay men.

From one perspective, it seems that Blanca reads Rupert's 'emotional meltdown' as evidence of his strength of character rather than proof of his inability to do his job. Submitting to that interpretation, Blanca's evaluation of Rupert's behaviour appears to be informed by her own negatively gendered experiences of work life in the organisation. Rupert's commentary suggests that Blanca attempts to link her experiences of workplace sexism with his experiences of organisational homophobia. In a similar way to how gay men have in the past laid claim to understanding the oppression of women by knowing their own oppression (Jay and Young 1972), Blanca establishes a connection based on the same principle of knowing that helps to engender affinity (Tillmann-Healy 2001).

Such points of reference between gay men and women are possible and important. One benefit from establishing workplace friendships where each friend recognises how the other friend is *Othered* is the opportunity to explore and undermine heteronormativity in the workplace (Andrew and Montague

1998). This can have a positive effect on a friend's well-being at work, as Rupert indicated later in our interview. But it is crucial to state that gay men do not have 'special knowledge about women that make them less inclined to hold sexist attitudes' (Ward 2000: 172). Applied in reverse, women do not have insider knowledge about how gay men are affected by homophobia and heterosexism (Maddison 2000). However, workplace friendship is not without the potential to unlock opportunities for gay men and women to reflect on the reproduction of homophobic and patriarchal discourses within relationships and institutions. Admiring Blanca for her willingness to identify with an organisational *Other*, Rupert reciprocated and, over time, learned about Blanca's experiences of sexism at work. Part of this process may involve friends confronting their own sexism or homophobia (Tillmann-Healy 2001; White 2008), in order to think critically about how certain forms of oppression impact on themselves and each other. Crucially gay men and women stand to benefit from this, particularly in terms of developing an action-based commitment towards challenging patriarchal and heteronormative discourse and practice in the workplace.

What if? Sexual desire and attraction between gay men and heterosexual women

As mentioned earlier, sexual attraction is often constructed as a reason why heterosexual men and women cannot – or should not – be friends. Indeed, populist discourse constructs heterosexual men and women as compatible romantic partners rather than friends (Werking 1997). A corollary of this is that gay men and heterosexual women make good friends on the basis that sexual attraction is assumed to be absent. In that respect, friendships between gay men and heterosexual women can be represented positively, as an ideal construction of friendship between men and women. Put differently, it might be said that where heterosexual men and women have often failed to become close friends due to the issue of sexual desire, so gay men and heterosexual women have triumphed in being able to form platonic friendships. This sounds convincing but it is a somewhat crude simplification of a complex relationship between sexual desire, sexual identities and friendship. Not least because previous research shows that gay men and heterosexual women can experience mutual sexual attraction, developing friendships that resist normative classification (de la Cruz and Dolby 2007; Tillmann-Healy 2001; Whitney 1990).

With this in mind, it was noticeable that many participants tended to construct their friendships with heterosexual women as non-sexual. For those participants who adopted this position, it was common for them to define and reduce sexuality to a sexual encounter, rather than a fluid discursive field of desire, identities, values, fantasies, relations, and so on (Brewis and Linstead 2000; Gherardi 1995). Great emphasis is therefore placed on the discursive regulation of sexuality and friendship, keeping the two separate. As Chapter 5 demonstrated, some participants were receptive to the idea of incorporating sex into workplace friendships with other men, but they were far less open to the notion of introducing sex into a friendship with a woman. For these participants particularly, the idea of finding a woman sexually attractive was inconceivable, employing discourse on gay sexuality as an absolute to explain the absence of sexual attraction and desire in their friendships with women.

As such, the majority of participants vigorously asserted that gay men and heterosexual women could develop platonic friendships more easily than heterosexual men and women, on the basis that, as Sam remarked, 'nothing is going to happen as far as sex is concerned'. Sam is an example of someone who firmly believes sexual attraction is absent from his friendships with heterosexual women. It is entirely plausible that some of Sam's female friends might disagree, but what is interesting is how the fluidity of sexuality is considered problematic, in that it opens up alternative possibilities for exploring the relationship between sexualities and identities. Sam was typical of those participants who sought to stabilise a link between sexuality and identity by relying on a heteronormative model of fixed sexual desire (Butler 1990). Within such a framework, heterosexuality is regarded as 'natural' and allows individuals like Sam to articulate cultural norms on what type of men and women have sex. From one perspective, this is problematic since it reinforces the 'naturalness' of heterosexuality, with the effect of positioning homosexuality as inferior to heterosexuality. From another angle, it appears that reifying and essentialising the boundary separating homosexuality and heterosexuality helps participants to understand friendships with heterosexual women as rewarding relationships.

By subscribing to discourses on friendships between gay men and heterosexual women as non-sexual, participants claimed they enjoyed an enlarged scope for developing intimacies with women in ways heterosexual men could not. For example, Austin was one of a number of gay men who felt they were able to enjoy physically intimate friendships with heterosexual women. Austin greets his female friends at work with a kiss each morning; other times they hug or hold hands to display affection. Other examples of physical intimacy described by participants included forms of physical contact that might be labelled risqué. Callum and Alex said they had affectionately 'prodded' their 'girlfriend's tits' and 'bums' at work. It is important to state that this kind of body contact might not be deemed by some individuals as 'intimacy' but considered within the context of friendship, acts such as slapping each other's buttocks, rubbing thighs and caressing women's breasts were constructed as intimate encounters that signified the exclusivity afforded to friends to touch each other's bodies in particular ways. For some gay men, such opportunities were a first for letting them touch specific, sometimes erogenous, parts of the female body. For instance, Michael was invited by one female friend to stroke her breasts after commenting he had never felt a woman's bosom.

In similar fashion, female friends were accorded opportunities to touch gay men's bodies. Stafford described a situation where he had come into work sunburnt. Several female friends went to the local chemist and bought some

Aloe Vera lotion, then escorted Stafford into a side room in the office, stripped him down to his underpants and rubbed in the lotion. This appeared to generate much laughter and pleasure for both Stafford, who was flattered by the attention, and his female friends who apparently revelled in touching Stafford's taught, muscular body. Participants experiencing such physical intimacy typically made the point that friends can touch each other where strangers cannot (Suttles 1970), emphasising that such acts were permissible due to the shared understanding that sexual desire is absent in friendships between gay men and heterosexual women. In this way the mutual exploration of each other's bodies is constructed by friends as a 'safe' pastime. Saying as much does not recognise the subtext of sexual desire that might underpin some of this body contact, particularly if such acts are labelled as 'jocularity' or occasions when friends are 'just messing about', as several participants did. The erotic energy that might motivate body contact also goes unremarked upon, although some participants were aware of these erotic undercurrents.

Philippe is one such example:

> Being a gay man, I never thought I could find women sexually attractive … I was of that opinion for many years until I met Dawn. I've known and worked with Dawn for about ten years. She is very sexy actually, very, very, very sexy. She has a wonderful figure and she is incredibly physical with me … she will sit on my lap and stick her hand up my shirt to feel my chest because she knows she can … and because she's so attractive there is a kind of physical attraction and I actually find it quite sexually intimate.

In line with the study findings of Tillmann-Healy (2001) and others (de la Cruz and Dolby 2007; Whitney 1990), the excerpt above suggests that sexualised components can be present within friendships between gay men and heterosexual women. More than this, however, is that voicing the possibility of sexual desire in friendships with women holds potential to disrupt normative constructions of these friendships. As in Shepperd et al. (2010), what is noticeable in such instances is the potential power of sex to redefine relationships. Experiencing friendship as sexual, potentially gives rise to questions about where and how it might be positioned on a continuum of human relations extending from friendship to sexual relationships (Sedgwick 1985; Werking 1997). There are no clear-cut answers to such questions, as friends themselves must work together to inscribe meaning onto friendships that are non-normative. In Philippe's example, there might not be any incentive to tell Dawn he finds some of their physical contact sexual. In cross-sex friendships, physical attraction and sexual activity can play out in different ways (Rawlins 2008), but against a plethora of media representations of how women often find gay men physically and sexually attractive, this example is notable for outlining a reverse scenario. Equally striking in this example is that gay sexuality is not represented as a unitary and unchanging category. Yet for many of the men I interviewed, gay sexuality was constructed as a fixed entity, which enabled them to speak about the benefits of getting intimate with women at work in ways that were problematic for heterosexual men. Unlike those heterosexual men in Elsesser and Peplau's (2006) study for whom gestures of friendship directed at women were considered risky, in that they might be read by women as sexual harassment, most of the gay men I interviewed felt they were secure from such accusations. Understood in this way, where forms of physical intimacy and bodily contact are disassociated from sexual harassment, a pathway to friendship with women can be established, one that is heavily trodden by gay rather than heterosexual men.

That being said, a small number of participants said they had explored the idea of sexual desire with their female work friends. In discussing this further, it is worth making a broader observation about the pleasure participants seemed to experience talking about sex with their female work friends. This can be explained in several ways, not the least of them being the tendency participants displayed in constructing such conversations as a 'naughty pastime' within the workplace. Talking about sex at work is not unheard of. Previous studies show that sexual banter between workers can be an important and pleasurable activity in the workplace (Erickson 2004; Pringle 1989; Williams et al. 1999), but it can also be a powerful way of promoting highly sexualised views of women (Messner 1992; Collinson 1992). Whatever one's view of sexual banter in the workplace, it is clear from these studies show that sexuality and work interweave, even if sexuality has been discursively constructed as belonging to the private sphere of life (Gherardi 1995). It is precisely because the subject of sex is heavily associated with the private domain that makes talking about it, according to one study participant, a 'titillating experience' in an office environment. As such, discussions about sex were often conducted behind closed doors, in deserted corridors and stairwells, out of the earshot of colleagues. Callum illustrates this point:

> Late last night at work Susannah comes down the stairwell … so I looked up at her and said: 'Look at you with your flip-flops and vagina'. And she went: 'you can't say flip-flops, you can't say vagina'. And I say: 'Yes I can, it's only you'. We both have a hyper sexualised way of talking to each other … it amuses me that we are always talking about bums and tits, and this and that, to each other. These moments seem quite transgressive because we do say things like: 'Oh, if only people could hear us now'. There is a kind of knowingness that this might be problematic to others and, therefore, feeling quite smug about it.

Pondering the potential consequences of being overheard is to contemplate the danger of incorporating sex/uality into organisation in such a way that shows up its existence as a thread within the fabric of everyday work life. However, it is not enough to simply say that possibilities exist for gay men and their heterosexual female friends to talk about sex, draw on a sexualised vocabulary and to explicitly refer to each other's body parts as conceivable foci of sexual pleasure. As significant as the examples above are for demonstrating how sexual banter is a source of pleasure at work, they also underline the importance of what friends talk about for helping them to understand friendship as a non-normative relationship.

Callum and Susannah have discussed what it might be like to 'have sex' together. Rather like Tillmann-Healy (2001), who also considered the sexual potential of some of her friendship ties to gay men, Callum and Susannah contemplate the same potential without feeling they must commit themselves to a sexual encounter. Unlike the participants in Shepperd et al.'s (2010) study, Callum and Susannah do not rely heavily on alcohol as a lubricating agent for loosening their tongues to discuss this topic. Nor do they feel alcohol would be required for them to engage in sexual relations. From Callum's interview account, they appear open and comfortable debating how they might find sex together an enjoyable activity. Of interest is what these explorations of alternative ways of relating might suggest about the potential for such workplace friendships to denaturalise biological sex differences between men and women. Here, Callum and Susannah can be seen to exercise creative agency in how they fashion their own relational expectations of friendship that complicate heteronormative discourses on what men and women are supposed to feel and do in cross-sex friendships. In that sense, we might begin to understand these examples of workplace friendships as holding political potential, in the scope they offer for performing gender and sexuality differently, in ways that engender new ways of organising. I consider this issue in Chapters 7 and 8.

Constructing emotionally supportive and intimate friendships with women

The fact that more women have entered the workforce has often been cited as one important precondition of cross-sex friendships in the workplace (Elsesser and Peplau 2006). Organisational settings that featured large numbers of women were often the best contexts for participants to befriend female colleagues. For some participants, female dominated professions such as nursing, human resources and social work were considered attractive workplaces because women were seen to be 'naturally more accepting of homosexuality than men', as Tom suggested. Although not all participants agreed with stereotypical, albeit positive, representations of women, the study data revealed plenty of examples of workplace friendships involving heterosexual women that were characterised by warmth, affection and emotional support. Indeed, many participants said it was much easier to establish emotionally intimate workplace friendships with women, even though some had experienced emotionally close friendships with men. As discussed above, claiming a 'gay' identity helps to allay the concerns of their female friends about the sexual intentions of male friends. Not surprisingly, some participants admitted that coming out to female friends during the earlier stages of friendship development had a positive impact on developing emotionally supportive and intimate friendships. Lee, for example, indicated that after disclosing as gay to his female work friends his friendships seemed to 'go up a gear':

Now they're friendlier, they share things with me, they touch me more, they let me comfort them. Like walking along one day my friend said to me she wasn't coping at work and couldn't face going back to the office. She let me put my arm round her, I gave her a hug and listened to her talk about why she was sad ... and I don't think that would have happened if I had been straight.

As in other examples provided in this chapter, workplace friendships can exhibit the cherished qualities of human relationships such as a concern for the welfare of one friend for their own sake. Participants attached much value to this dimension of friendship, noting how female work friends had been there for them at times of need.

It is important to state that participants frequently acknowledged the vital role played by women in providing practical as well as emotional support, such as assistance to complete tasks at and outside work. These examples were varied and included forms of practical aid stereotypically associated with men, such as solving IT problems, moving office furniture, completing DIY projects and helping with car maintenance (McGuire 2007). However, the perceived capacity of heterosexual women to listen and act as trusted confidantes figured prominently as an advantage of having a female work friend, with some participants admitting this had a positive effect on their emotional well-being at work.

For instance, Kris, introduced in Chapter 4, had moved from his hometown to take up an administrative post in a university on the south coast. Kris found himself working in a female dominated department, which he initially experienced as a constraint on his preference for befriending gay men. However, over time he became friendlier with the women with whom he shared an office, recalling numerous incidents of having fun together, sharing gossip and airing complaints about managers, academic staff, partners and boyfriends. Kris and two women in particular began to grow closer to each other, which affected how and what types of support they provided for one another. At the time of interview, Kris had recently split up with his boyfriend, describing moments at work when it was difficult to 'put on a brave face' to disguise his distress. His female work friends rallied, providing Kris with a sympathetic ear and a shoulder to cry on. Discussing 'man troubles' with his female work friends, some of who had experienced relationship breakdowns with their male partners, appeared to comfort Kris enormously, helping him to cope with the demands of work. Here we can see how work friends can help each other to speak directly about how they feel and where they stand in regard to others in their lives. Such qualities are not to be underestimated in workplace friendships, particularly as friendships characterised in this way remain susceptible to being colonised by discourse that emphasises the utility of work friends as a means to self-serving ends.

Given the empirical examples above, many of which bear testimony to the emotional closeness of some gay men's workplace friendships with heterosexual women, it is to be expected that these friendships might attract attention from onlookers. Chapter 5 revealed how gay men's workplace friendships with other men, notably those who identify as heterosexual, are vulnerable to the constraining and normative discourses on men's friendships. As some participant accounts demonstrated, these friendship ties can arouse suspicion about the potential homosexual nature of the friendship. In direct contrast, gay men's workplace friendships with heterosexual women received far less idle speculation and criticism. What is more, unlike the type of homophobic reactions friendships between men may inspire in others, negative reactions to participants' friendships with women centred on their exclusivity. Yet these friendships could be bathed in a positive light by onlookers who construct them as normatively acceptable.

It was apparent that some onlookers found the emotional closeness of some workplace friendships off putting. Damien explains:

> I think people at work are threatened by my friendship with Monica because we are very close … something will happen in a meeting and we'll look at each other. We don't have to speak because we know what the other is thinking … it's been picked up because one member of our team has made it clear to my manager that he feels excluded.

Damien highlights how colleagues can draw on a discourse of friendship that emphasises its exclusivity as a problem within a work context. When friends are seen to be particularly close, to the point that they are in synch with each other, this can generate a sense of exclusion among those who surround the friendship. In Damien's workplace, where value is attached to the importance of team work, the exclusivity that comes with being in friendship is seen by some to have an inimical effect on team dynamics. Significantly, examples of where workplace friendships attracted this kind of disapproval were mostly related to close friendships between gay men and heterosexual women. Some participants felt that such criticism was sometimes structured by an implicit desire for participation. Damien again:

> I think one reason [he] feels excluded is that [he's] not part of our friendship. I think [x] struggles with befriending women, and I get the distinct impression he feels frustrated by the fun and affection that Monica and I share together.

From one perspective, it might be that outsiders covet the types of friendships others manage to develop, especially if they struggle to develop similar friendships themselves (Rawlins 2008). Cross-sex friendships are particularly challenging to construct at work, as research shows (Elsesser and Peplau 2006). Those who are successful in forging these friendships may inspire others to do the same, or incite feelings of jealousy in those who secretly wish they could participate in the same friendships. Since gay men are often constructed as better than heterosexual men at befriending women, this might generate envy among some heterosexual men. Whatever the motive might be, it is possible that onlookers may engage in a discourse that allows them to criticise such friendships on the grounds they represent a risk to team cohesion.

In contrast, the emotionally intimate and supportive friendships participants developed with women also attracted admiration. Michael recalled a situation where a colleague had remarked to his friend Lucy: 'you're very close to him aren't you?' According to Michael, Lucy asked if their closeness was a 'problem', to which the colleague replied: 'Oh no, it's so lovely to see people really close at work. It makes the workplace feel less impersonal'. This example, not unlike the one provided in Chapter 5, typified the positive evaluations gay men's friendships with heterosexual women tended to generate. We can see how such friendships stand out against work cultures that are felt to embody the impersonal nature of bureaucratic work practices, or where attempts by employers to manufacture friendliness and intimacy between workers feel synthetic (Kerfoot 1999). In this sense, the idea of friendship as an organising element in people's work lives is readily apparent (Grey and Sturdy 2007), exerting a positive influence on people's experience of organisational life.

Indeed, other participants felt their friendships with heterosexual women had attractive positive comments from observers on the basis that they had succeeded in befriending women where other men had not. For example, one of Philip's male colleagues congratulated him on developing a close friendship with one particular woman at work. Philip's colleague told him he was 'pleased' to see a man and woman getting on well together as friends. This seemed to generate good feeling between Philip and his male colleague, who shared with Philip his frustration at having to explain and defend the non-sexual nature of a former friendship with a female employee to colleagues, friends outside work and his wife. Another participant, Tom, told a similar story:

> I can't fool anyone at work because I'm as gay as the hills, and yet so many people at work have asked me if Helena and I are a couple ... they say we're inseparable, like a married couple in love ... sometimes we play on it, acting like a married couple for effect ... we've have never had any complaints about how openly intimate we are with each other in the office.

One practice that renders friendships between gay men and heterosexual women normatively acceptable is making sense of them in heteronormative discourse of male-female coupling (Werking 1997; Rawlins 2008). Employing Butler's (1990) concept of the heteronormative matrix, the heterosexual romantic relationship is installed as the standard by which all other relationships are judged. Here, then, we can see how the matrix structures a heteronormative gaze, one that positions Tom and Helena as a man and woman who are romantically involved with each other. Looked at in this way, Tom and Helena's relationship is viewed through all but the narrowest of apertures, restricting the possibilities for understanding their relationship as a different type of cross-sex friendship. At the same time, the friendship appears to be accepted by many of Tom's colleagues, affording him a much welcome opportunity to maintain their emotionally close friendship at work. As such, there may be little incentive for the pair to resist this reading of their friendship, in case the good will surrounding the pair evaporates. In fact, what is striking is the complicity displayed by both friends in reinforcing the interpretation of their relationship as a romantic one, by playing out a normative script associated with how married couples behave. Such discursive playfulness leaves unchallenged the idea that men and women should be romantically involved.

Summary

The friendships studied in this chapter show variation in how gay men and women identify with each other, how sexual and gender norms influence the development of these friendships and how these friendships are understood to be important. The foregoing analysis underscores the complexity in how gay men and women negotiate normative discourses on friendships, particularly those that suggest men and women who are close often have to deal with the tensions that arise from sexual desire and attraction. Many of the examples above reveal how friendships between gay men and women, especially women who identify as heterosexual, are constructed as being free from sexual tension and, thus, as important friendships for developing emotional intimacies and forms of support in the workplace. Of particular interest is the discursive strategies used by gay men and their female friends to essentialise workplace friendships along these lines, although some examples challenge normative assumptions that friendships between gay men and women are non-sexual.

What emerges from this chapter is a sense of how gay men and women can develop supportive workplace friendships. For some participants, female friends have demonstrated empathy and a desire to identify with the plight of gay men as organisational *Others*. In these and other instances described above, work friends can be seen to shape each other's experience of organisational life and of themselves. In this way, gay men's workplace friendships with women are similar to some of the friendships participants established with other men, presented in Chapter 5. In both chapters we can observe how workplace friendships can enhance the opportunities for friends to explore who they are. However, both chapters also reveal that gay men's workplace friendships may be colonised by normative discourses that influence how they should be organised. Subscribing to normative discourses risks essentialising differences along the lines of sexuality and gender, constraining the imaginations of friends to explore how they might relate differently in friendship. This is a crucial issue, one that warrants further analysis. In pursuing this, closer attention must be paid to the capacity of workplace friendships to enable gay men to perform sexualities and genders differently, in ways that challenge how they are intelligible through a heteronormative matrix (Butler 1990). Equally, while sexuality and gender may form a solid basis for organising friendship, other differences matter such as class, age, parental status and ethnicity. Acknowledging this is to recognise the importance some gay men attach to cultivating a sense of self that is nuanced at the level of identity. How friendships in the workplace can support gay men in that regard is one area of concern in the next chapter.

Chapter 7
Workplace Friendships, Normativity and Identities

Introduction

It is apposite at this point in the book to dig more deeply into the ways workplace friendships condition possibilities for gay men to explore who they are. In that respect, friendships at work perform an important identity-building role for gay men. This is a robust finding of the study, as the previous two chapters have already indicated, providing insights into how the negotiation of friendship can open up discursive spaces for friends to recognise and support each other's sense of self. In these instances, it is possible to see how workplace friendships can help friends to understand differences and similarities between each other. Looked at in this way, friendship is, in large part, about recognition and affirmation. This raises questions of equality and acceptance, about how far and in what ways friends accept and dignify different identities and ways of living.

In the last two chapters, we have seen work friends question gender and sexual norms that influence how friendships should be organised and experienced. Within workplace friendships, gay men may find opportunities to perform gender and sexuality differently, in ways that go against the grain of heteronormativity. Gay men's gay workplace friendships can function in this way, setting norms that transfer to friendships between heterosexual men. At the same time, we have been witness to how binary understandings of gender and sexuality can impede the meaningful variations in how workplace friendships are lived out among differently gendered and sexually identified people. Where differences between friends become polarised they risk becoming essentialised, underlining the capacity of gay men's friendships to (re)produce problematic discourses of heteronormativity (Nardi 1999). Indeed, heteronormativity is a powerful and commonly used lens through which friendships, identities and human differences and similarities are understood (Shepperd et al. 2010; Rawlins 2008). This is one reason why it is useful to consider further how gay men might use workplace friendships to embrace and contest normative constructions about what it is to be human.

To begin, the first section of this chapter examines why some study participants mobilised heteronormative discourses to construct themselves as 'normal' gay subjects, taking advantage of the opportunities to do so within friendships involving heterosexual men and women. For some gay men, there are benefits associated with workplace friendships that help them to identify as 'normal', such as inclusion and a sense of belonging at work. However, one of the troubles with claiming normality as a gendered and sexual subject is that it entails embracing a normative standard grounded in idealised heterosexuality. As the second part of this chapter shows, workplace friendships can play a vital role in helping gay men to challenge the normalising tendency to construct them as particular kinds of gendered and sexual subjects. This is no small matter, which can put a strain on friendships, revealed in some of the examples of friendship presented. The final segment of discussion focuses on the role workplace friendships play in providing gay men with occasions to construct multiple identities, whereby sexuality can be seen to diminish in priority as a core identity. Identities that relate to ethnicity, gay fatherhood and class are touched on in this section of analysis, illuminating the supportive role of work friends in helping gay men to resist the established cultural tradition of defining LGBT people solely by their sexuality.

Establishing friendship, claiming normality

Gay men, it is argued, want to identify and be identified as 'normal'. As Andrew Sullivan (1996) reasons, being branded 'abnormal' means that gay men are (re)consigned to the margins of mainstream society. Neoconservative gay male commentators like Andrew Sullivan have lent a powerful voice to efforts to downplay the differences between heterosexuals and homosexuals, thereby constructing gay men and lesbians as 'normal' citizens. Opportunities for gay men and lesbians to understand themselves as equal and similar to heterosexuals have opened up in recent years. As Seidman (1998) argues, increased visibility of LGBT people is having a positive cultural effect, although the spread and consequences of the normalisation of lesbians and gay men is uneven and incomplete. However, from Warner's (1999) queer theory perspective, the assimilationist political tenet of gay and lesbian normalisation encourages these subjects to cleanse themselves of any intolerable whiff of homosexuality. For example, those individuals who put distance between themselves as gay men who link love with sex in a domestic setting, and those gay men who are sexually promiscuous, are a step closer to claiming normality. In this way, the idea of the 'normal gay' serves as a narrow social norm. Steven Seidman explains:

> This figure is associated with specific personal and social behaviors. For example, the normal gay is expected to be gender conventional, link sex to love and a marriage-like relationship, defined family values, personify economic individualism, and display national pride. (2002: 133)

The problem here, at least for Seidman and others (Warner 1999: 60), is that being normal is to blend and have no visible difference with those heterosexuals regarded as 'respectable'. Commenting in the same vein, Richardson (2005: 522) notes that in the effort to be recognised as 'normal', gay men and lesbians (re)draw 'new boundaries in relation to sexuality, ones that constitute *Other* sexualities that can be figured as problematic and in need of control'. Expressed differently, the construction of the 'normal gay', like the 'normal heterosexual', requires the invocation of the *Other* in order to signify what is 'abnormal'. Gay men who do not embody the qualities of the 'normal gay' risk being (re)positioned as the *Other*, and therefore least likely to benefit from the process of normalisation. From this angle, discourses of normalisation privilege a particular construction of gay sexuality that constitutes little if any threat as a transgressive and subversive assault on heteronormativity. Thus operating within a politics of normalisation is a discourse of recognition that turns on a notion of difference imagined through a set of comparisons and (dis)connections (Butler 2004).

These debates are relevant in this study because one theme to emerge from the data is the role workplace friendship performs as a context for laying claim to a sense of being 'normal'. It is already apparent from some interview accounts that friendship can allow gay men to affirm and sustain unconventional lives, but it is also the case that friendships can help gay men to construct and maintain conventional lives. It is no coincidence that the types of workplace friendships which conditioned possibilities for participants to understand themselves as 'normal' were those involving heterosexuals. Before considering the dynamics of these friendships, it is important to acknowledge the strength of feeling among some participants on the desirability of claiming normality. Douglas is one such example:

> My dream is to live in a detached house and live a regular life with all its ups and downs … for me it's about wanting to be part of the anonymous mass of people who enjoy comfortable suburban living … I don't want to stick out in any way, just think of the sitcom *Terry and June*, that's what I want.

Speaking from a similar point of view, Ryan remarked:

> I'm a professional who drives a Mercedes, has a partner at home, has holidays abroad, wears nice clothes … and what's wrong with that? I have no ambition to be political about my sexuality as some do … I don't wear my sexuality like a chip on my shoulder. It's a very small part of who I am … I'm a man who just happens to be gay.

The two quotes above are illuminating of the shifts that have taken place in how men may identify as 'gay'. Unlike those gay men for whom sexuality is pivotal in framing their identities (Nardi et al. 1994), both Douglas and Ryan treat sexuality as one part rather than the core of their identities. In so doing, Douglas and Ryan normalise their homosexuality by drawing on a discourse of normality, underpinned by heteronormativity. As the interview excepts demonstrate, gay men might require the help of friends to (re)construct themselves as 'normal'. Both Douglas and Ryan frame their aspirations and lives in terms of an affluent, middle-class domestic setting. This is represented nicely by Douglas's cultural reference to the long-running British sitcom *Terry and June* (broadcast from 1979 to 1987), that has come to be regarded, though often abraded, as an archetypal representation of English middle-class suburbanism (Wagg 1998).

By locating gay sexuality within a domain that has, historically, afforded it little if any accommodation, Douglas and Ryan reconstruct a 'respectable' version of gay sexuality that may be anchored in the context of everyday life. However, as Richardson (2004) suggests, this is not to say that tensions arising from (re)locating gay sexuality within the sphere of domestic life are resolved. In order to represent gay sexuality as compatible with domesticity and family life, it must be (re)fashioned to display certain qualities, as outlined by Seidman above (2002: 133).

From this point of view, the normalisation of homosexuality appears achievable only for a select number of gay men. For one thing, the construction of the 'normal gay' is classed, and some participants had an acute sense of this. For example, Gordon indicated his desire to 'live a professional lifestyle', denoted by a 'nice detached house … with a posh car on the drive', but felt this was beyond his means as a 'working-class gay man living on a paltry salary'. The desire to live a 'professional lifestyle', read here as an identification with a way of life that embodies a sense of normality (Rumens and Kerfoot 2009), requires resources to fund and sustain its (re)construction. Participants such as Gordon feel at a disadvantage to affluent gay men, reminding us that although it is possible to choose ways of life that are organised around norms of 'professionalism' and a discourse of normalisation, the ability to live out these choices is constrained by the material conditions of individual lives. However, the resources gay men may use to claim normality vary, with friendships being one such example. The study data revealed how heterosexual work friends could help some participants to legitimate their claims to normality in the workplace.

James, introduced in Chapter 4, spoke to me at some length about his workplace friendship with a heterosexual married couple, Vanessa and Robert. Explaining the appeal of this friendship, James started by providing a detailed account of his life history, emphasising his working-class family background and origins. For James, his upbringing in a working-class family was not characterised by the concern some working-class families exhibit to ensure their children are able to cope with the instability and hardship that might mark their lives (Gillies 2005). James described a childhood blighted by domestic violence and limited opportunities to shape his future path in life. Overcoming the disadvantaged circumstances of his formative years, James used work as a means of fashioning a middle-class way of life. Securing himself a job and lodgings as a teenager, and then by advancing up the career ladder, James has built a network of friends and colleagues who have supported his progress. In many ways James feels he has constructed a middle-class identity, being keen to point out that he lives in a large detached house in an affluent suburb, is employed as a sales director, drives a sports car and has a wardrobe of designer clothes. All of this symbolises a corrective against those people for whom James was 'never going to amount to much'.

Equally important to James is that he feels established within a network of friendships with other middle-class people. While James has a number of friendships with other gay men who appear to live out similarly middle-class urban lifestyles, James was keen to forge friendships with middle-class heterosexuals, taking advantage of opportunities to do so at work:

> Over a period of time Vanessa and Robert came into the showroom to buy caravans from me. Because I liked them, I did put myself out a bit to help them ... but what I saw in them was this amazing picture of normality. They had a perfect family life, something that I knew I'd never have, but the closest I could get to it was by being friends with them. The hardest thing was becoming friends. I had to wait every other year to see them, since the only time I actually saw them was when they popped into the showroom to buy another caravan. So I decided to step it up a bit. I phoned them up and asked them if they wanted some caravan equipment. It all started from there. We got to know each other really well...all of this sounds like a lot of effort over a lot of years, and it was. But it's through having these kinds of friends that I feel perfectly normal at work, at home, in all areas of my life.

It is noticeable how James constructs the value of his friendship with of Vanessa and Robert in terms of how they are considered to lead a normatively better way of life. It was clear from James's interview that the three of them enjoy a very sociable and close friendship. They socialise together outside work and often go caravanning as a threesome. Striking is that Vanessa and Robert's relationship and home life is discursively constructed as a heteronormative ideal, one that James covets but believes is out of his reach. One major benefit for gay men from establishing friendships with heterosexuals who are socially respectable is the cultural legitimacy they may gain from forging such connections. Through these friendships, gay men may have entry points into heterosexual worlds that might otherwise be closed to them (Rawlins 2008). Vanessa and Robert have incorporated James at the heart of their social and family life, enabling James to feel included within a sphere of heterosexual domestic life. In this example, friendship may be understood as a process of relating and identity making, in which James fashions a 'normal' gay identity. As this example shows, there are positive outcomes associated with the identity building role of friendship but there are problems. James might be understood as a contentious figure, someone who settles for recognition at the cost of sacrificing transgressive and subversive possibilities for undermining heteronormative values and practices. In other words, James valorises conventional heterosexual relations as being the most 'normal' and desirable way of life. Queer theorists such as Michael Warner (1999) might bristle here because, in elevating the heterosexual couple relationship over all others, James reinforces a hetero-homo binary that constitutes a hierarchical gender and sexual order.

Be that as it may, the desire among other participants to connect with heterosexuals in order to claim a sense of normality in the workplace is strong. For example, Grant remarked that forging friendships with heterosexuals was crucial to 'keeping it real': feeling included within society rather than solely relying upon friendships with other gay men in order to feel 'good about being gay'. For Grant, like many other men I interviewed, the practice of befriending LGBT people only is short-sighted. Grant criticised such a strategy for putting gay men at risk of feeling 'isolated', confined to 'gay ghettos' and thus disconnected from wider society. Another example is Ryan, who suggested that being 'cut off' from heterosexuals would have a damaging effect on the extent to which gay men could be integrated within the workplace:

> Friendships with straight people are very important … you don't have much choice about what types of people you work with, and loads of workplaces are full of straight people anyway … so if you're unskilled at relating to straight people, then you might be seen as being something of an outsider. You're not going to fit in. Having straight friends at work is important because it's through these types of relationships that I feel like a fully functioning employee.

As Ryan points out, workplace friendships have the capacity to facilitate the development of a sense of belonging. Of interest here is that organisational integration is expressed using a discourse of normative commonality. When Ryan says that having heterosexual work friends help him to feel like a 'fully functioning employee', he does perhaps mean gaining acceptability among work friends and colleagues. However, as research shows, to be accepted at work some gay men must demonstrate adherence to conventional gender norms, conservative politics and patriotic, middle-class values (Seidman 2002). In other words, workplace acceptability is not granted arbitrarily, since there needs to be commonality between individuals in terms of values and outlooks that go beyond those espoused in, for example, organisational mission statements. Workplace friendship might be a vehicle for gay men to be identified as acceptable individuals, as illustrated in Ryan's understanding of friendship as playing a key role in the establishment of shared values that can be used as a basis for laying claim to being simultaneously 'normal' and 'gay'. Indeed, for many participants, being 'normal' was constructed as an aspiration, as a way of defending themselves against organisational discourse that might construct them in pathological terms (Humphrey 1999). Yet in the bid to measure the quality of work life by a particular yardstick of normalcy, friendship might reinforce the importance of specific taken-for-granted norms as the only criteria of value (Warner 1999). Expressed differently, workplace friendship might inadvertently constrain the possibility for gay men to explore alternative ways of constructing and valuing the self.

The trouble with normal

For Warner (1999), one of the troubles with claiming normality is that it entails embracing a normative standard grounded in idealised heterosexuality. As stated previously, the lure of the normal for gay men is located in its impulse to blend, to have no visible difference with 'respectable' heterosexuals. From participants' accounts, there is already a sense of how (re)constructions of a 'normal' gay identity are problematic, insofar as they uphold heteronormative ideals of normality. While some men like James struggle to forge a 'normal' gay identity, using workplace friendships as a resource in that endeavour, other participants experienced discomfort when work friends tried to normalise them. Kris recalled one such incident:

> When Carla said to me in the office that it's nice to work with such normal people, I said to her: 'Don't you ever call me normal. That's the greatest insult ever!' I'm not normal because I don't think I am … I guess I was a bit rough with her, but I thought Carla knew that because she's a close friend. I have such an unorthodox approach to being gay and being at work … constantly pushing the boundaries to the limit, so it felt like Carla was putting me in a straight box that's very claustrophobic.

Kris's account offers a glimpse into how friendships between individuals who identify differently in terms of gender and sexuality often require friends to negotiate differences and similarities carefully, so neither friend loses a sense of their own individuality (Rawlins 2008). In this case, Kris resists being discursively tagged as 'normal' because he reads Carla's statement as having a heterosexualising effect on his sense of identity as a gay man. In contrast to some other study participants, sexual identity is central to how Kris constructs a positive sense of individual difference, one that gives him distinctiveness in the workplace. In an occupation and office environment dominated by women, Kris protects his 'novelty value' as the only openly gay man in the administration department by drawing on discourses of gay sexuality to support and reward an unconventional identity. Thus he rebukes Carla for positioning him within a discourse of normalisation that minimises his sense of difference from his office colleagues and friends.

In Foucault's terms (1979), this example carries an acknowledgement that the self is a site of discursive power, where different ways of being identified can be jeopardised. As well, the example illustrates that the process of getting to know someone in friendship is not always smooth, even when friends have known each other for many years. For example, Philippe has been a close friend to Clint, a gay man employed in the same organisation, for 15 years or more. Recently, Clint invited Philippe to attend his forthcoming civil ceremony. The invitation dealt an unexpected fatal blow to their friendship, as Philippe explains:

Clint and his boyfriend have been together for over twenty-three years and I've been looking forward to it for some time. Clint is a special friend, we've known each other for a long time, we have supported each other through all sorts of things, particularly at work … I got this phone call from Clint who says: 'I don't know how to put this to you but you have to behave yourself at the ceremony, you're going to have to stop being camp and outrageous, because there will be three hundred people there, lots of whom will be straight'. I was gobsmacked. What did he think I was going to do? Shag my boyfriend on the wedding table and sit on the cake? The one place I would have expected to be accepted is at a gay civil partnership ceremony. I think, if he was honest about it, Clint feels I symbolise everything he doesn't like in gay men … like when I camp it up, that I'm unafraid to be out and proud, unapologetic to be myself. It's been a fatal blow to the friendship, particularly as I've found this out after fifteen years. To have a gay friend not accept your sexuality after all these years of knowing you is devastating, and it's going to be very difficult to work together professionally.

One issue of interest from the quotation above is how one friend seeks to discipline the other friend's performance as a gendered and sexual subject. Clint's concern that Philippe might camp it up with gusto, at a ceremony that may be read as an act that normalises the 'right way' to live intimacy for gay men and lesbians (Weeks 2007), can be seen as part of a new form of regulation surrounding the normalisation of same-sex couples. Put differently, in making such a request of his friend, Clint invokes a crude dualism that separates the 'respectable gay' from the 'unrespectable'. What is emphasised here and in earlier examples, is the particular signification of masculinity that expels the feminine *Other*, with the effect of (re)producing harmful gender hierarchies in how gay men understand and perform masculinities. In that respect, Clint's apprehension is structured by a concern that Philippe's gendered performance of camp will bolster a discourse of homosexuality as deviant. It is in this sense that this example underlines the strained circumstances under which friendships operate, enmeshed as they are within gender and sexual power relations. The effects of this are evident in the upset experienced by Philippe and the subsequent deterioration in his friendship with Clint, with potentially negative consequences for how they will continue to work together in a professional capacity (Sias et al. 2004; Sias and Perry 2004).

In contrast, other participants provided accounts of how they sought to challenge the normalising tendency to construct gay men as particular kinds of gendered and sexual subjects, with notable effects on how they and their friends were able to perform gender and sexuality in the workplace. Callum thought his friendship with his line manager, Armand, a heterosexual male university academic, exemplified this point. Callum and Armand have known each other for some years, and they enjoy the exchange of scholarly ideas, perspectives and values that are part and parcel of the everyday activities and interactions as academics. This has helped the two men to establish a form of intellectual closeness, which has influenced how they relate to each other at work. Significant, then, is that both men are situated within a discipline of the social sciences receptive to articulations of gender and sexuality in terms of performance, contradiction, play and incoherence (Butler 1990, 2004).

Callum suggested that Armand's interest and utilisation of queer theory in his academic writing has prompted him not only to contest heteronormative discourses on gender and sexuality, but also to generate confusion over how he might be identified. Friendship helps to facilitate this type of experimentation:

> Having knowledge of queer theory makes [Armand] more able to experiment with ideas about sexuality, drag and camp in our friendship. It gives us some space to think about creating those ways of doing sexuality. At the same time, working in an academic environment that gives some license to that kind of play helps a lot. But access to that knowledge gives us much more scope for generating these possibilities than someone who lays bricks for a living ... it's allowed Armand a bucket load of space to do all sorts of things ... like writing outrageous journal articles on queer theory, making provocative arguments, being polemic and flamboyant.

It is worth scrutinising how these public activities illustrate a mode of engagement for using queer theory to challenge normative constructions of gender and sexuality in the workplace. From one perspective, Armand's commitment to 'queering things up a bit' in the workplace can potentially generate gender trouble for how men and men's relationships are understood:

> I think Armand is really taken by the idea of parody ... how camp and drag can show up the performativity of management and work life ... when it comes to drag, I think Armand plays around with me and other people at work, by moving from one subject position to the next. In one moment he can present in one way, like being very affectionate. Quite a lot of the time we kiss each other on the lips when we see each other ... in my office, in his office, or in public. But on one occasion, he planted a kiss on me as I was walking across the campus. Normally, I wouldn't give a rat's arse about what other people would think about that, but I noticed some of my first year students close by and it made me think whether it was entirely appropriate. In another moment, he can be quite serious. Other times, he'll try to make us aware of how being a manager is performative ... like the time we were in an executive meeting and he deliberately got everyone talking about whether some people were mingers. Not appropriate behaviour in a business meeting, is it? For me, these are all queer moments ... they confuse people's expectations about who he actually is, and how the day-to-day stuff of work gets done.

Certainly, the open expression of affection between these male friends is notable within the public arena of work for its potentially destabilising effect on organisational discourses that promote largely instrumental ways of relating at work (Kerfoot and Knights 1993, 1998). Witnessing such acts of intimacy between the two men, colleagues of Armand have questioned Callum about whether Armand is 'gay', revealing again how vulnerable men's relations are to being understood within discourses of heteronormativity. Indeed, rather than letting such confusion go unchallenged, Callum has felt compelled at times to defend his friend against assertions of homosexuality, suggesting that Armand is undermining normative constructions about how people should relate to each other. Demands made by others for recognition, using a heteronormative matrix (Butler 1990), can produce moments of difficulty, as Callum's example demonstrates. Constructing multiple identities and (re)configuring how relations between men are understood in gendered and sexual terms is not always effortless, sometimes requiring men to face dilemmas about how to deal with the expectations of others that shape the organisational contexts in which they interact. As the example above reveals, friendship may provide a relational context to develop and support men's action-based commitments to expanding narrow views of gender and sexuality.

Yet, from another perspective, the interview extracts highlight the potential pitfalls associated with this kind of experimentation. For instance, encouraging members of staff to evaluate the physical appearance of other colleagues is a dubious act of subversion. Such behaviour from a senior academic might be construed as cruel, fuelling the anger of critics who feel that queer theory in the hands of men can lead to intellectual posturing with aggressive and sexist overtones (Jeffreys 2003). Furthermore, Callum's discomfort at being embraced by Armand on campus exposes a valid concern about how public displays of affection might jeopardise his sense of self as professional. Callum positions himself as a reluctant partner in some of these intimate moments, raising questions about whether he feels obliged to participate because Armand is his line manager. Negotiating the expression of intimacy must be participative if they are to avoid reinforcing power relations that (re)produce hierarchy and inequality (White 2008). While Callum is supportive of Armand's unconventional gender performances, he also appears constrained at times to share his doubts with Armand about their consequences.

Taking this further, an uncomfortable parallel can be drawn, one informed by feminist research about how senior organisational men can 'do' intimacy with junior females in ways that reinforce their subordinate position (Cockburn 1991; Gherardi 1995). Looked at from a feminist point of view, Armand's outbursts of affection are exercised within gendered power relations that (un)wittingly (re)position Callum as a subordinate male, and thus (re)produce the very gendered forms of organising Armand seeks to undermine. Notable, therefore, is that doubt appears to collect in Callum's mind about the motives behind Armand's desire to perform 'gender trouble' at the level of identity:

> I do think sometimes that he gives nothing away, particularly as he moves from one identity to the next, making himself ambiguous in terms of gender and sexuality … So he moves between those things and I find it intriguing in

one sense, but sometimes I wonder if he's performing for my benefit or at my expense ... it's a conversation I've yet to have with him.

As Callum's narrative continues, we learn more about how his friendship with Armand is positioned within discourses that contain competing and contradictory elements. On the one hand, Callum draws upon discourses on the performativity of gender and sexuality to intellectualise Armand's performances of intimate friendship as 'intriguing'. Armand's discursive activities underline the constructed and performative qualities of gender and sexuality, and are certainly not out of place against a cultural backdrop of postmodern sexualities and genders (Roseneil 2000). A gender-as-performative discourse informs how Callum understands his friendship with Armand as 'novel' and 'experimental', not least because in the context of work the performance of masculinities is often seen to be 'purposive-rational' in their orientation (Kerfoot and Knights 1993).

On the other hand, Callum struggles to understand if Armand's performances of gender are for his benefit or at his expense. On this matter, it is no small thing that friendships are often constructed as relationships in which people can be themselves, without pretence or dishonesty (Allan 1989). A friendship-as-performance discourse, which emerges from Callum's example, underlines how Armand's discursive manoeuvring reveals more about playing with and off a multiplicity of selves, and less about revealing a deeper sense of self. This is not to imply that individuals have a fixed authentic self that can be accessed through friendship. Instead it is to recognise that one of the pleasures of friendship is about being able to explore who and what you wish to be, as studies on gay men's friendship poignantly illustrate (Nardi 1999). In this vein, Callum's example encourages us to see the potential in cross-sexuality workplace friendship for this kind of discursive activity, but also reminds us that friends need to negotiate and understand each other's discursive performances of gender and sexuality in ways that are intelligible and acceptable to them. One lesson that can be drawn here is that it requires friends to actively confront and reflect on each other's discursive performances as well as their own.

Gay men, workplace friendship and the intersection of identities

So far we have seen how workplace friendships bear the potential to help gay men and their friends challenge normative discourses about how they should be understood as gendered and sexual subjects. However, it is crucial to acknowledge the identity-building role of friendship does not operate on the axes of sexuality and gender alone. Workplace friendships can help gay men to construct multiple identities, where in some situations sexuality and gender may be given less emphasis than other aspects of the self. Saying as much is to recognise that many gay men, like many lesbians and bisexuals, regard sexuality as peripheral rather than core to the identification process (Seidman 2002). This theme emerged from the interview data, evident in accounts of how work friends had helped participants to resist what Weeks (2007) describes as the long standing cultural tradition of defining LGBT people solely by their sexuality. In that sense nothing can be taken-for-granted in terms of how gay men wish to identify, already illustrated by the differences between some participants in how they feel about discourses of gay/lesbian normalisation. As we shall see in some of the examples presented below, while workplace friendships can facilitate a range of possible identities for individuals to construct, it is unwise to assume friends will always experience mutual acceptance regarding all identities and ways of life.

Exploring how work friends can help gay men to understand themselves not merely as sexual and gendered subjects, it is useful to return to Theo. Theo said he experienced difficulty forming some cross-race friendships at work, referring to one work friend who repeatedly relaxed into Asian stereotyping. What started as a promising friendship gradually faded, after Theo's friend joked that he must be disappointed, as a general manager of a small theatre company, to have bucked the Asian trend of overachieving in education and work. This lamentable occurrence highlights how friends can struggle to negotiate the racialised discourses that shape the development of emerging cross-race friendships, with some friends reinforcing the very discourses of race and ethnicity their friendships hope to transcend. Recalling his experiences here gave Theo an opportunity to voice his wider frustrations about living and working in a white-dominated seaside town on the south coast, with limited opportunities to make friends who recognise his Asian identity but who understand him as a person.

From another angle, it is interesting also that some participants who identified as 'white' bemoaned the absence of cross-race friendships in their lives. Pursuing cross-race friendships was constructed by several gay men as a potentially culturally enriching experience, for adding nuance to their perspectives on people and the world around them. Yet the prevailing friendship practices of the majority of participants were consistent with previous research, in that most befriended others who were similar in race and ethnicity (DeMott 1995; McCullough 1998), even in workplaces that were described as multi-racial.

In that sense we can see how workplace relations can be characterised by constraint and misunderstanding, but they can also open up opportunities for acceptance and support. Theo is fortunate to have developed several close cross-race workplace friendships, where friends do not treat him as a racial token or pretend racial differences do not exist at all. He provided an illustration of this, where work friends rallied to his defence after being pinned with negative racial stereotypes:

> I was attending a management meeting when the external auditor, unaware that I was the general manager, quipped that I must be the accountant because I'm Asian ... I was dumbfounded by his remark, it was so blatantly racist, I was left speechless, although my friends jumped on the auditor's comments instantly. They were marvellous. It pays to have friends like mine because they treat me

as a person, and not as a gay man or a gay manager or an Asian or a gay-Asian, or whatever.

What comes to the fore in Theo's example is the importance of friendship in supporting identities that are threatened by the narrow confines of stereotypes. As such examples demonstrate, it is a noble deed performed by one work friend when they confirm the other's sense of self in meaningful ways. Theo's friends play an empowering role here, defending him from racial stereotyping that threatens to rob Theo of the possibilities to sustain a meaningful but contingent sense of personhood.

Commitments made by friends to help each other build identities are not obligatory but negotiated, motivated by concern about understanding each other as a person rather than the occupant of specific identity categories. Put differently, this is to recognise that in exploring different ways of being human, individuals may construct all manner of identities, with some new identities coming to the fore at specific moments in time. However, this does not mean that the process of constructing and sustaining new identities is entirely unproblematic, noticeable when some participants tried to make sense of themselves as gay parents.

To illustrate, it is useful to refer again to Jack, someone who has come out as gay later on in life. Jack is divorced, having been married for a number of years before disclosing his gay identity to his wife, with whom he has parented three children. Although Jack has remained in the same job, he has moved to a different town, and currently lives on his own. Still the needs of his children are a priority, and Jack maintains regular contact with his teenage offspring, which he feels is important not only for his children but also for himself, as a 'committed father'. Indeed, it became apparent in our interview conversations that Jack's identity as a father was more meaningful to him than his new identity as a gay man. However, fathers who later identify as gay are confronted with complex issues surrounding the future of their relationships with female partners, living arrangements and negotiating access and care provision for children, to mention just a few.

Another set of issues relate to the difficulties gay fathers experience when they are discursively positioned within heteronormative discourses on parenting, which frequently articulate grave concerns about the impact of gay parents on the children themselves (Weeks 2007; Wilton 2004). At worst, discourses of homophobia routinely align gay men with paedophilia, making identities as gay fathers hard to develop and maintain. Still, as Chapter 2 demonstrated, gay discourses have run counter to this, promoting and granting legitimacy to new forms of parenting, thereby undermining discourses of reproductive heterosexuality and the family (Weeks et al. 2001; Weston 1991). Study participants such as Jack had an acute sense of this as a backdrop to laying claim to an identity as a 'dad who just happens to be gay'. Yet, unlike many of the gay men in studies by Weston (1991) and Weeks et al. (2001), Jack did not have a set of gay friends to rely on for support in negotiating these conflicted elements within his identities.

Disconnected from an established circle of family friends outside of work, many of whom have 'sided with [his] ex-wife', Jack has found comfort and support in a small number of women he has befriended since the break-up of his marriage. These female work friends, all mothers with teenage children, have been more receptive than most others to the change in how Jack identifies in terms of sexuality. In contrast, other work friends have struggled: 'some of them can't see beyond the gay thing, it's like they've forgotten that I'm a dad with three kids, but just no longer married to [X]'. For Jack, coming out has placed too much emphasis on his sexuality as a marker of identity, overshadowing his identity as a father. Here, then, commonalities formed between some of his work friends have weakened, as perceived differences intensify, placing some long-standing workplace friendships under strain. In contrast, his new female work friends have helped Jack where others have faltered, by providing opportunities to discuss parenting and affirm his identities as a father and gay divorcee. Conversations about divorce, parenting teenage children and living as a single person have given Jack fresh perspectives on his situation and sense of self:

> I was pretty desolate when I moved out of the marital home, having come out to my wife and friends. Most people didn't want to know me ... then I started to panic about what my kids would think of their dad being gay, breaking up the family. I just felt like a monster ... I felt guilty, regretting my decision, wondering whether it was all worth it, that my kids were the victims of my selfishness to come out. Cathy and some of the other mums didn't start from that position. They approached me with a sympathetic ear, telling me that divorce and being gay was not the end of the world but the start of something new. It took me a while to appreciate this, but then we starting talking about run-of-the-mill stuff like coping with stroppy teenage kids and being a single again. They gave me the strength to see that being a dad is really important to me, and that being gay needn't get in the way of that.

The more we discussed the supportive role played by Cathy, the more Jack's commentary betrayed his previously low expectations of women as friends. Jack is an example of a gay man who has had few female friends in the past, when he was part of a heterosexual couple, having conformed to strict cultural norms that tend to limit the formation of individual cross-sex friendships outside marriage (Werking 1997). He spoke with real feeling about the help he had received from Cathy and his other female work friends, valued all the more given his initial attempts to rely on his male friends at and outside work were largely unsuccessful. Some struggled to empathise with Jack's emotional difficulties leaving his children, while others refused to accept his newly adopted gay identity.

Although components of this account might be present in the narratives of any parent who leaves one relationship for another, there are particular features in Jack's that relate to the problems gay men experience when they have been heterosexually active for a substantial period of time (Weeks et al. 2001). Other participants with children, like Lee, told similar heart-wrenching stories of ending marriages and negotiating custody arrangements for children, when forming new gay identities. A picture emerges in these accounts of existing work friends rallying to provide emotional support or, in the case of Jack, how new work friends perform that supportive role. Notable also from this example is that gay father identities can require considerable emotional support to nurture and sustain them, especially in situations that threaten to destabilise and undermine them.

Analysis of the interview data revealed also the significance of class as an important identity for some gay men. Although few participants described workplace friendships that cut across lines of class, Sam provided a typical account of friendship struck up, not on the basis of sexuality or gender but on sharing a similar working-class background. While this is not altogether surprising, as research shows that friendships are typically although not exclusively formed between people who share the same social class (Spencer and Pahl 2006), in the context of the study data, Sam's account is unique as an example of how class identity is negotiated differently in the company of work friends and colleagues.

For Sam, coming out as gay at work seemed to spark much less of a reaction from colleagues and friends than, as he put it, 'coming out as working-class'. Asked how colleagues responded to his identity claim as working-class, Sam mentioned that several thought he was having a joke with them, convinced of his 'middle-classness' from his 'nice house in a nice part of town, with a nice boyfriend in a middle-class profession'. Notably, one colleague suggested Sam ought to 'downplay' his working-class roots, if he was serious about climbing the organisation's career ladder. Feeling the pressure to fit in at work, Sam adopted a particular identity strategy:

> I put on an acceptable middle-class gay persona ... to a degree, but it doesn't always sit comfortably with me. I'm from solid working-class stock. It's an important part of who I am, although I need to tone it down ... like not talking about my family background or political beliefs, or I just conceal it when I'm working alongside management, most of whom are Oxbridge educated, middle-class straight men.

This is a striking account of how naming one's self as 'working-class' is to make a public statement about identity, that is first not taken seriously and then must managed by strategies such as those based on concealment. Like other examples provided above, opportunities emerge within friendship to counter organisational discourses that inform normative standards about the class identities of senior managers.

Sam's close friendship with Morag, who is similarly positioned within the company as an 'outsider' because of her class, but also by her gender as one of very few women in management, can be seen as a process of overcoming the limits of organisational expectations about what it means to be a 'model worker':

We went to one of those company barbeques and I heard Morag talking about growing up in a working-class family in Scotland. We've chatted quite a bit about coming from working-class families, and how you can't really get ahead here if you're working-class. Talking about it doesn't change how the company is but it does reduce that feeling of isolation that comes from being the only gay working-class kid in this place. I don't lose that side of me when I'm with Morag … I can be comfortable with just being myself, and not some model worker the company insists I ought to be.

This is a striking account of how friendships can be formed on the basis of *Otherness* that relate not just to sexuality and gender, as seen in earlier chapters, but also to class. There is a strong impression running through these accounts, of understanding the significant role work friends can play in providing respite from expressing the self in ways that might be experienced as forced, false and narrow. Here, workplace friendships are constructed by gay men as relationships that allowed them to 'be themselves'. Friendships that afforded participants such opportunities were often prized above other types of amicable, informal workplace relations, since they facilitated freedoms that enabled the men to transcend the confines of stereotypes in their identity making. In Sam's example, the construction of a middle-class identity is felt to be 'inauthentic', since it raises questions in Sam's mind about whether he is being 'true' to himself. Of course organisational scholars might argue that Sam is no different to many people who feel their identities are circumscribed within the workplace, but so few of them acknowledge the role of workplace friendship in providing a space for friends to address this issue. Here, then, Sam's example, like others documented previously, hints at the potential for friendship to provide protective spaces for identity making within contexts that levy discursive closure on how individuals may locate themselves within and across identities.

Summary

Workplace friendships can perform an important identity-development role for gay men. Instances of how participants have re-interpreted their lives during moments of change, such as claiming an identity as a gay father, are strikingly powerful accounts about how friends can support and shape each other's lives. In these interview extracts we get a sense of how one work friend can identify with the plight of another, offering much needed support to sustain new identities and ways of living. In some cases, this may involve speaking up on the behalf of friends when they are threatened, illustrated nicely by Theo's work friends. But the capacity work friends have for expanding our sense of self is not uniform. As we have seen in Jack's example, the stance of some work friends towards his adopted identity as a gay man reminds us that some new identities are vulnerable to censure in changing circumstances. In this regard, workplace friendships can make a positive difference to how gay men understand themselves within and across different identities. At the same time, this chapter has shown that it is important to raise certain questions about how gay men's workplace friendships can buttress and transcend discourses that divide and reduce who they are, and limit what and who they might become. In order to realise the potential for gay men's workplace friendships to condition the possibilities for human flourishing, then those involved in these friendships must address these questions, which is one way of saying that friends must come to learn about each other. I have more to say on this in the concluding chapter.

Chapter 8
On the Significance of
Gay Men's Workplace Friendships

Introduction

For the gay men who participated in this study, workplace friendships matter. As explored in this book, the role and meaning of workplace friendships is far from uniform, but these relationships are generally important in terms of support, goodwill, identity and intimacy. In this concluding chapter I comment further on some of the themes and issues that have emerged from previous chapters about the importance of workplace friendships for gay men. Workplace friendships are clearly significant to gay men at an individual level, but we may also understand these friendships having wider significance, especially in terms of the social. This warrants discussion as does the issue of what lessons individuals can draw from the study for developing friendships in the workplace. Since workplace friendships are of interest to practitioners, I outline some implications for management before signalling directions for future research.

Significance of workplace friendships: For gay men

Analysis of the study data reveals that the importance of having work friends is experienced keenly in the micro-level actions of participants' everyday lives. The work friends of gay men can help them to enhance the potential for experiencing pleasure, joy, intimacy, happiness and the extremes, both positive and negative, of organisational life. Friends can provide many different forms of support, from acting as confidantes to offering practical assistance and advice. Notably, workplace friendships do not have to be long standing and durable in order for gay men to understand them as significant relationships. Contrary to some popular and academic wisdom, casual friendships can be intensely pleasurable as sources of sociability and even intimacy. Compared to friendships established over long periods of time, short-lived friendships are equally capable of helping gay men to find meaning in their work lives. At the same time, the study findings reveal that complex workplace friendships, those which are multi-stranded, multi-functional and often transcend hierarchies and inequalities, generally take time to develop. The significance of these workplace friendships often relates to the opportunities for gay men to construct identities and selves. Participants attach special value to those friendships that enable them to fashion identities and selves that help them to feel fully human. In other words, those friendships that permit friends to explore and cherish their own and each other's singularity as human beings at the same time as treating each other as a whole.

The different ways gay men make sense of their workplace friendships as significant is conditioned by all manner of things, not the least of them being that countless people spend much of their waking day engaged in paid employment. The workplace is not merely a location for undertaking the activities associated with fulfilling a contract of employment or a job description. It is a potentially fertile context for meeting other people with whom we might wish to establish friendships. Crucially, we may come into contact with people we might not ordinarily meet outside work, so some work settings harbour potential for individuals to enrich the diversity of existing friendship circles. While many study participants prize friendships with individuals with whom they share a lot in common, other participants have spoken, with real feeling, about the joy of friendships with people who identify differently in terms of sexuality and gender. One major area of empirical analysis in this book has been the discursive sense making activities among participants, which enable them to understand particular friendships as significant in specific ways. Here, then, study findings show how identities can shape people's eligibilities as friends, revealed in participants' friendship preferences. The interview accounts also highlight the influence exerted on gay men's workplace friendships from the structural dimensions of organisational environments, jobs and work activities. As this book has revealed, workplace friendships can be significant because they have been hard to establish, whether this is due to limited opportunities for socialising at work, rigid hierarchies, inequalities and oppressive work cultures. Developing workplace friendships in these environments can represent a personal victory against organisational discourses and practices that, for example, marginalise certain social groups and target the individual as an organisational resource.

At this stage it is useful to make some specific points about how we might theorise the significance of gay men's workplace friendships. What emerges from the study data is a sense of how workplace friendships are significant in two broad ways. First, workplace friendships can be conceptualised as circles of safety for gay men, offering protection against oppressive structural conditions that contribute to the heteronormativity of everyday life. These types of workplace friendships can perform a crucial role, blunting the effects of organisational homophobia and heterosexism. In that respect, workplace friendships hold a similar capacity to those formed outside work, as noted in research by Weeks et al. (2001) and others (Nardi 1999; Gottlieb 2008). Friendship is a critical relationship for equipping gay men with the fortitude and courage to come out as gay, secure themselves from the effects of negative gay stereotyping and confront the challenges of living against the grain of heteronormativity. As argued in Chapter 2, friendship has long been understood and cherished by gay men as a personal strategy for self-protection and preservation.

Defined in this way, it appears the significance of friendship has not lost its salience. Although there is an increasing acceptance of LGBT people (Weeks 2007), it is uneven and the workplace continues to be one arena in which gay men, and other sexual minority groups, are particularly vulnerable to discrimination (Bowring and Brewis 2009; Burnett 2010). Even in a context characterised by an explosion of postmodern sexualities and genders (Weeks 2007; Simon 1996) and at a time when notions of 'gay-friendliness' are gaining more than a toehold in many organisations (Colgan et al. 2007; Williams et al. 2009), workplace friendships can serve as crucial sites for helping gay men to openly participate in organisational life. Heteronormativity continues to be a feature of a wider postmodern landscape of sexualities and organisational settings in which gay sexualities are 'promoted' and 'celebrated' (Chapter 3). Against this backdrop, workplace friendships may help gay men to 'be themselves', if by that we refer to gay men rather than organisations about what this might mean. From the point of view of some participants, 'being yourself' is to be 'out and proud' about a gay identity in the workplace. Work friends play supportive roles here, emotionally and practically. But the study data also reveals that at a time when more LGBT people appear willing to be open about their sexuality (Weeks 2007), certain workplace friendships are more likely to emerge, such as those involving individuals who identify differently in terms of sexuality. One robust finding of this study is that these friendships afford opportunities to learn about gay lives and identities. Likewise, gay men may find opportunities to connect with heterosexuals. It is here that we may conceptualise gay men's workplace friendships as holding the capacity to bridge between socially divided groups and networks of people.

My second point builds on the first. What emerges clearly from this study is the creative agency exhibited by gay men in forming workplace friendships that are multi-dimensional and multi-functional, many of which defy neat classification. As noted in Chapter 2, friendship research on LGBT people in a post-AIDS era is focusing on the creative possibilities that reside within friendship for constructing new senses of belonging and ways of relating to others (Nardi 1999; Weeks et al. 2001; Weston 1991). Weeks (2007) cites these unconventional relationalities, that blur discursive boundaries between other human relations such as sexual, romantic and familial relationships, as a colourful illustration of the growing cultural significance of friendship in people's everyday lives. In that sense, it is not enough to state that workplace friendship provides a haven for gay men in an unfeeling heteronormative world of work. Such an interpretation would be plausible, were it not for the accounts of how participants exercise agency in developing and sustaining workplace friendships that defy normative constraints. As such, the study data contributes to the growing literature that argues friendship offers alternatives, in terms of identities, selves, human relations and intimacies (Roseneil and Budgeon 2004; Spencer and Pahl 2006; Weeks et al. 2001; Weston 1991). Remarkably, workplace friendships remain largely under the radar of these researchers, but there is no reason to discount these relationships from bearing the potential to provide opportunities to raise new questions and pursue fresh directions for organising and understanding the self and others at and outside work. Saying as much has broad implications for how we might use different theories to study gay men's workplace friendships.

As outlined in the Introduction, a multi-pronged approach to drawing on theory is merited, one that derives insights from poststructuralism and the sociology of friendship, in order to theorise gay men's agency within specific historical, social, cultural and organisational contexts. Poststructuralist theories place emphasis on the discursive, useful for conceptualising workplace friendship not as a fixed and stable variable or phenomenon, but as a subjective set of interactions and activities. As the study data reveals, the meanings attached to activities and everyday interactions are contingent and fluid, made by those involved in these relationships. Adopting a discursive approach helps us to keep an eye on the horizon of possibilities for viewing gay men's workplace friendships as localised sites of creative resistance, in that they might facilitate the generation of identities, relationships and actions that violate heteronormative assumptions. It also allows us to understand how the construction of friendship is related to the performance of gender and sexuality. For example, we can examine the creative agency of gay men demonstrated in (re)shaping gender relations to establish close friendships with heterosexual men at work.

At the same time as a focus on agency is maintained, attention can be paid to how the construction and upkeep of friendship is influenced by the contexts in which it is constituted. The study data illustrates this to some degree, affording glimpses into how relations within gay men's male workplace friendships are shaped by organisational environments and wider social change and practices around sexualities. The sociology of friendship has been particularly robust at theorising friendship as a relationship that is marked by contextual contingency (Adams and Allan 1998; Allan 1989). In that regard, what comes to the fore is an appreciation of the resources, discursive and material, required by participants to develop friendships in ways, more or less, of their choosing. At work, participants may need to acquire time, energy and space, among other things, to forge friendship ties. The cultural constituency of organisations will be of influence here, as will people, events and relationships in other contexts. As one might expect, individuals, including participants of this study, do not have equal access to the resources that may be required for building and conserving friendships. Nor are they inoculated from the influence of context, in shaping how their workplace friendships are organised and patterned.

In short, I argue that the findings of this research serve to demonstrate gay men's workplace friendships as processes of organising. So, while I am at pains to point up the agency in how gay men might form workplace friendships to satisfy their needs and interests, they do not have *carte blanche* to do whatever they want. Indeed, this is what makes friendship special. This is so, insofar as study participants reveal that workplace friendship is negotiated, sometimes under demanding circumstances and constraints, involving commitment, flexibility, reflexivity and risk-taking on the part of friends themselves.

The wider significance of gay men's workplace friendships

This book has placed emphasis on the significance of gay men's workplace friendships at the level of the individual and self, but this does not mean to say these friendships do not have wider significance politically and within the field of organisation studies. With this in mind, there is a strong impression, running throughout many of study participants' accounts, of how the 'personal is political'. This is to say, in Rawlins's words (2008: 193), that the daily actions of friends can 'promote freedom and justice in small and large ways'. This idea is one of several that are fundamental to Peter Nardi's (1999) perspective on the politics of gay men's friendships. As discussed in Chapter 2, Nardi suggests that gay men's friendships can act as 'mechanisms of social reproduction in which gay masculinities, gay identities, gay cultures, and gay communities get created, transformed, maintained, and passed on' (1999: 7). Crucially, some of these identities, cultures and values may destabilise cultural norms that contribute to the heteronormativity of everyday life, thereby denaturalising its taken-for-granted and normative status. As argued previously, heteronormativity is often legitimised by reference to a 'natural' order and 'necessity', and gay men's friendships provide a context for questioning these false associations.

One pertinent question to raise here is: do gay men's workplace friendships hold the capacity for (re)producing, nurturing and sustaining gay identities, selves, sexualities, masculinities and intimacies? Within limits gay men's workplace friendships bear the potential to function in this way. Study findings show how gay men's gay workplace friendships can facilitate the (re)production of gay identities that are meaningful, less in terms of self-closeted understandings mired in shame and guilt, but more in terms of pride. Networks of gay male friendships, where they occur, can provide the emotional and practical support to affirm gay identities in the workplace and generate positive organisational discourses on gay sexualities. These networks of friendship ties appear promising for effecting organisational change, in combating the oppressive structural conditions of heteronormative work environments. In these situations, there is no reason why gay men's friendship networks cannot support the development of non-corporate identities and selves at odds with a heteronormative sexual order. Analysis of the study data hints at the possibilities here, although it also underscores how workplace friendships between gay men can be self-serving both politically and personally, failing to address the injustices such friendships create when they privilege the needs of one social group over others. It is noteworthy also that the study data underlines how gay men's identities are divided and multiple, with many gay men choosing to disassociate themselves from other gay men in the workplace.

It is crucial that we do not blithely assume gay men flock together in friendship due to the perceived power of sexuality as a bonding agent in the process of friendship development. This is a rather obvious point to make, but a raft of research suggests that sexuality is an important basis on which close friendships among gay men are likely to be formed (Nardi 1999; Sullivan 1998;

Weeks et al. 2001; Weston 1991; Chapter 2). In contrast, this study paints a different picture of the friendship patterns of gay men, in which heterosexual figure prominently as cherished work friends. To explain this, we might assume that because heterosexuals often outnumber LGBT people in the workplace that gay men must make do with heterosexuals as friends. That this is not so, evident in how study participants desire such friendships, underscores the significance of friendships with heterosexuals as not only relationships that facilitate gay men's smooth passage in organisational domains, but as relationships for making sense of themselves in alternative ways. For some gay men, sexuality may suffice initially as a basis for friendship but other identities may be of equal or more salience as defined points of similarity and attraction in friendship making. It is clear from the study that gay men identify in multiple ways, particularly at a time when it appears many gay men and lesbians are not ascribing sexuality priority as a core identity (Seidman 2002).

Another reason for the great significance attached by many participants to cross-sexuality friendships is that gay men might feel exposed by openly associating with other gay men, risking workplace discrimination. This is a plausible explanation, but it is not the story told by those study participants for whom integrating themselves into organisations requires establishing connections with heterosexuals. One striking finding of this study is the strength of feeling among many participants about the value and joy of befriending heterosexuals in the workplace. This adds a new dimension to extant research on cross-sex workplace friendships, which has typically focused on heterosexual men and women (Elsesser and Peplau 2006; Markiewicz et al. 2000; Fritz 1997; Sapadin 1988). Empirical insights into participants' friendships with heterosexual men and women reveal how these friendships can mount a challenge against cultural and organisational norms about how these friendships should be organised. In some cases, these friendships compensate friends for the deficiencies of other relationships, contest the privileging of romantic love over friendship and blur the discursive boundaries between sexual relations and friendship. In these instances, friendships are politically-edged, in that they can help friends to overcome the relational constraints of heteronormative discourse and institutions (Rawlins 2008). Both gay men and their heterosexual friends stand to benefit from this.

For the heterosexual friends of gay men, workplace friendship can bear potential as a relational context for guarding against sexual stereotyping, and opening up possibilities for performing friendship, gender and sexuality differently. For some gay men, cross-sexuality friendships can help them to not only understand themselves as gendered and sexual subjects, but also in terms of ethnicity and as fathers, working-class and so on. Constructing multiple identities is a powerful process of exposing social injustice and its effects on the most vulnerable identities of each friend. We have seen in some friendship accounts the willingness of heterosexuals to stand up for their gay friends at work, which carries its own risks for those who do so from positions of privilege. It is here that we can see the potential for heterosexuals to act as 'straight allies' in co-constructing organisational worlds that are much less influenced by the strictures of heteronormative patterns of organising and being. Workplace friendships can act as the seed beds for organisational change in that respect although as indicated in the study, such change is typically localised, visible in the discursive activities involved in the process of fashioning identities, selves and relationships. For other gay men, cross-sexuality friendships permit them to feel 'normal' and to build a sense of belonging within the workplace. But this is so, insofar as gay men who report that their own sense of being 'normal' draw upon discourses of heteronormativity. However much some gay men may welcome opportunities to reinvent themselves as 'normal' within such discourses, they limit other possibilities for making sense of themselves as fully human.

Despite this, one particularly notable instance of the political potential of gay men's workplace friendships lies in the opportunities they occasion for setting norms that transfer to friendships between other gay and non-gay men and women. There is some evidence to support this in Chapter 5, regarding how gay men's gay workplace friendships can inspire heterosexual men to reconstruct intimate relations within their own workplace friendships. Striking, then, is how Michel Foucault anticipated these aspects of gay men's friendships in a number of interviews, published in the concluding years of his life:

> ... the question of gay culture – which not only includes novels written by pederasts about pedastry, I mean culture in the large sense, a culture that invents ways of relating, types of existence, types of values, types of exchanges between individuals which are really new and are neither the same as, nor superimposed on, existing cultural forms. If that's possible, then gay culture will be not only a choice of homosexuals for homosexuals – it would create relations that are, at certain points, transferable to heterosexuals. (1982/1997: 159–60)

Like other commentators such as Nardi (1999) and Vernon (2000), I take Foucault to mean here that gay friendships can function as a model for a way of life for LGBT people and heterosexuals. Part of the attraction of gay men's friendships for heterosexual men and women is their capacity to transcend normative relational constraints. Indeed, in a published interview that appeared in the French magazine *Gai Pied* in 1981, titled 'Friendship as a Way of Life', Foucault suggested that gay people have, out of necessity, been inventive in order to experience same-sex intimacies. For our purposes here, 'friendship as a way of life' is a compelling call for people to explore alternative ways to structure and conduct their lives. There is no reason to doubt the capacity of gay men's workplace friendships to stimulate those who participate in them and others who surround them into reinventing selves, identities and relations. The question for me becomes, then: how might gay men's workplace friendships be significant within the field of organisation studies?

To reiterate an earlier point, one contribution of this study is the knowledge it generates about how gay men's workplace friendships can underwrite and undermine the on-going construction of organisational discourses of gender and sexuality. Study participants are constructed as active in how they respond to narrow gendered stereotypes of men's workplace friendships. Yet research on how men may reshape gender relations within organisational relationships and prioritise their own well-being over the cultural restraints of heteronormativity is scarce, despite an explosion of critical scholarship on men, masculinities and organisation (Kerfoot and Knights 1993, 1998; Collinson and Hearn 1996). From this stream of literature, an understanding is obtained of the inimical effects of 'purposive-rational' modes of masculinity for both the subjects who perform such masculinities and those who are marginalised by them. These studies are both necessary and illuminating, but they tend to present an overly bleak perspective on organisational masculinities. For example, Deborah Kerfoot contends that as a consequence of a 'concern to maintain control, masculine subjects disavow the possibility of relationships and forms of intimacy that are non-instrumental' (1999: 196–7), but this assertion does not recognise fully the potential for men's workplace friendships to develop non-instrumental intimacies and alternative genders and sexualities. Roper's (1996) study adds nuance to Kerfoot's (1999) analysis of the link between intimacy and managerial forms of masculinity, by showing how male homosocial forms of intimacy or, as Hearn (1992: 205) puts it, 'circuits of desire' can thrive between male managers in organisational contexts where instrumental forms of masculinity are well established. Roper's (1996, 1994) research is part of a small and important body of literature that considers how different types of men organise and relate to each other, in ways that disrupt heteronormative discourses of gender and sexuality (Pullen and Simpson 2009; Kaplan 2006; Martin 2001).

In that regard, this study adds a new dimension to this scholarship. Many interview accounts problematise a worn-out argument that men's friendships outside and at work are more instrumental and less intimate than women's friendships. The interview findings help to supplant dominant perspectives on men's friendships in particular, showing how men can establish workplace friendships that embody qualities such as intimacy, trust and acceptance. Such friendships can enable gay men to (re)produce empowering identities and selves, suggesting that organisational discourses of heteronormativity cannot fully colonise gay sexualities and genders. Indeed, study findings indicate that gay men's workplace friendships can encourage men to question and explore the limits of heteronormative discourses of gender and sexuality. For some men, the supportive and emotional expressive nature of some friendships between gay men might be used as a discursive schema for remodelling depersonalised male-to-male relations in the workplace. Here, then, the study prompts a review of how men's friendships are understood.

Still, it is not enough that by showing how gay men's workplace friendships might be understood in terms associated with femininity (i.e. support, emotional intimacy), stereotypes of men's friendships are sufficiently debunked. We might inadvertently fall into the essentialist trap of using a 'feminine ruler' to measure the 'value' of men's friendships (Wood and Inman 1993). One way of getting round this problem is to adopt a poststructuralist approach, which discourages the treatment of gender and sexuality as static variables, allowing us to interrogate and potentially move beyond the confines of gender dichotomies for understanding men's (and women's) friendships. As some study participant accounts demonstrate, acknowledging the restrictions of gender and sexual dichotomies can prise open new possibilities for understanding men's workplace friendships. While it is premature to suggest that gendered stereotypes of men's friendships have collapsed, they are being undermined and not just by gay men, as this study reveals. The cumulative effect of discursive activities can help to (re)shape the gendered and sexual contours of organisational domains as well as wider social and cultural landscapes.

That being so, we might speak also of the potential that resides in those workplace friendships outside the parameters of this book. This includes workplace friendships between and among women. This is a crucial observation because women's friendships have been at the vanguard of sexual and gender politics for some time, as feminist scholars have been at pains to point out (Faderman 1981; Friedman 1993; Raymond 1986; Weinstock 1998). The intellectual weight of feminist research on friendship cannot be underestimated, not least because it reminds us that, no matter how gay men's workplace friendships might incite others to reshape gender and sexual relations, they do not hold universal appeal in that endeavour. Gay men's friendships are quite capable of supporting the very discourses of heteronormativity they might otherwise undo. As this study has shown, gay men occupy positions of gender privilege, allowing some to reinforce gendered social and cultural divisions between men and women (Ward 2000). As such, I do not elevate gay men's workplace friendships over all other forms of friendship in the workplace as a relationship template for others to emulate. Gay men's friendships cannot be universalised. They do not provide solutions or propose a 'right way' to oppose normalising regimes or live meaningful lives. Moreover, my point is that gay men's workplace friendships, like other workplace friendships not covered in this book, can offer ideas into the possibility of creating alternatives. Here we can delve deeper into the different possibilities certain workplace friendships may occasion, demonstrated in Chapters 5 and 6. In that sense, gay men's workplace friendships are about showing others the potential for experimenting in the invention of identities, selves, intimacies and relationships. At the very least, this is something we all need to think about because it can have a positive effect on how we understand ourselves and relate to others in the business of organisational life.

Drawing lessons from gay men's workplace friendships: For individuals

Although gay men's workplace friendships do not offer prescriptions on creating better ways of organising in the workplace, we may still draw lessons from the study data about what friends might need to consider if they wish to explore the possibility of any 'becoming' that transcends normative constraints. In that respect, many of the interview accounts provided by study participants reveal their agency, in how they think, make choices and undertake actions in the processes of friendship. From a Foucauldian perspective, this is an engagement with ethics, in that it involves creating and enacting new ways of life. As noted in Chapter 2, Foucault defines ethics as the 'conscious practice of freedom', insofar as it is the 'considered form that freedom takes when it is informed by reflection' (1997: 284). Looked at in this way, ethics is not about adhering, unthinkingly, to a particular set of codes. Rather, and put simply, ethics is an on-going activity that involves choices and actions about forging new ways of life. Like Weeks et al. (2001), I see an important association between ethics (as practices of freedom) and friendship. For those who participate in friendship, there are opportunities for friends to experiment in the creation of new ways of life. Here, then, establishing a set of ethical relations with other people is an on-going process that involves caring for the self.

In light of the study findings, caring for the self can be understood as the cultivation of potential, qualities and skills required by friends to constitute themselves as human. For many of the gay men who participated in this study, this entails exploring the possibility of being different or 'normal' rather than deviant. Caring for the self can be an important part of friendship, whereby friends can develop and sustain commonalities, respect and promote caring for others. Essentially, caring of the self should not lead to the abuse of others. However, commentators such as McNay (1992) suggest that caring for the self is problematic within contexts where relations are ordered in hierarchies. Under these circumstances, caring for the self can turn into the domination of others. The workplace, it is often argued, is one such example of a context in which human relations are structured hierarchically, cultivating self-interest and utility (Vernon 2005). In this vein, there might be limited scope within organisations for caring for the self to incite people to reflect and scrutinise how their positions of privilege are contingent on the subordination of others. A related concern is again voiced by McNay (1992), who rightly notes that Foucault is not forthcoming on the matter of distinguishing between what is and is not a legitimate exercise of power in caring for the self. The lack of guidance here is problematic, particularly for men. Men have often been chided by feminists, with good reason, for their gender blindness, for seldom acknowledging their gender and the privilege it carries (Jeffreys 2003). However, men might look to gay men and men who identify as 'feminist' or 'pro-feminist' for vision and inspiration here. Although gay men can be gender blind, they have been constructed as a good example of a group of men who have defined and developed a new way of life, helping some men to 'become gay' and experience same-sex intimacies (Nardi 1999; Blasius 1994; Weeks et al. 2001). The study findings suggest there might be a role for gay men to play here, and friendship is a good example of a relationship that can potentially foster caring for others and for thinking and living differently. At the same time, the interview data reveals the challenges gay men and their friends face when engaged with the creative dimension to caring for the self. Several lessons may be drawn from this.

First, there is no predetermined shape that workplace friendships must take for them to serve as relational contexts for experimenting with the self. However, experimental work on the self requires, as McWhorter (1999: 198) argues, trying out new things, thinking new thoughts and developing new ways of seeing ourselves and others. Study findings show that when gay men's workplace friendships embody trust, mutual respect and care giving, friends stand a better chance of being able to experiment with caring for the self. Saying as much is to recognise that friends must be open to each other people's lives and points of view. In so doing, friends may be exposed to alternative ideas about how identities and lives can be lived, helping friends to gauge to what extent it might be possible to think and act differently. This is a process of learning, as the study data suggests. Where there is a willingness among friends to learn about each other there is a greater chance for friends to create new identities and selves. Of course there are people who do not wish to engage in that sort of activity in friendships outside and at work. As the study shows, some gay men have no desire to use workplace friendships for testing the discursive limits of normative constructions of sexuality and gender. While friendship may bear the potential for self-transformation, it cannot be forced onto people.

From another angle, many men do not wish to befriend men who identify as gay. For American essayist Joseph Epstein, the idea that gay men might be able to offer heterosexual men lessons in the art of supportive and intimate friendship is neither desired nor required. Confessing that he has no wish to 'be like women, or gay men, or successful therapy patients', Epstein (2006: 118) makes light of the efforts made by other men seeking to develop intimacy based on self-disclosure. Constructing himself as someone who does not give hugs but accepts hearty handshakes, Epstein is an example of a man who draws on a masculine discourses that assigns a low value to how many men wish to relate, using more expressive forms of intimacy, to other men. In a context when stereotypes of men who disclose less and have fewer friendships than women are being destabilised, Epstein's comments are a sober reminder of the backlash against men's efforts to gain legitimacy and acceptance for new ways of relating and becoming. As this book demonstrates, simply having a gay friend does not magically make friendship an intimate or politically subversive relationship. It requires a desire and commitment on the part of friends themselves to explore living differently, despite the risks of being discredited and constrained by others.

Second, if gay men's workplace friendships are to function as a context for disrupting normative discourses of gender and sexuality, friends must be prepared to provide alternative perspectives that might be critical of each other's point of view. As Steve Garlick asserts, a 'friend is one who makes you aware of where your limits lie. He or she directs your attention towards the boundaries that enclose us, and thus towards possibilities of freedom' (2002: 570). If friends are determined to overcome forms of heteronormativity, they must interrogate the cultural imperatives that assert heterosexuality is a normatively better way of life. This is no small matter, as aspects of the empirical chapters demonstrate. Some gay men still rely on discourses of sexual orientation that essentialise gay and heterosexual identities, in order to construct friendship. It appears from the study data that when friends mobilise such discourses the opportunities for contesting the facticity of sexual identities as natural occurrences dry up. However, when one friend draws on discourses of sexuality that recognises its fluidity and provisional qualities, there is more hope for producing new capacities for living sexuality, gender and friendship differently. Understandably, there might be a clash of perspectives between friends, giving rise to conflict and argument. But if friends are to work against discourses of sexual or gender normalisation, disagreement is likely – particularly if one friend has a greater stake than the other in the regime of heteronormativity. When friends are able to confront each other about the limitations of their views and actions, there is greater opportunity for both friends to help each other become better people.

This kind of work is complicated by other issues, not the least of them being where friends are positioned in organisational hierarchies. Differentials between friends in terms of hierarchy, organisational status and capacity to exercise power can all compromise the potential workplace friendships hold for thinking and living differently. One friend may be reluctant to challenge the other friend's point of view or be unsure about how to tackle a friend's behaviour if it causes discomfort and offense. There is some evidence in this study to illustrate these challenges, but there is data also that suggests friendships can straddle organisational hierarchies, providing friends are open to treating each other as equals and as a whole person, not just as occupants of a job role (Bridge and Baxter 1992). A strong theme to emerge from the interviews was the benefit of doing this kind of friendship work. When gay men and their friends appear open and receptive to each other's ideas and viewpoints, they appear more willing to explore the process of becoming other than what they are.

Drawing lessons from gay men's workplace friendships: For practitioners

If lessons can be drawn for individuals who exercise a will to friendship, then there are lessons that can be drawn for practitioners. As discussed in Chapter 3, the attention given to workplace friendships by employers can be linked to a desire to improve organisational performance. Academic research that indicates how perceived opportunities for employees to develop workplace friendships can positively influence levels of job satisfaction, and that being in friendship can help to reduce employee turnover and increase productivity, has confirmed what some employers have long suspected, that informal workplace relations matter in the business of organisation. Indeed, some employers have gone to great lengths to foster informality in the workplace, such as Google and Microsoft, in the hope that employees will be more committed to performing work tasks and duties (Fleming and Sturdy 2009). My concern, shared by others (Grey and Sturdy 2007; Sias 2009), is that in the pursuit of organisational efficiency gains, some employers have turned workplace friendships into commodities. In Chapter 3 I argued that the construction of workplace friendships as organisational resources leaves little, if any, room for understanding how these friendships are important for their own sake. As such, I wished to lift the diverse voices of gay men in workplace friendships because it seemed to me that they could reveal particular insights into the significance of these relationships from the perspectives of those who participate in them. In light of this empirical data, the merit of this book for practitioners lies not in a set of lessons about how gay men's workplace friendships might be managed, but in a cautionary note regarding the temptation to view workplace friendships as organisational resources.

It stands to reason that a book on gay men's workplace friendships might hold appeal to practitioners, especially as much of the empirical data presented reveals insights into how individuals use friendship as a process a becoming at work. To some participants this role of friendship is articulated as 'being yourself', a concept that might be attractive to employers, in that it represents an opportunity to treat people's personal everyday identities and selves as corporate resources (Fleming and Sturdy 2009; Fleming 2007). Of course, as the study data shows to some degree, in organisational settings that encourage informality there are benefits for those participants who wish to engage in the process of befriending. Having work friends can help draw out the sociable and fun side of organisational life. They can provide support, intimacy and help to affirm identities. However, the capacity for some employers to use friendship as another means at their disposal to improve productivity is troubling. As Fleming and Sturdy (2009: 213) argue, more aspects of the private self enter the purview of management, making it harder to maintain a 'preserve of private selfhood' that separates employees from their employers. This is not to say that the call for employees to 'be themselves' is a case of 'anything goes'. When organisations embark on the appropriation of workplace friendship as an organisational resource, they are not giving free reign to employees to cultivate friendships of entirely their own choosing. One of the managers in Hochschild's (1997) study of a Fortune 500 company explains:

> … in a workshop for Human Resource managers that I observed, participants explored ways to make friendship work for the benefit of the company. As one manager told me, The company can reduce mistakes by pooling problem-solving skills. You piggyback on ordinary friendships. Joe calls up Bill and talks about the family, the ballgame. Then at the end, Joe says, 'By the way, I'm also having problems with [some work-related dilemma] … Do you know anyone who can help me with that?' We need to educate our workers to do that. (1997: 54)

Managing workplace friendships to keep them on the right course will involve educating employees about what counts as the 'right' type of friendship as well as how such relationships are to be sustained and used. Not surprisingly, business press pundits and academics have provided guidance for organisations, with some developing friendship management 'strategies' (Berman et al. 2002). I am not particularly interested in conjuring up more of the same here, but to establish that in the quest to manage friendships productively, employers risk choking out the opportunities for friends to attach significance to these relationships. As well, if we are to imagine alternative forms of organising, we scupper our chances of being able to do so by fashioning workplace friendships according to the designs of management. As Parker (2002: 210) poignantly remarks, 'co-ordination, in the sense of bringing people and things together in productive ways, is not necessarily managerial'. In workplace friendships, some practitioners and organisation studies scholars might gain insights into how people can come together to do things at work in ways that are not managerial. The trouble, however, as I see it, is that I suspect some employers are aware of this but still act on the urge to tidy up the informality of work life, as one might prune over an overgrown rose bush. But in so doing, it seems that many are simply trying to bend workplace friendships to the will of management, rather than learning lessons about what it is to be human at work and the construction of organising and organisations (Grey 1996; Parker 2002). This is not to say I think workplace friendships should be, or can be, secure from the gaze of management. Just as some rose bushes become unruly, so some workplace friendships can become dysfunctional, for both friends and management. Some type of organisational intervention might be required, and it is here that practitioners would benefit from understanding how workplace friendships develop, function and deteriorate. For example, giving consideration to how workplace friendships are significant to those who participate in them can help to fashion more sensitive organisational responses, in situations like those I described in the Introduction, such as when a friend dies. This might sound incredibly well-intentioned, but if we do not pay greater attention to issues like these we risk letting the organisational experiences that make us human slide further out of view.

Limitations and directions for future research

This exploratory study has a number of limitations which I have chosen to address as areas for future research. First, the decision to draw the study sample exclusively from gay men is a recognised shortcoming in terms of those men and women who are excluded. For example, the absence of bisexual men is lamentable, as research on bisexuality in cross-sexuality friendships complicates further the current picture of how friendships are developed and sustained (Galupo 2007a, 2007b). Bisexual men might make different decisions about who they wish to befriend, how they understand themselves and others as gendered and sexual subjects and how they rely on friends in the workplace. Future research is encouraged in this area, especially studies that examine how bisexual men might problematise accepted practices of cross-sex and same-sex intimacies between friends. Indeed, empirical studies on the organisational lives of bisexual men and women would certainly shed a different light on the discursively patterned opportunities and constraints for friendship making in the workplace.

Taking this further, a range of other people might also qualify as desirable study participants. As I have mentioned above, the scholarship on men's workplace friendships could be enriched by research on how men can develop friendships that are characterised by care-giving, emotional support, intimacy as well as instrumentality. Similarly, women's friendships command an engaging and laudable literature but it is apparent that scholarly knowledge about women's friendships in the workplace is underdeveloped. Just as men's workplace friendships have suffered from the tendency among academics to use a 'feminine ruler' to measure their 'value' as friendships (Woods 1993), so too have women's workplace friendships. Researchers are encouraged to investigate the diversity within women's friendships in the workplace, examining how constructions of gender and sexuality shape normative modes of caring and support among women. Perspectives from bisexual and lesbian identified women are invaluable here, not least for helping to undermine heteronormative stereotypes of women's friendships.

Second, this study has touched upon issues concerning the intersections of sexuality and gender with class, race, ethnicity and parental status but the limitations of the study data prevent further exploration. This is a vital area for future research because identity-based acronyms such as LGBT, commendable for moving beyond homogenous notions of a 'gay community', do not reference the intersection of other social identities (Cronin and King 2010). Understanding how workplace friendships might satisfy the diverse needs and interests of LGBT persons who identify within and across other social identity categories can only enhance existing knowledge about the complex lives of these people. We stand to gain greater insights into how identity categories should be understood as multiple and the role workplace friendship might play here. In that respect, research that draws on intersectionality theory would build on the particular findings of this study, such the friendship experiences of gay men who identify as fathers. Here sexuality and fatherhood may intersect in ways that are empowering and inhibiting. Intersectionality theory examines social divisions and exposes multiple inequalities, useful for understanding how workplace friendships might provide opportunities for those who participate in them to explore the full range of experiences identity categories incorporate.

Third and finally, the decision to exclude those individuals named by study participants as 'work friends' could also be viewed as a limitation. There are robust practical and ethical methodological reasons for adopting this approach (see Appendix 1). Nevertheless, there might be plenty of mileage in pursuing this possibility, particularly in terms of investigating the following research questions:

- How do heterosexual men and women experience and understand workplace friendships with gay men?
- How do heterosexual men and women construct themselves as gendered

and sexual subjects within workplace friendships involving gay men?

- Can workplace friendships with gay men enable heterosexual men and women to become 'straight allies'?
- How can friendships between gay men and heterosexual men and women help to create 'gay-friendly' work environments?

As research on gay men's friendships shows (Shepperd et al. 2010), both members of a friendship dyad can be out of synch with each other when it comes to understanding the role and meaning of friendship. There may be important differences in how each friend learns about and identifies with the other, allowing us to delve deeper into the construction of friendship.

Drawbacks notwithstanding, in view of the paucity of empirical material on gay men's workplace friendships, the strength of this study lies in its exploratory quality. Presenting in-depth qualitative insights into the roles and meanings of friendship in gay men's work lives marks a significant departure from the standard fare of LGBT issues and themes studied within the field of organisation studies. Empirical research on any of the areas outlined above would help others to refine the exploratory nature of my study data.

Closing remarks

As I write these closing remarks, shortly after starting a new academic job at a new university, a new friendship is unfolding. I am reminded again of the joy of emerging friendships with people at work. Currently in the early stages of getting to know one female colleague – let me call her Miranda – we have over a short period of time exchanged text messages, emails, several gifts, indulged our fondness for gin-based cocktails and disclosed copious snippets of personal information. For me, at least, all of this has hastened a developing sense of intimacy. Of course one can never be entirely sure, especially in the early stage of friendship making, if there is shared understanding or consensus about the broad meaning of the relationship and its future course. The work of friendship is a risky and sometimes unpredictable business, no matter what sorts of different situations and settings individuals become friends. While concerns about creating friends out of colleagues are valid, though prone to exaggeration, this book has helped to show that things can be different, undermining facile stereotypes not just about men in friendship but also about friendships in the workplace. Like many of the gay men who participated in the study, workplace friendships have connected me to other people, offering fresh opportunities to understand and better myself and others as human. I find it hard to imagine my work life without friends.

Appendix 1:
Researching Gay Men's
Workplace Friendships

The broad aim of this study was to generate in-depth qualitative insights into the role and meaning of friendship in gay men's work lives. Given that there is no extant body of empirical research on this subject, which might be used as a baseline from which to work, the study is exploratory. As such, I needed to gather data that would allow me to analyse a wide range of issues regarding the development, maintenance, roles and meanings of workplace friendships from the perspectives of gay men. In this appendix, I sketch out some of the methodological decision-making that underpins this study. It is not intended to be an exhaustive account but an overview of the approach taken, outlining some of the challenges that confronted me when carrying out the research.

Sampling

Gay men are one example of a social group often characterised as 'hidden' and 'hard to reach' because, in large part, sexuality is not always 'visible' or 'obvious' to the researcher. I used a snowball sampling procedure to overcome some of the difficulties here, following in the footsteps of other researchers who have constructed samples involving LGBT people (Browne 2005; Ward and Winstanley 2003; Weston 1991; Wilton 2004). I sent out email flyers advertising my interest in recruiting gay men in a study on workplace friendships. Several personal contacts in different organisations kindly disseminated information about my study to employees via email, on staff notice boards and approached potential study participants in person. The information contained on the flyers and notices did not exclude gay men who had little or no experience of workplace friendship. It was my intention to elicit a range of perspectives on these relationships including those for whom friendship might not be an important feature in their work lives.

To participate in the study, the men had to identify themselves as predominately or exclusively 'gay', and be willing to talk about their experiences of workplace friendship. Several points are worth making here. Although my intention was to build upon the research on gay men's friendships, which influenced my initial decision to exclude bisexual men, had bisexual males approached me they would have been included in the study. Research on bisexual men's friendships is rare, so eliciting these viewpoints would have been useful. Indeed, if this study were to be carried out again, I would actively encourage bisexual men to participate. Another point concerns the requirement that participants did not have to be 'openly gay'. Participants who were not 'out' in the workplace to colleagues and friends would have provided different perspectives on workplace friendships. However, all study participants identified as 'openly gay' at work, although in some accounts of past friendships this did not appear to be the case. There is a strong impression running throughout many of the interviews about the variation in the number of people who appeared to know the sexual identity of participants. Unless stated otherwise, the sexual identities of each friend are known to each other in the empirical content of this book.

Regarding responses, I initially received 12 expressions of interest from gay men who wished to be involved in the study. Of these, five set time aside to be interviewed and I was able to commence my first batch of interviews. However, as is the case with snowball sampling, the pace at which the referral chains developed was found to be very uneven. After a promising start, interest seemed to dry up, and anxieties welled up in my mind as to whether I would be able to drum up further interest. I emailed the five men I had already interviewed with a plea for their assistance in helping me to recruit study participants. They responded magnificently. I soon received enquiries of interest from a number of gay men. This method of recruiting participants seemed to work extremely well. In the main, participants approached other men they knew were gay such as friends, friends of friends, colleagues and family members. The bulk of the data was collected over a 12-month period but recruiting further gay men and conducting follow-up interviewing extended the data gathering process by another 12 months. In that sense, interviewing and recruiting for study participants often occurred concurrently. Thirty-three gay men participated in the study, whose demographic details (based on how they chose to identify in terms of sexuality, ethnicity, class, age, etc.) are contained in Appendix 3. The geographical reach of the study was the UK, although all the participants resided in mainland Britain in urban, semi-rural and rural locations. This involved travelling extensively across some parts of the UK to interview participants. It is noted that snowballing sampling has its pitfalls (Browne 2005). The sample displays some degree of bias towards inclusion of individuals who wish to participate in the study and the tendency for participants to recruit others similar to themselves. The study sample is not as rich and diverse as it could be in terms of ethnicity, race, age and other aspects of individual difference. These limitations notwithstanding, I follow Biernacki and Waldorf (1981) who argue that snowball sampling is particularly relevant and useful in situations where participants are members of hard to find populations and when the subject matter is sensitive and of a private nature.

Who to interview?

In order to generate data on workplace friendships of a qualitative and exploratory nature, I followed a well-established tradition of using interviewing techniques to research friendship (Reeder 2000; Spencer and Pahl 2006; Walker 1994a, 1994b; White 2008). Semi-structured interviews were considered to be the most appropriate research method since these would allow the exploration of the topic area in a flexible and adaptive manner. However, gathering interview data on friendship is not straightforward. There are many perspectives on any given friendship that not only originate from those involved in them, but also from the people who surround a friendship dyad. Recognising this is to appreciate that collecting rich descriptive data on friendship can benefit from eliciting a range of viewpoints (Allan 1989). For example, some commentators on friendship, noting the tendency among researchers to interview one rather than both members of a dyad, strongly recommend interviewing both friends (Duck and Pond 1989). Thus some scholars have made a point of interviewing each member of a specific friendship dyad to overcome the one-sidedness that is said to characterise many interview-based studies on friendship (Werking 1997). But exploring friendship dyads in this way is tricky, not least in practical terms, as Oliker (1989) maintains.

I encountered problems in my initial attempts to interview each member of a particular friendship dyad. First, several interviewees said they did not feel comfortable about me potentially interviewing friends they had mentioned during our conversations. This was not because they had spoken about them in disparaging terms. In some cases they had disclosed information and viewpoints they had not previously shared (or had no intention of sharing) with their friends. For instance, one interviewee remarked that he would not have provided me with the same level of intimate detail about his feelings on a complex friendship with a female colleague, had either his friend been present in the interview or been interviewed separately. Ill at ease with the idea of confiding in his female friend about his uncertainties over the strength of his feeling towards her, he found it easier to talk to me (as someone outside the dyad) about the emotional complexities of this friendship. Indeed, when I broached the possibility of interviewing some of the workplace friends we had talked about, several interviewees went so far as to say they would have to reconsider their involvement in the study. This alarmed me. It was apparent that some interviewees felt uncomfortable knowing that I might carry into the interview specific interpretations of the friendship unbeknown to the other friend. Second, because I asked the interviewees to describe current and past workplace friendships, interviewees were not always in a position to put me in touch with work friends they had made some years ago but with whom they had lost contact. Indeed, in one case the friend talked about had died some years ago.

Taking into account the issues outlined above and the sluggish start to recruiting study participants, I decided early on in the research process not to gather the perspectives of the work friends mentioned during our interview-based conversations. As such, I recognise the limitations this might impose on the richness of the data collected. However, like other friendship researchers (White 2008), I reason also that there is no need to verify participants' accounts of workplace friendships by interviewing the work friends they described. Triangulating data in this way might be useful for delving into the discrepancies and similarities in how two friends understand and experience the same friendship, but there is no 'right' or 'wrong' version of accounts waiting to be discovered. Interview data on friendship is partial, situated and constructed (Holstein and Gubrium 1995; Rubin and Rubin 2005). Put differently, the research interview is a localised context of discursive activity from which texts are generated and ascribed meaning.

A poststructuralist position recognises that meaning making within the interview situation is contingent and partially constructed between the interviewer and the interviewee (Davies and Thomas 2003; Linstead and Thomas 2002). As such, the interview data is not treated as being 'unblemished', since the interviewer does not have unmediated access into the minds of interviewees. Like Davies and Thomas (2003: 686), I regard interview data as 'living social texts' insomuch as the meanings attached to concepts such as friendship, gender and sexuality are not only fluid and multiple, but also emerge out of co-produced interview-based conversations. Viewed in this way, participant accounts of past and current friends and friendships are (re)constructions, so there may be omissions, embellishments and alternative perspectives embedded and applied in the process of (re)construction. The incompleteness of the study data in that respect is not read as a failing, since the strength of in-depth interview data lies in its focus on the messiness of human subjectivities and its conceptual creativity, evident in its capacity for generating theoretical insights.

Semi-structured interviewing

As mentioned above, a semi-structured interview format was used to provide interviewees every opportunity to talk expansively about their experiences of workplace friendship. This particular type of interview was chosen as the most appropriate method of obtaining information about past and current experiences of workplace friendships. Since semi-structured interviews are particularly good at allowing interviewees to determine what topics of conversation are discussed (Johnson 2001; Kvale 1996; Rubin and Rubin 2005; Wengraf 2001), participants had freedom to decide which work friends and workplace friendships they wished to discuss. In that respect, they could feel involved as active participants in the interview process (Holstein and Gubrium 1995), rather than sense that they were being treated by the interviewer as repositories of knowledge. By comparison, over-structured approaches to interviewing, often used in the study of friendship (Allan 1989: 8), were rejected because they can result in participants providing 'information about the ideology of friendship, rather than about the way friendship actually is'. Following Rubin and Rubin's (2005: 30–38) model of 'responsive interviewing', characterised by its focus on depth of understanding, flexibility and rootedness in constructionist and critical theory philosophy, I found interviewees open to disclosing the detail of how workplace friendships are experienced as complex and profoundly rewarding relationships.

Interview questions were open-ended and focused on a number of themes that covered experiences of workplace friendships throughout participants' work lives. The themes included: (1) the role workplace friendship played in their lives; (2) the significance of particular work friends; (3) the place of friendship in relation to other friendships and relationships with partners and families; (4) the different ways in which work friends provide forms of support and intimacy; (5) how workplace friendships were initiated and sustained; (6) and the influence of sexuality and gender on workplace friendships. Further information is contained in Appendix 2, which provides an abridged interview protocol with a select sample of interview questions.

Typically, I opened each interview by restating the study's aim and that the interview would be tape-recorded. I also reiterated reassurances about anonymity and confidentiality. Potential themes for discussion were mentioned to give some indication of what we might talk about. Next, I asked interviewees for a description of their current place of employment including details about their job. This initial line of questioning was more or less free of any demand on interviewees to discuss sensitive issues, and yielded rich contextual data about organisational life against which current workplace friendships could be located. Once participants appeared comfortable talking to me, we then pursued some of the themes described above. Not all the themes were covered in each interview or in the same level of detail, given the flexible and participant-centred approach to interviewing. Interview-based conversations often continued after the interviews had been concluded, which prompted me to invite participants to participate in a second interview. These interviews followed the same protocol: they were semi-structured, largely conducted in the interviewees' homes and tape-recorded. They lasted between one and a half to two hours.

One particular issue deserves mention here. The terms 'friend' and 'friendship' can cover a multitude of people and relationships that are not always distinct from other relationships such as those familial in nature (Allan 1989). Finding out what gay men understood by the terms 'work friend' and 'workplace friendship' was crucial. I did not approach the interviews with an a priori definition of friendship. To do so would potentially exclude different meanings participants assigned to friendship (Wood 1993). In line with a poststructuralist theoretical framing, which places emphasis on a refusal to fix the meaning of such things, participants were actively encouraged to provide different accounts of friendship derived from their everyday experiences of these relations in the workplace. As such, I found that asking participants to define 'workplace friendship' was not the best way to gain insights into how these relationships are understood. Many participants appeared to flounder when confronted with the question of defining friendship. Instead, I checked participants' interpretations of the term throughout the interviews by, for example, asking them to tell me why certain friends were called 'work friends'.

Like Spencer and Pahl (2006: 214), I was less interested in creating a typology of friendship, and more concerned with exploring how participants liberated themselves from received wisdom about different categories of friendship.

Lastly, the discussion of methodological procedure in qualitative research can give the impression of a process free of mistakes and errors of judgement. As such, I feel it is important that I admit to some gaffes, particularly in the interviews. For instance, in some interviews I had become so enthralled by what I was hearing that I forgot to ask some very obvious questions, and duly kicked myself afterwards for not listening actively (Rubin and Rubin 2005). On two occasions I failed to collect enough personal data about the work friends described to me. Despite making a point at the end of each interview to ask the interviewee if there was anything else they wanted to talk about, I forgot to do so in four interviews. Fortunately, I was able to rectify this by email or on the telephone. On another two occasions, I forgot to press the record button on the tape recorder, thereby losing over six hours of interview data. Rather than reconstruct the interviews from memory, I contacted the participants in question and confessed my clumsiness. In each case, the interviewees kindly agreed to be re-interviewed. Despite making every effort to be sensitive to the potential pitfalls of conducing qualitative research, my experiences bear testimony to the sometimes unpredictable and messy nature of generating qualitative data, an intensely pleasurable and frustrating process.

Some ethical issues

Some of the interviews were emotionally charged, as participants disclosed very personal information. Emotional reactions and relationships can seldom be predicted with accuracy, or managed fully, not least because intimacy and friendliness can arise spontaneously. I needed to be vigilant of, rather than seeking to control, the shifting interpersonal relations between the interviewees and myself (Kong et al. 2001). Some participants were aware of and commented on the shifting emotionalities in the research process. Several commented on the distinctions between friendship and friendliness not only in regard to relations in their work lives, but also in the context of our research interview. These observations prompted me to reflect on the emotional attachments I had formed with some participants. From my perspective, the research process was largely characterised by relations of friendliness rather than friendship. As Kirsch (2005) suggests, to acknowledge this is to come to hold realistic expectations about the research relationship. Even when the boundary between the researcher and the study participant is blurred by friendliness or friendship, it is important not to lose sight of, or stop talking with participants about, the underpinning rationale of the research process.

Another ethical issue that confronted me was how to develop trust in the research process. Indeed, taking on board the issues discussed above, I felt it was more appropriate to develop an 'ethic of trust'. Following Kong et al. (2001) on this endeavour, I worked at constructing an ethical identity in order to establish relations of trust with the study participants. Wherever possible, I spent time getting to know the men before we met in an interview situation. Telephone calls, email correspondence and face-to-face conversations helped me to explain the aim of the study, the method and style of gathering data and how the interview data might be used. This allowed participants time to form their own judgements of me and of the merit in participating in a study on gay men's workplace friendships.

One of the most important issues I needed to cover here concerned protecting the men in terms of anonymity and confidentiality. There is a risk of discrimination for LGBT people taking part in scholarly research that stems from self-identifying as 'gay' (Ward and Winstanley 2006b; Wilton 2004). With this in mind, I asked each participant to select a name I could use when referring to him in the written analysis. They obliged accordingly but four participants insisted that I use their 'real' names, telling me they did not wish to be cloaked in anonymity. However, acting out of an ethical duty to protect their identities alongside the men who opted for pseudonyms, I have not distinguished between the two. Furthermore, the names of work friends and organisations have all been changed to ensure anonymity.

Relatedly, on the matter of consent, I adopted an approach similar to that used by Wilton (2004). All study participants volunteered verbally to be involved in the research process. In the spirit of informed consent, I explained to the participants that they could withdraw from the study at any point without prejudice. Ensuring anonymity and confidentiality was not the only way in which I constructed myself as someone who could be trusted. Disclosing my sexuality was an important way in which I could help facilitate rapport. Many participants said they felt more comfortable talking to another gay man about sexuality, gender and friendship. This observation is not unusual, as gay and lesbian researchers have noted of their own experiences in the field (Weeks et al. 2001). However, it is important to state that disclosing sexual identity is not a licence to accessing deeper insights into others' experiences. It can help but, as some sexuality scholars aver, it is not be to be taken-for-granted as being singularly sufficient for developing trust and rapport (Browne 2005). That being said, sharing a common sexuality did seem to help recruiting participants as well as providing a common frame of reference at various points throughout the interview. Still I noted also that, as I got to know participants during the interview process, I found we could identify points of reference that formed a stronger sense of mutual affinity between us beyond that based on sexuality alone.

Data analysis

As a final methodological point, it is important to indicate how the study data was analysed. Analysing the interview data started as soon as I had finished each interview. At this point, I penned my initial reactions and thoughts about how well I thought the interview went, noting among other things ideas, topics and quotes that seemed relevant and noteworthy (Rubin and Rubin 2005). These field notes served as 'memos' throughout the data process analysis. They not only helped me to remember the salient points and themes of each interview, but they also enabled me to sketch out preliminary thoughts about how to analyse the data thematically.

The next stage was transcribing the interview data. This activity consumed more hours than I care to remember, producing hundreds of pages of transcription. As Tilley (2003) and others note (Lapadat and Lindsay 1999; Kvale 1996; Rubin and Rubin 2005), transcribing interview data is a key part of the analysis process. As I transcribed each interview, I highlighted emerging themes. I also made further notes about discussion points and quotes that appeared unusual, striking and surprising. Again, these memos assisted me in guiding the next stage of the data analysis process.

My analytical emphasis was both thematic, focusing on what was said by participants and discursive, focusing on how discourses made it possible for participants to speak in particular ways about their friendships. In practice, this entailed constructing data-driven categories based on multiple readings of the interview transcripts. Pre-existing categories were also used, informed by reading the relevant subject literature. This combination afforded some degree of structure to organise the data while letting some categories emerge from the data analysis process. This work was undertaken manually, allowing me to submerge myself in the data quite literally, surrounded as I was at times by billowing piles of coded interview transcripts.

In view of my concern to examine how participants could talk about certain things in particular ways, discourse analysis techniques were used at various stages of the data analysis process. Adopting a Foucauldian conception of discourse, language is not taken to be a simple reflection of what it claims to represent. Rather, language enables individuals to construct realities of everyday life (Fairclough 1992). Throughout the analysis of each transcript, I searched for evidence of discourses used by interviewees to construct and understand their workplace friendships with other men. This part of the process involved analysing the components of different discourses, also noting how they overlap and shift.

The process of selecting relevant interview excerpts to illustrate the empirical analysis was informed by my own interpretations and the theories used to frame the book. As such, I spent many hours deciding which data extracts were most striking, important and illuminating. Crucial, then, is that this process of selection is not to be regarded as a definitive interpretation of the data. Acts of interpretation are partial, multiple and contingent, and should be treated as such.

Appendix 2:
Abridged Interview Protocol

Introduction

Pre-interview issues: introduce self and interest in gay men's workplace friendships, reiterate statements about the purpose of the study, reaffirm confidentiality, anonymity, explain audio recording procedure and indicate length of interview.

Interviewee background – questions asked to gather information on: age, ethnicity, class, marital status, children, present employer, job role and location within the UK.

Find out from interviewee what length of time they have identified as gay and how 'open' they are in their current workplace.

Interview questions

The questions below are some examples of those used in regard to interview theme 5: the influence of sexuality and gender on workplace friendships.

Characteristics of workplace friendships with other men/women

Do you have any workplace friendships with other men/women?
Do you prefer workplace friendships with other men or with women?
Do these men/women identify as 'gay', 'heterosexual', 'lesbian', 'transgender' or 'bisexual'?
How would you describe this/these workplace friendships?
(Potential probes: What do you talk about? Has the friendship developed or changed? How? Why?)
Are there any rules or expectations of workplace friendships with other men/women?

Dynamics of gender and sexuality within workplace friendships with other men/women

Have you ever talked to your friend about how you both identify differently in terms of sexuality?

Can you describe what you have talked about in these conversations?

Have you ever found it hard to discuss differences in sexual identities?

Were they any particular turning points or circumstances when you acknowledged differences in sexuality? What are they?

What are your experiences of sexual attraction in workplace friendships with men/women?

How do certain types of male/female work friends compare to others – e.g. a gay work friend compared to a heterosexual male work friend?

Importance of workplace friendships with other men/women

Think of one workplace friendship involving another man/woman that is or has been important to you. How would you describe how important this friendship is or was?

(Potential probes: How do you feel towards this person? What does it mean to have a male/female work friend?)

Has the importance of this workplace friendship changed? Is it the same or different from when you first met?

Close

Ask interviewee if they wish to discuss anything not covered in the interview.

Ask interviewee if there is anything they wish to revise or reflect on any aspect of the interview.

Ask interviewee how they felt about being interviewed.

Reassure interviewee that further discussion can take place regarding any aspect of the interview process.

Reaffirm confidentiality and anonymity, ask interviewee to select a pseudonym.

Ask interviewee to recruit another gay man to participate in the study.

Appendix 3:
Profiles of Study Participants

The information provided below was accurate at time of interview.

Table A3   List of research participants

Pseudonym	Age	Ethnicity	Class	Relationship	Occupation
Alex	Early 30s	White	Middle class	Single	Advertising
Austin	Mid 30s	White	Middle class	Partnered	Occupational Therapist
Callum	Early 30s	White	Middle class	Single	University Lecturer
Carl	Mid 40s	White	Middle class	Partnered	IT Manager
Ciaran	Early 40s	White	Middle class	Partnered	Training
Conor	Early 40s	White	Middle class	Partnered	University Lecturer
Danny	Mid 30s	White	Middle class	Single	Hospital Registrar
Damien	Early 30s	White	Middle class	Single	IT Officer
Darren	Mid 30s	White	Working class	Partnered	Police Officer
Denton	Late 20s	White	Middle class	Partnered	Project Manager
Dion	Mid 40s	White	Middle class	Partnered	Senior Health Care Manager
Douglas	Early 40s	White	Working class	Single	Paramedic
Finlay	Late 30s	White	Middle class	Partnered	Business Consultant
Gordon	Late 30s	White	Working class	Single	Paramedic
Grant	Early 30s	White	Middle class	Partnered	Finance Director
Hugo	Late 50s	White	Middle class	Partnered	Principal Lecturer (University)
Jack	Early 50s	White	Middle class	Single, three children	Director
James	Late 30s	White	Middle class	Single	Sales Director
Kris	Late 20s	White	Middle class	Single	Administrator

Table A3   (Continued)

Pseudonym	Age	Ethnicity	Class	Relationship	Occupation
Lee	Early 40s	White	Middle class	Single, three children	Occupational Therapist/ Lecturer
Michael	Mid 30s	White	Middle class	Partnered	University Lecturer
Morgan	Late 30s	White	Middle class	Single	Senior Health Care Manager
Oscar	Early 40s	White	Middle class	Single	Research Scientist
Philip	Late 20s	White	Middle class	Single	Civil Servant
Philippe	Late 40s	White	Middle class	Partnered	IT/Research
Rupert	Late 40s	White	Middle class	Single	University Lecturer
Ryan	Early 30s	White	Middle class	Single	Hospital Doctor
Sam	Early 30s	White	Working class	Partnered	Project Manager
Stafford	Mid 30s	White	Working class	Partnered	Community Support Worker
Steve	Early 30s	White	Middle class	Partnered	Department Head (Higher Education)
Theo	Late 20s	Asian	Middle class	Single	General Manager
Tom	Early 30s	White	Middle class	Single	Human Resources Assistant
Tony	Late 20s	White	Middle class	Single	Hospital Doctor

References

Acker, J., Barry, K. and Esseveld, J. 1981. Feminism, Female Friends, and the Reconstruction of Intimacy, in *Research in the Interweave of Social Roles: Families and Jobs*, Volume 3, edited by H.Z. Lopata and J.H. Pleck. Greenwich CT.: Jai Press, 75–108.

Adams, R.G. 1985. People Would Talk: Normative Barriers to Cross-Sex Friendships for Elderly Women. *The Gerontologist*, 25(6), 605–11.

Adams, R.G. and Allan, G. (eds) 1998. *Placing Friendship in Context*. Cambridge: Cambridge University Press.

Allan, G. 1977. Class Variation in Friendship Patterns. *British Journal of Sociology*, 28(3), 389–93.

Allan, G. 1989. *Friendship: Developing a Sociological Perspective*. Hemel Hempstead: Harvester-Wheatsheaf.

Allan, G. 1996. *Kinship and Friendship in Modern Britain*. Oxford: Oxford University Press.

Allan, G. 1998. Friendship, Sociology and Social Structure. *Journal of Social and Personal Relationships*, 15(5), 685–702.

Allan, G. 2008. Flexibility, Friendship, and Family. *Personal Relationships*, 15(1), 1–16.

Altman, I. and Taylor, D. 1973. *Social Penetration: The Development of Interpersonal Relationships*. New York: Rinehart and Winston.

Alvesson, M. and Billing, Y.D. 1997. *Understanding Gender and Organizations*. London: Sage.

Andrew, A. and Montague, J. 1998. Women's Friendship at Work. *Women's Studies International Forum*, 21(4), 355–61.

Antcliff, V., Saundry, R. and Stuart, M. 2007. Networks and Social Capital in the UK Television Industry: The Weakness of Weak Ties. *Human Relations*, 60(2), 371–93.

Argyle, M. and Henderson, M. 1985. *The Anatomy of Relationships*. London: Heinemann.

Aristotle 2004. *The Nicomachean Ethics*, translated by J.A.K. Thomson. London: Penguin.

Ashcraft, K.L. 2000. Empowering "Professional" Relationships: Organizational Communication Meets Feminist Practice. *Management Communication Quarterly*, 13(3), 347–92.

Ashcraft, K.L. 2007. Appreciating the 'Work' of Discourse: Occupational Identity and Difference as Organizing Mechanisms in the Case of Commercial Airline Pilots. *Discourse & Communication*, 1(1), 9–36.

Bank, B.J. 1995. Friendships in Australia and the United States: From Feminization to a More Heroic Image. *Gender & Society*, 9(1), 79–98.

Barrett D. and Pollack L. 2005. Whose Gay Community? Social Class, Sexual. Identity, and Gay Community Involvement. *The Sociological Quarterly*, 46(3), 437–56.

Bech, H. 1997. *When Men Meet: Homosexuality and Modernity*. Cambridge: Polity.

Beck, U. 1992. *Risk Society: Towards a New Modernity*. London: Sage.

Beck, U. and Beck-Gernsheim, E. 1995. *The Normal Chaos of Love*. Cambridge: Polity.

Beer, C.R., Jeffrey, R. and Munyard, T. 1983. *Gay Workers: Trade Unions and the Law*. London: NCCL.

Bell, R. 1981. *Worlds of Friendship*. Beverly Hills: Sage.

Bell, S. and Coleman, S. (eds) 1999. *The Anthropology of Friendship*. London: Berg.

Berman, E.M., West, J.P. and Richter, M.N. 2002. Workplace Relations: Friendship Patterns and Consequences (According to Managers). *Public Administration Review*, 62(2), 217–30.

Bird, S.R. 1996. Welcome to the Men's Club: Homosociality and the Maintenance of Hegemonic Masculinity. *Gender & Society*, 10(2), 120–32.

Biernacki, P. and Waldorf, D. 1981. Snowball Sampling: Problems and Techniques of Chain Referral Sampling. *Sociological Methods and Research*, 10(2), 141–63.

Blackshaw, T. 2003. *Leisure Life: Myth, Masculinity and Modernity*. London: Routledge.

Blasius, M. 1994. *Gay and Lesbian Politics: Sexuality and the Emergence of a New Ethic*. Philadelphia: Temple University Press.

Booth, A. 1972. Sex and Social Participation. *American Sociological Review*, 37, 183–92.

Bowring, M. and Brewis, J. 2009. Truth and Consequences: Managing Lesbian and Gay Identity in the Canadian Workplace. *Equal Opportunities International*, 28(5), 361–77.

Boykin, K. 1996. *One More River to Cross: Black and Gay in America*. New York: Anchor.

Bray, A. 1982. *Homosexuality in Renaissance England*. London: Gay Men's Press.

Bray, A. 1990. Homosexuality and the Signs of Male Friendship in Elizabethan England. *History Workshop Journal*, 29(1), 1–19.

Bray, A. 2003. *The Friend*. Chicago: Chicago University Press.

Bray, A. and Rey, M. 1999. The Body of the Friend: Continuity and Change in Masculine Friendship in the Seventeenth Century, in *English Masculinities, 1660–1800*, edited by T. Hitchcock and M. Cohen. London: Longman, 65–84.

Brewis, J. and Linstead, S. 2000. *Sex, Work and Sex Work: Eroticizing Organization*. London: Routledge.

Bridge, K. and Baxter, L. 1992. Blended Relationships: Friends as Work Associates. *Western Journal of Communication*, 56(3), 200–25.

Bristow, J. 2007. Remapping the Sites of Modern Gay History: Legal Reform, Medico-Legal Thought, Homosexual Scandal, Erotic Geography. *Journal of British Studies*, 46(1), 116–42.

Browne, K. 2005. Snowball Sampling: Using Social Networks to Research Non-heterosexual Women. *International Journal of Social Research Methodology*, 8(1), 47–60.

Buchanan, D.A. and Badham, R.J. 1999. *Power, Politics, and Organizational Change: Winning the Turf Game*. Thousand Oaks, CA: Sage.

Budgeon, S. 2006. Friendship and Formations of Sociality in Late Modernity: The Challenge of 'Post Traditional Intimacy'. *Sociological Research Online*, 11(3) [Online]. Available at: http://www.socresonline.org.uk/11/3/budgeon.html [accessed: 15 September 2010].

Burke, M. 1993. *Coming Out of the Blue: British Police Officers Talk About Their Lives in 'The Job' as Lesbians, Gays and Bisexuals*. London: Cassell.

Burnett, L. 2010. Young Lesbians Explore Careers and Work Landscapes in an Australian Culture. *Journal of Lesbian Studies*, 14(1), 36–51.

Burt, R. 1992. *Structural Holes: The Social Structure of Competition*. Cambridge, MA: Harvard University Press.

Butera, K.J. 2008. Neo-mateship in the 21st Century: Changes in the Performance of Australian Masculinity. *Journal of Sociology*, 44(3), 265–81.

Butler, J. 1990. *Gender Trouble: Feminism and the Subversion of Identity*. London: Routledge.

Butler, J. 1993. *Bodies that Matter: On the Discursive Limits of "Sex"*. New York: Routledge.

Butler, J. 2004. *Undoing Gender*. London: Routledge.

Button, S. 2004. Identity Management Strategies Used by Gay and Lesbian Employees: A Quantitative Investigation. *Group & Organization Management*, 29(4), 470–94.

Caldwell, M. and Peplau, L. 1982. Sex Differences in Same-sex Friendships. *Sex Roles*, 8(7), 721–32.

Cancian, F.M. 1986. The Feminization of Love. *Signs*, 11(4), 692–709.

Chan, D.K.S. and Cheng, G.H.L. 2004. A Comparison of Offline and Online Friendship Qualities at Different Stages of Relationship Development. *Journal of Social and Personal Relationships*, 21(3), 305–20.

Christian, H. 1994. *The Making of Anti-sexist Men*. New York: Routledge.

Cockburn, C. 1991. *In the Way of Women: Men's Resistance to Sex Equality in Organizations*. London: Macmillan.

Colgan, F., Creegan, C., McKearney, A. and Wright, T. 2007. Equality and Diversity Policies and Practices at Work: Lesbian, Gay, and Bisexual Workers. *Equal Opportunities International*, 26(6), 590–609.

Colgan, F., Creegan, C., McKearney, A. and Wright, T. 2008. Lesbian Workers: Personal Strategies Amid Changing Organisational Responses to Sexual Minorities in UK Workplaces. *Journal of Lesbian Studies*, 12(1), 65–86.

Colgan, F., Wright, T., Creegan, C. and McKearney, A. 2009. Equality and Diversity in the Public Services: Moving Forward on Lesbian, Gay and Bisexual Equality? *Human Resource Management Journal*, 19(3), 280–301.

Collinson, D.L. 1992. *Managing the Shopfloor: Subjectivity, Masculinity and Workplace Culture*. London: Sage.

Collinson, D.L. and Hearn, J. (eds) 1996. *Men as Managers, Managers as Men*. London: Sage.

Connell, R.W. 1995. *Masculinities*. Berkeley: University of California Press.

Creed, W.E.D. and Scully, M.A. 2000. Songs of Ourselves: Employees: Deployment of Social Identity in Workplace Encounters. *Journal of Management Inquiry*, 9(4), 391–412.

Cronin, A. and King, A. 2010. Power, Inequality and Identification: Exploring Diversity and Intersectionality amongst Older LGB Adults. *Sociology*, 44(5), 876–92.

D'Augelli, A.R. 1998. Developmental Implications of Victimization of Lesbian, Gay, and Bisexual Youths, in *Stigma and Sexual Orientation: Understanding Prejudice against Lesbians, Gay Men, and Bisexuals*, edited by G.M. Herek. Thousand Oaks, CA.: Sage, 187–210.

Dalton, M. 1959. *Men Who Manage*. New York: Wiley.

Daly, M. 1978. *Gyn/Ecology*. London: The Women's Press.

Davies, A. and Thomas, R. 2003. Talking COP: Discourses of Change and Policing Identities. *Public Administration*, 81(4), 681–99.

Day, N.E. and Schoenrade, P. 1997. Staying in the Closet versus Coming Out: Relationships between Communication about Sexual Orientation and Work Attitudes. *Personnel Psychology*, 50(1), 147–63.

Day, N.E., and Schoenrade, P. 2000. The Relationship among Reported Disclosure of Sexual Orientation, Anti-discrimination Policies, Top Management Support and Work Attitudes of Gay and Lesbian Employees. *Personnel Review*, 29(3), 346–63.

de la Cruz, M. and Dolby, T. 2007. *Girls Who Like Boys Who Like Boys: True Tales of Love, Trust, and Friendship between Straight Women and Gay Men*. New York: Dutton.

de Montaigne, M. 1580/1993. *Essays*. London: Penguin Books.

de Vries, B. and Hoctel, P. 2007. The Family Friends of Older Gay Men and Lesbians, in *Sexual Inequalities and Social Justice*, edited by N. Teunis and G. Herdt. Berkeley: University of California Press, 213–32.

DeMott, B. 1995. *The Trouble with Friendship: Why Americans Can't Think Straight about Race*. New York: Atlantic Monthly Press.

Deverell, K. 2001. *Sex, Work and Professionalism: Working in HIV/AIDS*. London: Routledge.

DiGangi, M. 2003. How Queer was the Renaissance?, in *Love, Sex, Intimacy and Friendship between Men, 1550–1800*, edited by K. O'Donnell and M. O'Rourke. Basingstoke: Palgrave/Macmillan, 126–45.

Duck, S.W. 1991. *Understanding Relationships*. New York: Guilford Press.

Duck, S.W. (ed.) 1993. *Social Context and Relationships*. Newbury Park, CA.: Sage.

Duck, S.W. and Pond, K. 1989. Friends, Romans, Countrymen, Lend Me Your Retrospective Data: Rhetoric and Reality in Personal Relationships, in *Close Relationships Vol. 10*, edited by C. Hendrick. Newbury Park, CA.: Sage, 17–38.

Duck, S.W. and Wright, P.H. 1993. Re-examining Gender Differences in Same-gender Friendships: A Close Look at Two Kinds of Data. *Sex Roles*, 28(11–12), 709–27.

Dyer, R. 1979. *Stars*. London: British Film Institute.

Dyer, R. 2002. *The Culture of Queers*. London and New York: Routledge.

Eisenberg, S.A.J. 1994. Friendship or Fraternization? *Credit Union Management*, 17(7), 22–3.

Elsesser, K. and Peplau, L.A. 2006. The Glass Partition: Obstacles to Cross-sex Friendships at Work. *Human Relations*, 59(8), 1077–100.

Embrick, D.G., Walther, C.S. and Wickens, C.M. 2007. Working Class Masculinity: Keeping Gay Men and Lesbians Out of the Workplace. *Sex Roles*, 56(11–12), 757–66.

Epstein, J. 2006. *Friendship: An Exposé*. New York: Houghton Mifflin Harcourt.

Erickson, K. 2004. Bodies at Work: Performing Service in American Restaurants. *Space and Culture*, 7(1), 76–89.

Faderman, L. 1981. *Surpassing the Love of Men: Romantic Friendship and Love between Women from the Renaissance to the Present*. New York: William Morrow.

Fairclough, N. 1992. *Discourse and Social Change*. Cambridge: Polity Press.

Fee, D. 2000. One of the Guys: Instrumentality and Intimacy in Gay Men's Friendships with Straight Men, in *Gay Masculinities*, edited by P.M. Nardi. Thousand Oaks, CA.: Sage, 44–65.

Feeley, T., Hwang, J. and Barnett, G. 2008. Predicting Employee Turnover from Friendship Networks. *Journal of Applied Communication Research*, 36(1), 56–73.

Fehr, B. 1996. *Friendship Processes*. Thousand Oaks, CA.: Sage.

Ferrin, D.L., Dirks, K.T. and Shah, P.P. 2006. Direct and Indirect Effects of Third-party Relationships on Interpersonal Trust. *Journal of Applied Psychology*, 91(4), 870–83.

Ferris, G.R., Liden, R.C., Munyon, T.P., Summers, J.K., Basik, K.J. and Buckley, M.R. 2009. Relationships at Work: Toward a Multidimensional Conceptualization of Dyadic Work Relationships. *Journal of Management*, 35(6), 1379–403

Fielding, H. 1996. *Bridget Jones's Diary*. London: Picador.

Fine, G.A. 1986. Friendship in the workplace, in *Friendship and Social Interaction*, edited by V.J. Derlega and B.A. Winstead. New York: Springer-Verlag, 185–206.

Fischer, J.L. and Narus, L.R., Jr 1981. Sex Roles and Intimacy in Same Sex and Other Sex Relationships. *Psychology of Women Quarterly*, 5, 444–55.

Fleming, P. 2007. Sexuality, Power and Resistance in the Workplace. *Organization Studies*, 28(2), 239–56.

Fleming, P. and Sturdy, A. 2009. Bringing Everyday Life Back into the Workplace: Just Be Yourself!, in *The Management of Everyday Life*, edited by P. Hancock and M. Tyler. Basingstoke: Palgrave Macmillan, 199–216.

Foucault, M. 1979. *The History of Sexuality, Vol. I: An Introduction*. London: Allen Lane.

Foucault, M. 1982/1997. The Social Triumph of the Sexual Will, in *Ethics: Subjectivity and Truth*, edited by P. Rabinow. New York: New Press, 1157–62.

Foucault, M. 1984/1997. Sex, Power and the Politics of Identity, in *Ethics: Subjectivity and Truth*, edited by P. Rabinow. New York: New Press, 163–74.

Foucault, M. 1985. *The Use of Pleasure: The History of Sexuality, Vol. II*. Pantheon: New York.

Foucault, M. 1986. *The Care of the Self: The History of Sexuality, Vol. III*. Pantheon: New York.

Foucault, M. 1997. The Ethics of the Concern for Self as a Practice of Freedom, in *Ethics: Subjectivity and Truth, Vol. 1 of The Essential Works of Foucault, 1954–1984*, edited by P. Rabinow. New York: New Press, 281–301.

Francis, D.H. and Sandberg, W.R. 2000. Friendship within Entrepreneurial Teams and its Association with Team and Venture Performance. *Entrepreneurial Theory and Practice*, 25(2), 5–25.

French, R. 2007. Friendship and Organization: Learning from the Western Friendship Tradition. *Management and Organizational History*, 2(3), 255–72.

Friedman, M. 1993. *What are Friends For?: Feminist Perspectives on Personal Relationships and Moral Theory*. Ithaca, NY: Cornell University Press.

Fritz, J.H. 1997. Men's and Women's Organizational Peer Relationships: A Comparison. *Journal of Business Communication*, 34(1), 27–44.

Fritz, J.M.H. and Omdahl, B.L. (eds) 2006. *Problematic Relationships in the Workplace*. New York: Peter Lang.

Galupo, M.P., Sailer, C.A. St John, S.C. 2004. Friendships Across Sexual Orientations: Experiences of Bisexual Women in Early Adulthood. *Journal of Bisexuality*, 4(1–2), 37–54.

Galupo, M.P. 2007a. Friendship Patterns of Sexual Minority Individuals in Adulthood. *Journal of Social and Personal Relationships*, 24(1), 5–17.

Galupo, M.P. 2007b. Women's Close Friendships across Sexual Orientation: A Comparative Analysis of Lesbian-Heterosexual and Bisexual-Heterosexual Women's Friendships. *Sex Roles*, 56(7–8), 473–82.

Galupo, M.P. 2009. Cross-category Friendship Patterns: Comparison of Heterosexual and Sexual Minority Adults. *Journal of Social and Personal Relationships*, 26(6–7), 811–31.

Garlick, S. 2002. The Beauty of Friendship: Foucault, Masculinity and the Work of Art. *Philosophy & Social Criticism*, 28(5), 558–77.

Gherardi, S. 1995. *Gender, Symbolism and Organizational Cultures*. London: Sage.

Gibbons, D.E. 2004. Friendship and Advice Networks in the Context of Changing Professional Values. *Administrative Science Quarterly*, 49, 238–62.

Gibbons, D.E. and Olk, P.M. 2003. Individual and Structural Origins of Friendship and Social Position Among Professionals. *Journal of Personality and Social Psychology*, 84, 340–51.

Giddens, A. 1991. *The Consequences of Modernity*. Stanford, CA: Stanford University Press.

Giddens, A. 1992. *The Transformation of Intimacy: Sexuality, Love and Eroticism in Modern Societies*. Cambridge: Polity.

Gillies, V. 2005. Raising the Meritocracy: Parenting and the Individualization of Social Class. *Sociology*, 39(5), 835–53.

Giuffre, P., Dellinger, K. and Williams, C.L. 2008. No Retribution for Being Gay?: Inequality in Gay-friendly Workplaces. *Sociological Spectrum*, 28(3), 254–77.

GLC 1985. *Danger! ... Heterosexism at Work*. London: GLC.

Goldthorpe, J.H., Lockwood, D., Bechhofer, F. and Platt, J. 1968. *The Affluent Worker in the Class Structure*. Cambridge: Cambridge University Press.

Gottlieb, A.R. (ed.) 2008. *On the Meaning of Friendship between Gay Men*. London: Routledge.

Gough, B. and Edwards, G. 1998. The Beer Talking: Four Lads, a Carry Out and the Reproduction of Masculinities. *The Sociological Review*, 46(3), 409–35.

Granovetter, M. 1973. The Strength of Weak Ties. *American Journal of Sociology*, 78(6), 1360–80.

Green, E. 1998. Women Doing Friendship: An Analysis of Women's Leisure as a Site of Identity Construction, Empowerment and Resistance. *Leisure Studies*, 17(3), 171–85.

Green, E. and Singleton, C. 2009. Mobile Connections: An Exploration of the Place of Mobile Phones in Friendship Relations. *The Sociological Review*, 57(1), 125–44.

Green, I.A. 2007. On the Horns of a Dilemma Institutional Dimensions of the Sexual Career in a Sample of Middle-class, Urban, Black, Gay Men. *Journal of Black Studies*, 37(5), 753–74.

Greenberg, D.F. 1988. *The Construction of Homosexuality*. Chicago: Chicago University Press.

Grey, C. 1996. Towards a Critique of Managerialism: The Contribution of Simone Weil. *Journal of Management Studies*, 33(5), 591–611.

Grey, C. and Sturdy, A. 2007. Friendship and Organizational Analysis: Toward a Research Agenda. *Journal of Management Inquiry*, 16(2), 157–72.

Grigoriou, T. 2004. *Friendship between Gay Men and Heterosexual Women: An Interpretative Phenomenological Analysis*. London: Families and Social Capital ESRC Group Working paper No5.

Grossman, A.H. and Kerner, M.S. 1998. Support Networks of Gay Male and Lesbian Youth. *International Journal of Sexuality and Gender Studies*, 3(1), 27–46.

Hacker, H.M. 1981. Blabbermouths and Clams: Sex Differences in Self-disclosure in Same-sex and Cross-sex Dyads. *Psychology of Women Quarterly*, 5, 385–401.

Halford, S., Savage, M. and Witz, A. 1997. *Gender, Careers and Organisations – Current Developments in Banking, Nursing and Local Government*. Basingstoke: Macmillan.

Hall, E. 1995. *We Can't Even March Straight*. London: Vintage.

Halperin, D.M. 1990. *One Hundred Years of Homosexuality: And Other Essays on Greek Love*. New York: Routledge.

Hammond, D. and Jablow, A. 1987. Gilgamesh and the Sundance Kid: The Myth of Male Friendship, in *The Making of Masculinities: The New Men's Studies*, edited by H. Brod. Boston: Allen and Unwin, 241–58.

Hansen, K.V. 1992. Our Eyes Behold Each Other: Masculinity and Intimate Friendship in Antebellum New England, in *Men's Friendships*, edited by P. Nardi. Newbury Park, CA.: Sage, 35–58.

Harrison, K. 1998. Rich Friendships, Affluent Friends: Middle-class Practices of Friendship, in *Placing Friendship in Context*, edited by R.G. Adams and G. Allan. Cambridge: Cambridge University Press, 92–116.

Hart, G., Fitzpatrick, R., McLean, J. and Dawson, J. 1990. Gay Men, Social Support and HIV Disease: A Study of Social Integration in the Gay Community. *AIDS Care*, 2(2), 163–70.

Harvey, S.J. 1999. Hegemonic Masculinity, Friendship, and Group Formation in an Athletic Subculture. *The Journal of Men's Studies*, 8(1), 91–108.

Hassett, C. and Owen-Towle, T. 1994. *Friendship Chronicles: Letters Between a Gay and a Straight Man*. San Diego, CA.: Bald Eagle Press.

Hays, R.B., Catania, J.A., McKusick, L. and Coates, T.J. 1990. Help-seeking for AIDS-related Concerns: A Comparison of Gay Men with Various HIV Diagnoses. *American Journal of Community Psychology*, 18(5), 743–55.

Heaphy, B. 2009. The Storied, Complex Lives of Older GLBT Adults: Choices and its Limits in Older Lesbian and Gay Narratives of Relational Life. *Journal of GLBT Family Studies*, 5(1–2), 119–38.

Heaphy, B., Yip, A.K.T. and Thompson, D. 2004. Ageing in a Non-heterosexual Context. *Ageing and Society*, 24(6), 881–902.

Hearn, J. 1992. *Men in the Public Eye: The Construction and Deconstruction of Public Men and Public Patriarchies*. London: Routledge.

Hearn, J. and Parkin, W. 1987. *Sex at Work: The Power and Paradox of Organisation*. Brighton: Wheatsheaf.

Hearn, J., Sheppard, D.L., Tancred-Sheriff, P. and Burrell, G. (eds) 1989. *The Sexuality of Organization*. London: Sage.

Henderson, S. and Gilding, M. 2004. I've Never Clicked this Much with Anyone in My Life: Trust and Hyperpersonal Communication in Online Friendships. *New Media and Society*, 6(4), 487–506.

Herek, G., Cogan, J.C. and Gillis, J.R. 2002. Victim Experiences in Hate Crimes Based on Sexual Orientation. *Journal of Social Issues*, 58(2), 319–39.

Herek, G., Gillis, J.R., Cogan, J.C. and Glunt, E.K. 1997. Hate Crime Victimization among Lesbian, Gay, and Bisexual Adults: Prevalence, Psychological Correlates, and Methodological Issues. *Journal of Interpersonal Violence*, 12(2), 195–215.

Hochschild, A.R. 1997. *The Time Bind: When Work Becomes Home and Home Becomes Work*. New York: Metropolitan Books.

Hoffmann, S.L. 2001. Civility, Male Friendship, and Masonic Sociability in Nineteenth-century Germany. *Gender & History*, 13(2), 224–48.

Hollinger, K. 1998. *In the Company of Women: Contemporary Female Friendship Films*. Minneapolis: University of Minnesota Press.

Holstein, J.A., and Gubrium, J.F. 1995. *The Active Interview.* Newbury Park, CA: Sage.

Homans, G. 1951. *The Human Group*. London: Routledge & Kegan Paul.

Homer. 2003. *The Iliad*, translated by E.V. Rieu. London: Penguin Books.

Hopcke, R.H. and Rafaty, L. 1999. *Straight Women, Gay Men: Absolutely Fabulous Friendships*. Berkeley, CA: Wildcat Canyon Press.

Hultin, M. and Szulkin, R. 2003. Mechanisms of Inequality: Unequal Access to Organizational Power and the Gender Wage Gap. *European Sociological Review*, 19(2), 143–59.

Humphrey, J. 1999. Organizing Sexualities, Organized Inequalities: Lesbians and Gay Men in the Public Service Occupations. *Gender, Work & Organization*, 6(3), 134–51.

Ibarra, H. 1992. Homophily and Differential Returns: Sex Differences in Network Structure and Access in an Advertising Firm. *Administrative Science Quarterly*, 37(3), 422–47.

Ibarra, H. 1993. Personal Networks of Women and Minorities in Management: A Conceptual Framework. *Academy of Management Review*, 18(1), 56–88.

Ibarra, H. 1995. Race, Opportunity and Diversity of Social Circles in Managerial Managers' Networks. *Academy of Management Journal*, 38(3), 673–703.

Jamieson, L. 1998. *Intimacy: Personal Relationships in Modern Societies*. Cambridge and Malden, MA: Polity.

Jay, K. and Young, A. 1972. *Out of the Closets: Voices of Gay Liberation*. New York: Pyramid.

Jeffreys, S. 2003. *Unpacking Queer Politics: A Lesbian Feminist Perspective*. Cambridge: Polity Press.

Jehn, K.A. and Shah, P.P. 1997. Interpersonal Relationships and Task Performance: An Examination of Mediating Processes in Friendship and Acquaintance Groups. *Journal of Personality and Social Psychology*, 72(4), 775–90.

Johnson, J.M. 2001. In-depth Interviewing, in *The Handbook of Interview Research: Context and Method*, edited by J.F. Gubrium and J.A. Holstein. London: Sage, 103–19.

Johnston, D., Stall, R. and Smith, K. 1995. Reliance by Gay Men and Intravenous Drug Users on Friends and Family for AIDS-related Care. *AIDS Care*, 7(3), 307–20.

Kakabadse, A. and Kakabadse, N. 2004. *Intimacy: An International Survey of the Sex Lives of People at Work*. Basingstoke: Palgrave/Macmillan.

Kanter, R.M. 1977. *Men and Women of the Corporation*. New York: Basic Books.

Kaplan, D. 2006. *The Men We Love: Male Friendship and Nationalism in Israeli Culture*. New York: Berghahn Books.

Kaplan, D. and Ben-Ari, E. 2000. Brothers and Others in Arms: Managing Gay Identity in Combat Units of the Israeli Army. *Journal of Contemporary Ethnography*, 29(4), 396–432.

Katz, F.E. 1968. *Autonomy and the Organization: The Limits of Social Control*. New York: Random House.

Kennedy, P. 2004. Making Global Society: Friendship Networks among Transnational Professionals in the Building Design Industry. *Global Networks*, 4(2), 157–79.

Kerfoot, D. 1999. The Organization of Intimacy: Managerialism, Masculinity and the Masculine Subject, in *Transforming Managers: Gendering Change in the Public Sector*, edited by S. Whitehead and R. Moodley. London: UCL Press, 184–99.

Kerfoot, D. and Knights, D. 1993. Management, Masculinity and Manipulation: From Paternalism to Corporate Strategy in Financial Services in Britain. *Journal of Management Studies*, 30(4), 659–79.

Kerfoot, D. and Knights, D. 1998. Managing Masculinity in Contemporary Organizational Life: A 'Man'agerial Project. *Organization*, 5(1), 7–26.

Kimmel, M.S. 1994. Masculinity as Homophobia: Fear, Shame and Silence in the Construction of Gender Identity, in *Theorizing Masculinities*, edited by H. Brod and M. Kaufman. Thousand Oaks, CA.: Sage, 119–41.

King, A.R. and Terrance, C. 2006. Relationships between Personality Disorder Attributes and Friendship Qualities among College Students. *Journal of Social and Personal Relationships*, 23(1), 5–20.

Kirsch, G.E. 2005. Friendship, Friendliness, and Feminist Fieldwork. *Signs*, 30(4), 2163–72.

Klesse, C. 2005. On the Road to Equality? Gender, Sexuality and Race in Sociological Meta-narratives on Transformations of Intimacy, in *Sexual Politics of Desire and Belonging*, edited by N. Rumens and A. Cervantes-Carson. Amsterdam: Rodopi, 59–80.

Komarovsky, M. 1967. *Blue-Collar Marriage*. New York: Random House.

Kong, T.S.K., Mahoney, D. and Plummer, K. 2001. Queering the Interview, in *The Handbook of Interview Research: Context and Method*, in J.F. Gubrium and J.A. Holstein. London: Sage, 239–58.

Konstan, D. 1997. *Friendship in the Classical World*. Cambridge: Cambridge University Press.

Korczynski, M. 2003. Communities of Coping: Collective Emotional Labour in Service Work. *Organization*, 10(1), 55–79.

Kram, K.E. and Isabella, L.A. 1985. Mentoring Alternatives: The Role of Peer Relationships in Career Development. *Academy of Management Journal*, 28(1), 110–32.

Kurth, S. 1970. Friendships and Friendly Relations, in *Social Relationships*, edited by G.J. McCall, M.M. McCall, N.K. Denzin, G.D. Suttles and S.B. Kurth. Chicago: Aldine, 136–70.

Kvale, S. 1996. *InterViews: An Introduction to Qualitative Research Interviewing*. Thousand Oaks, CA.: Sage.

Lapadat, J. and Lindsay, A. 1999. Transcription in Research and Practice: From Standardization of Technique to Interpretive Positionings. *Qualitative Inquiry*, 5(1), 64–23.

Lapota, H. 1971. *Occupation: Housewife*. New York: Oxford University Press.

Lea, M. 1989. Factors Underlying Friendship: An Analysis of Responses on the Acquaintance Description form in Relation to Wright's Friendship Model. *Journal of Social and Personal Relationships*, 6(3), 275–92.

Lehne, G. 1989. Homophobia among Men: Supporting and Defining the Male Role, in *Men's Lives*, edited by M. Kimmel and M. Messner. New York: Macmillan, 416–29.

Levin, S. 1999. *In the Pink: The Making of Successful Gay and Lesbian-owned Businesses*. New York: The Haworth Press.

Levine, M.P. 1979. Employment Discrimination against Gay Men. *International Review of Modern Sociology*, 9, 151–63.

Levine, M.P. 1989. The Status of Gay Men in the Workplace, in *Men's Lives*, edited by M.S. Kimmel and M.A. Messner. New York: Macmillan, 261–76.

Levine, M.P. and Leonard, R. 1984. Discrimination against Lesbians in the Work Force. *Signs*, 9(4), 700–710.

Levy, D.P. 2005. Hegemonic Complicity, Friendship, and Comradeship: Validation and Causal Processes among White, Middle-class, Middle-aged Men. *Journal of Men's Studies*, 13(2), 199–224.

Lewis, R.A. 1978. Emotional Intimacy among Men. *Journal of Social Issues*, 34(1), 108–21.

Lincoln, J.R. and Miller, J. 1979. Work and Friendship Ties in Organizations: A Comparative Analysis of Relational Networks. *Administrative Science Quarterly*, 24(1), 181–99.

Linstead, A. and Thomas, R. 2002. What Do You Want From Me? A Post-structuralist Feminist Reading of Middle Managers' Identities. *Culture and Organization*, 8(1), 1–21.

Litwak, E. 1989. Forms of Friendship among Older People in an Industrial Society, in *Older Adult Friendship: Structure and Process*, edited by R.G. Adams and R. Blieszner. Newbury Park, CA: Sage, 65–88.

Lupton, D. 1998. *The Emotional Self: A Sociocultural Exploration*. London: Sage.

Lupton, T. 1963. *On the Shop Floor: Two Studies of Workplace Organisation and Output*. Oxford: Pergamon Press.

MacFaul, T. 2007. *Male Friendship in Shakespeare and his Contemporaries*. Cambridge: Cambridge University Press.

Mccorkle, B.H., Dunn, E.C., Wan, Y.M. and Gagne, C. 2009. Compeer Friends: A Qualitative Study of a Volunteer Friendship Programme for People with Serious Mental Illness. *International Journal of Social Psychiatry*, 55(4), 291–305.

McCullough, M.W. 1998. *Black and White Women as Friends: Building Cross-Race Friendships*. Cresskill, NJ: Hampton Press.

McDowell, L. 1997. *Capital Culture: Gender at Work in the City*. Oxford: Blackwell.

McGuire, G.M. 2007. Intimate Work: A Typology of the Social Support that Workers Provide to their Network Members. *Work and Occupations*, 34(2), 125–47.

McNay, L. 1992. *Foucault and Feminism: Power, Gender and the Self*. Cambridge: Polity Press.

McWhorter, L. 1999. *Bodies and Pleasure: Foucault and the Politics of Sexual Normalization*. Bloomington, Indiana: Indiana University Press.

Maddison, S. 2000. *Fags, Hags and Queer Sisters*. Basingstoke: Macmillan Press.

Malone, J. 1990. *Straight Women/Gay Men: A Special Relationship*. New York: Dial.

Mao, H.Y. 2006. The Relationship between Organizational Level and Workplace Friendship. *The International Journal of Human Resource Management*, 17(10), 1819–33.

Markiewicz, D., Devine, I. and Kausilas, D. 2000. Friendships of Women and Men at Work: Job Satisfaction and Resource Implications. *Journal of Managerial Psychology*, 15(2), 161–84.

Marks, S.R. 1998. The Gendered Contexts of Inclusive Intimacy: The Hawthorne Women at Work and Home, in *Placing Friendship in Context*, edited by R.G. Adams and G. Allan. Cambridge: Cambridge University Press, 43–70.

Martin, P.Y. 2001. Mobilizing Masculinities: Women's Experience of Men at Work. *Organization*, 8(4), 587–618.

Messner, M. 1992. Like Family: Power, Intimacy, and Sexuality in Male Athletes' Friendships, in *Men's Friendships*, edited by P. Nardi. Newbury Park, CA.: Sage, 215–37.

Migliaccio, T. 2009. Men's Friendships: Performances of Masculinity. *The Journal of Men's Studies*, 17(3), 226–41.

Milardo, R.M. and Wellman, B. 1992. The Personal is Social. *Journal of Social and Personal Relationships*, 9(3), 339–42.

Miles, S. and Rofes, E. (eds) 1998. *Opposite Sex: Gay Men on Lesbians, Lesbians on Gay Men*. New York: New York University Press.

Miller, S. 1983. *Men and Friendship*. London: Gateway Books.

Monsour, M. 2002. *Women and Men as Friends: Relationships Across the Life Span in the 21st Century*. New York: Lawrence Erlbaum.

Moon, D. 1995. Insult and Inclusion: The Term Fag Hag and Gay Male Community. *Social Forces*, 74(2), 487–510.

Morgan, D. 2009. *Acquaintances: The Space between Intimates and Strangers*. Maidenhead: McGraw Hill/OUP.

Morrison, R.L. 2004. Informal Relationships in the Workplace: Associations with Job Satisfaction, Organisational Commitment and Turnover Intentions. *New Zealand Journal of Psychology*, 33(3), 114–28.

Morrison, R.L. 2009a. Are Women Tending and Befriending in the Workplace? Gender Differences in the Relationship Between Workplace Friendships and Organizational Outcomes. *Sex Roles*, 60(1–2), 1–13.

Morrison, R.L. 2009b. The Double-edged Sword: Organizational Outcomes of Workplace Friendships, in *Friends and Enemies in Organizations*, edited by R.L. Morrison and S.L. Wright. Basingstoke: Palgrave Macmillan, 122–38.

Morrison, R.L. and Nolan, T. 2007. Too Much of a Good Thing? Difficulties with Workplace Friendships. *University of Auckland Business Review*, 9(2), 32–41.

Morrison, R.L. and Wright, S.L. (eds) 2009. *Friends and Enemies in Organizations*, Basingstoke: Palgrave Macmillan.

Nahas, R. and Turley, M. 1979. *The New Couple: Women and Gay Men*. New York: Seaview.

Nardi, P.M. 1992a. Sex, Friendship, and Gender Roles among Gay Men, in *Men's Friendships*, edited by P.M. Nardi. Newbury Park, CA.: Sage, 173–85.

Nardi, P.M. (ed.) 1992b. *Men's Friendships*. Newbury Park, CA.: Sage.

Nardi, P.M. 1999. *Gay Men's Friendships: Invincible Communities*. Chicago: Chicago University Press.

Nardi, P.M. 2007. Friendship, Sex, and Masculinity, in *The Sexual Self: The Construction of Sexual Scripts*, edited by M.S. Kimmel. Vanderbilt: Vanderbilt University Press, 49–57.

Nardi, P.M. and Sherrod, D. 1994. Friendship in the Lives of Gay Men and Lesbians. *Journal of Social and Personal Relationships*, 11(2), 185–99.

Nardi, P.M., Sanders, D. and Marmor, J. (eds) 1994. *Growing Up before Stonewall: Life Stories of Some Gay Men*. New York: Routledge.

Nielsen, S., Jex, M. and Adams, G.A. 2000. Development and Validation of Scores on a Two-Dimensional Workplace Friendship Scale. *Educational and Psychological Measurement*, 60(4), 628–43.

Nestle, J. and Preston, J. (eds) 1994. *Sister & Brother: Lesbians and Gay Men Write About Their Lives Together*. New York: Harper.

Nolan, T. and Morrison, R.L. 2009. I Get By with a Little Help from My Friends … At Work. *Kotuitui: New Zealand Journal of Social Sciences Online*, 14, 330–44.

Nye, R.A. 2000. Kinship, Male Bonds, and Masculinity in Comparative Perspective. *American Historical Review*, 105(5), 1656–66.

O'Connor, P. 1992. *Friendships Between Women: A Critical Review*. Hemel Hempstead: Harvester-Wheatsheaf.

O'Connor, P. 1998. Women's Friendships in a Post-modern World, in *Placing Friendship in Context*, edited by R.G. Adams and G. Allan. Cambridge: Cambridge University Press, 117–35.

O'Meara, J.D. 1989. Cross-sex Friendship: Four Basic Challenges of an Ignored Relationship. *Sex Roles*, 21(7/8), 525–43.

Oliker, S.J. 1989. *Best Friends and Marriage: Exchange among Women*. Berkeley: University of California Press.

Oliker, S.J. 1998. The Modernisation of Friendship: Individualism, Intimacy, and Gender in the Nineteenth Century, in *Placing Friendship in Context*, edited by R.G. Adams and G. Allan. Cambridge: Cambridge University Press, 18–42.

Olk, P.M. and Gibbons, D.E. 2010. Dynamics of Friendship Reciprocity Among Professional Adults. *Journal of Applied Social Psychology*, 40(5), 1146–71.

Pahl, R. 2000. *On Friendship*. Cambridge: Polity.

Pahl, R. 2002. Towards a More Significant Sociology of Friendship. *European Journal of Sociology*, 43(3), 410–23.

Paine, R. 1969. In Search of Friendship: An Exploratory Analysis in Middle-class Culture. *Man*, 4(4), 505–24.

Parker, M. 2002. *Against Management: Organization in the Age of Managerialism*. Cambridge: Polity.

Parris, M.A., Vickers, M.H. and Wilkes, L. 2008. Friendships under Strain: The Work–Personal Life Integration of Middle Managers. *Community, Work & Family*, 11(4), 405–18.

Pettinger, L. 2005. Friends, Relations and Colleagues: The Blurred Boundaries of the Workplace. *The Sociological Review*, 53(2), 37–55.

Plummer, D. 1999. *One of the Boys: Masculinity, Homophobia, and Modern Manhood*. New York: Harrington Park Press.

Plummer, K. 2003. *Intimate Citizenship: Private Decisions and Public Dialogues*. Seattle: University of Washington Press.

Podolny, J.M. and Baron, J.N. 1997. Resources and Relationships: Social Networks and Mobility in the Workplace. *American Sociological Review*, 62(5), 673–96.

Pollert, A. 1981. *Girls, Wives, Factory Lives*. London: Macmillan.

Preston, J. and Lowenthal, M. (eds) 1996. *Friends and Lovers: Gay Men Write about Families they Create*. New York: Dutton.

Price, J. 1999. *Navigating Differences: Friendships between Gay and Straight Men*. New York: Harrington Park Press.

Pringle, J.K. 2008. Gender in Management: Theorizing Gender as Heterogender. *British Journal of Management*, 19(1), 110–19.

Pringle, R. 1989. *Secretaries Talk: Sexuality, Power, and Work*. London: Verso.

Pullen, A. and Simpson, R. 2009. Managing Difference in Feminized Work: Men, Otherness and Social Practice. *Human Relations*, 62(4), 561–87.

Quimby, K. 2005. *Will & Grace*: Negotiating (Gay) Marriage on Prime-time Television. *The Journal of Popular Culture*, 38(4), 713–31.

Raeburn, N.C. 2004. *Changing Corporate America Inside Out: Lesbian and Gay Workplace Rights*. Minneapolis: University of Minnesota Press.

Ragins, B.R., Cornwell, J.M. and Miller, J.S. 2003. Heterosexism in the Workplace: Do Race and Gender Matter? *Group and Organizational Management*, 28(1), 45–65.

Ragins, B.R. and Dutton, J.E. 2007. Positive Relationships at Work: An Introduction and Invitation, in *Exploring Positive Relationships at Work: Building a Theoretical and Research Foundation*, edited by J.E. Dutton and B.R. Ragins. Mahwah, NJ: Lawrence Erlbaum, 1–25.

Rauch, K. and Fessler, J. 1995. *Why Gay Guys are a Girl's Best Friend*. New York: Simon and Schuster Inc.

Rawlins, W.K. 1992. *Friendship Matters*. New York: Aldine de Gruyter.

Rawlins, W.K. 2008. *The Compass of Friendship: Narratives, Identities and Dialogues*. London: Sage.

Raymond, J. 1986. *A Passion for Friends*. London: The Women's Press.

Reeder, H.M. 2000. 'I Like You … As a Friend': The Role of Attraction in Cross-sex Friendship. *Journal of Social and Personal Friendships*, 17(3), 329–48.

Reid, H.M. and Fine, G.A. 1992. Self-disclosure in Men's Friendships: Variations Associated with Intimate Relations in *Men's Friendships*, edited by P. Nardi. Newbury Park, CA.: Sage, 132–54.

Remarque, E.M. 1929/1987. *All Quiet on the Western Front*. New York: Ballantine Books.

Richardson, D. 2004. Locating Sexualities: From Here to Normality. *Sexualities* 7(4), 391–411.

Richardson, D. 2005. Desiring Sameness? The Rise of a Neoliberal Politics of Normalisation. *Antipode*, 37(3), 515–35.

Riordan, C.M. and Griffeth, R.W. 1995. The Opportunity for Friendship in the Workplace: An Unexplored Construct. *Journal of Business and Psychology*, 10(2), 141–54.

Rocke, M. 1996. *Forbidden Friendships: Homosexuality and Male Culture in Renaissance Florence*. Oxford: Oxford University Press.

Roethlisberger, F.J. and Dickson, W.J. 1939. *Management and the Worker*. Cambridge, MA: Harvard University Press.

Roper, M. 1994. *Masculinity and the British Organization Man since 1945*. Oxford: Oxford University Press.

Roper, M. 1996. Seduction and Succession: Circuits of Homosocial Desire in Management, in *Men as Managers, Managers as Men*, edited by D.L. Collinson and J. Hearn. London: Sage, 210–26.

Rose, S. 2000. Heterosexism and the Study of Women's Romantic and Friend Relationships. *Journal of Social Issues*, 56(2), 315–28.

Roseneil, S. 2000. Queer Frameworks and Queer Tendencies: Towards an Understanding of Postmodern Transformations of Sexuality, *Sociological Research Online*, 5(3). [Online]. Available at: http://www.socresonline.org.uk/5/3/roseneil.htlm [accessed 20 September 2010].

Roseneil, S. 2004. Why We Should Care about Friends: An Argument for Queering the Care Imaginary in Social Policy. *Social Policy and Society*, 3(4), 409–19.

Roseneil, S. and Budgeon, S. 2004. Cultures of Intimacy and Care Beyond the Family: Personal Life and Social Change in the Early Twenty-first Century. *Current Sociology*, 52(2), 135–59.

Roy, D.F. 1959. Banana Time: Job Satisfaction and Informal Interaction. *Human Organization*, 18, 158–68.

Rubin, H.J. and Rubin, I. 2005. *Qualitative Interviewing: The Art of Hearing Data*, 2nd edn. London: Sage.

Rubin, L. 1985. *Just Friends: The Role of Friendship in Our Lives*. New York: Harper and Row.

Rumens, N. and Kerfoot, D. 2009. Gay Men at Work: (Re)constructing the Self as Professional. *Human Relations*, 62(5), 3–786.

Rust, P.C. 1995. *The Challenge of Bisexuality to Lesbian Politics: Sex, Loyalty, and Revolution*. New York: New York University Press.

Rutherford, J. 1997. *Forever England: Reflections on Masculinity and Empire*. London: Lawrence and Wishart.

Ryniker, M.R. 2008. Lesbians Still Face Job Discrimination. *Journal of Lesbian Studies*, 12(1), 7–15.

Sapadin, L.A. 1988. Friendship and Gender: Perspectives of Professional Men and Women. *Journal of Social and Personal Relationships*, 5(4), 387–403.

Sawicki, J. 1991. *Disciplining Foucault: Feminism, Power and the Body*. New York: Routledge.

Schilt, K. and Connell, C. 2007. Do Workplace Gender Transitions Make Gender Trouble? *Gender, Work & Organization*, 14(6), 596–618.

Sedgwick, E.K. 1985. *Between Men: English Literature and Male Homosexual Desire*. New York: Columbia University Press.

Sedgwick, E.K. 1990. *The Epistemology of the Closet*. Berkeley: University of California Press.

Segal, L. 1990. *Slow Motion: Changing Masculinities, Changing Men*. London: Virago.

Seibert, S.E., Kramer, M.L. and Liden, R.C. 2001. A Social Capital Theory of Career Success. *Academy of Management Journal*, 44(2), 219–2237.

Seidler, V.J. 1992. Rejection, Vulnerability, and Friendship, in *Men's Friendships*, edited by P. Nardi. Newbury Park, CA.: Sage, 15–34.

Seidler, V.J. 1997. *Man Enough: Embodying Masculinities*. London: Sage.

Seidler, V.J. 2007. *Young Men and Masculinities: Global Cultures and Intimate Lives*. London: Zed Books.

Seidman, S. 1997. *Difference Troubles*. Cambridge: Cambridge University Press.

Seidman, S. 1998. Are We All in the Closet? Notes Towards a Sociological and Cultural Turn in Queer Theory. *European Journal of Cultural Studies*, 1(2), 177–92.

Seidman, S. 2002. *Beyond the Closet: The Transformation of Gay and Lesbian Life*. New York: Routledge.

Seymour, J. and Bagguley, P. (eds) 1999. *Relating Intimacies: Power and Resistance*. Basingstoke: Macmillan Press.

Shah, P.P. and Jehn, K.A. 1993. Do Friends Perform Better than Acquaintances? The Interaction of Friendship, Conflict, and Task. *Group Decision and Negotiation*, 2(2), 149–65.

Shallenberger, D. 1994. Professional and Openly Gay: A Narrative Study of the Experience. *Journal of Management Inquiry*, 3(2), 119–42.

Shelton, J.N., Richeson, J.A. and Bergsieker, H.B. 2009. Interracial Friendship Development and Attributional Biases. *Journal of Social and Personal Relationships*, 26(2–3), 179–93.

Shepperd, D., Coyle, A. and Hegarty, P. 2010. Discourses of Friendship between Heterosexual Women and Gay Men: Mythical Norms and an Absence of Desire. *Feminism & Psychology*, 20(2), 205–24.

Sherrod, D. 1987. The Bonds of Men: Problems and Possibilities in Close Male Relationships, in *The Making of Masculinities: The New Men's Studies*, edited by H. Brod. Boston: Allen and Unwin, 213–39.

Shugart, H.A. 2003. Reinventing Privilege: The New (Gay) Man in Contemporary Popular Media. *Critical Studies in Media Communication,* 20(1), 67–91.

Sias, P.M. 2005. Workplace Relationship Quality and Employee Information Experiences. *Communication Studies*, 56, 375–95.

Sias, P.M. 2009. *Organizing Relationships: Traditional and Emerging Perspectives on Workplace Relationships*. Thousand Oaks, CA: Sage.

Sias, P.M. and Cahill, D.J. 1998. From Coworkers to Friends: The Development of Peer Friendships in the Workplace. *Western Journal of Communication*, 6(2), 273–99.

Sias, P.M. and Gallagher, E. 2009. Developing, Maintaining and Disengaging from Workplace Friendships, in *Friends and Enemies in Organizations*, edited by R.L. Morrison and S.L. Wright. Palgrave Macmillan, 78–100.

Sias, P.M., Heath, R.G., Perry, T., Silva, D. and Fix, B. 2004. *Narratives of Workplace Deterioration*, 21(3), 321–40.

Sias, P.M. and Perry, T. 2004. Disengaging from Workplace Relationships: A Research Note. *Human Communication Research*, 30(4), 589–602.

Sias, P.M., Smith, G. and Avdeyeva, T. 2003. Sex and Sex-composition Differences and Similarities in Peer Workplace Friendship Development. *Communication Studies*, 54(3), 322–40.

Siegel, D. and Epstein, J. 1996. Ethnic-racial Differences in Psychological Stress Related to Gay Lifestyle among HIV Positive Men. *Psychological Reports*, 79(1), 303–12.

Silver, A. 1990. Friendship in Commercial Society: Eighteenth-century Social Theory and Modern Sociology. *American Journal of Sociology*, 95(6), 1474–504.

Simon, W. 1996. *Postmodern Sexualities*. London: Routledge.

Sinfield, A. 1998. *Gay and After: Gender, Culture and Consumption*. London: Serpent's Tail.

Skidmore, P. 2004. A Legal Perspective on Sexuality and Organization: A Lesbian and Gay Case Study. *Gender, Work & Organization*, 11(3), 229–53.

Song, S.H. 2006. Workplace Friendship and Employee's Productivity: LMX Theory and the Case of the Seoul City Government. *International Review of Public Administration*, 11(1), 47–58.

Song, S.H. and Olshfski, D. 2008. Friends at Work: A Comparative Study of Work Attitudes in Seoul City Government and New Jersey State Government. *Administration and Society*, 40(2), 147–69.

Spencer, L. and Pahl, R. 2006. *Re-Thinking Friendship: Hidden Solidarities Today*. Princeton: Princeton University Press.

Stanley, L. 1982. Male Needs: The Problems and Problems of Working with Gay Men, in *On the Problem of Men: Two Conferences*, edited by S. Friedman and E. Sarah. London: The Women's Press, 190–213.

Stanley, J.L. 1996. The Lesbian's Experience of Friendship, in *Lesbian Friendships: For Ourselves and For Each Other*, edited by J.S. Weinstock and E.D. Rothblum. New York: New York University Press, 39–59.

Stonewall. 2008. *Peak Performance: Gay People and Productivity*. London: Stonewall.

Stuart, E. 1995. *Just Good Friends: Towards a Lesbian and Gay Theology of Relationships*. London: Mowbray.

Sullivan, A. 1996. *Virtually Normal: An Argument about Homosexuality*. London: Picador.

Sullivan, A. 1998. *Love Undetectable: Notes on Friendship, Sex and Survival*. New York: Knopf.

Suttles, G. 1970. Friendship as a Social Institution, in *Social Relationships*, edited by G.J. McCall, M.M. McCall, N.K. Denzin, G.D. Suttles and S.B. Kurth. Chicago: Aldine, 95–135.

Swain, S.O. 1989. Covert Intimacy: Closeness in Men's Friendships, in *Gender in Intimate Relationships: A Microstructural Approach*, edited by B.J. Risman and P. Schwartz. Belmont, CA: Wadsworth, 71–86.

Swain, S.O. 1992. Men's Friendships with Women: Intimacy, Sexual Boundaries, and the Informant Role, in *Men's Friendships*, edited by P. Nardi. Newbury Park, CA: Sage, 153–76.

Tadmor, N. 2001. *Family and Friends in Eighteenth Century England*. Cambridge: Cambridge University Press.

Taylor, V. and Raeburn, N. 1995. Identity Politics as High-risk Activism: Career Consequences for Lesbian, Gay and Bisexual Sociologists. *Social Problems*, 42(2), 252–73.

Tilley, S.A. 2003. Challenging Research Practices: Turning a Critical Lens on the Work of Transcription. *Qualitative Inquiry*, 9(5), 750–73.

Tillmann-Healy, L.M. 2001. *Between Gay and Straight: Understanding Friendship Across Sexual Orientation*. Walnut Creek, CA: AltaMira Press.

Tosh, J. 2005. *Manliness and Masculinities in Nineteenth Century Britain: Essays on Gender, Family and Empire*. London: Longman.

Trau, R.N.C. and Härtel, C.E.J. 2004. One Career, Two Identities: An Assessment of Gay Men's Career Trajectory. *Career Development International*, 9(7), 627–37.

Traub, V. 2002. *The Renaissance of Lesbianism in Early Modern England*. Cambridge: Cambridge University Press.

Tyler, M. 2009. Managing Under the Covers: Lifestyle Media and the Management of Sexuality in Everyday Life, in *The Management of Everyday Life*, edited by P. Hancock and M. Tyler. Basingstoke: Palgrave/Macmillan, 23–38.

Ueno, K. and Adams, R.G. 2007. Men's Friendships, in *International Encyclopedia of Men and Masculinities*, edited by M. Flood, J.K. Gardiner, B. Pease and K. Pringle. London: Routledge, 216–20.

Vargo, M.E. 1998. *Acts of Disclosure: The Coming-out Process of Contemporary Gay Men*. New York: The Haworth Press.

Vernon, M. 2000. What are Gay Men For? *Theology and Sexuality*, 7(13), 63–76.

Vernon, M. 2005. *The Philosophy of Friendship*. Basingstoke: Palgrave Macmillan.

Vicinus, M. 2004. *Intimate Friends: Same-sex Love between Women, 1780–1920*. Chicago: Chicago University Press.

Vincke, J. and Bolton, R. 1994. Social Support, Depression and Self-acceptance among Gay Men. *Human Relations*, 47(9), 1049–62.

Wagg, S. (ed.) 1998. *Because I Tell a Joke or Two: Comedy, Politics and Social Difference*. London: Routledge.

Walker, K. 1994a. I'm Not Friends the way She's Friends: Ideological and Behavioural Constructions of Masculinity in Men's Friendships. *Masculinities*, 2(2), 38–55.

Walker, K. 1994b. Men, Women and Friendship: What they Say; What they Do. *Gender & Society*, 8(2), 246–65.

Ward, J. 2000. Queer Sexism: Rethinking Gay Men and Masculinity, in *Gay Masculinities*, edited by P.M. Nardi. Thousand Oaks, CA: Sage, 152–75.

Ward, J. and Winstanley, D. 2003. The Absent Present: Negative Space within Discourse and the Construction of Minority Sexual Identity in the Workplace. *Human Relations*, 56(10), 1255–80.

Ward, J. and Winstanley, D. 2005. Coming Out at Work: Performativity and the Recognition and Renegotiation of Identity. *The Sociological Review*, 53(3), 447–75.

Ward, J. and Winstanley, D. 2006. Watching the Watch: The UK Fire Service and its Impact on Sexual Minorities in the Workplace. *Gender, Work & Organization*, 13(2), 193–219.

Ward, J. 2008. *Sexualities, Work and Organizations: Stories by Gay Men and Women in the Workplace at the Beginning of the Twenty-first Century*. London: Routledge.

Warner, M. 1999. *The Trouble with Normal: Sex, Politics, and the Ethics of Queer Life*. New York: The Free Press.

Watney, S. 2000. *Imagine Hope: AIDS and Gay Identity*. London: Routledge.

Weeks, J. 1977. *Coming Out: Homosexual Politics in Britain from the Nineteenth Century to the Present*. London: Quartet Books.

Weeks, J. 1995. *Invented Moralities: Sexual Values in an Age of Uncertainty*. London: Routledge.

Weeks, J. 2007. *The World We Have Won*. London: Routledge.

Weeks, J., Heaphy, B. and Donovan, C. 2001. *Same-sex Intimacies: Families of Choice and Other Life Experiments*. London: Routledge.

Weinstock, J.S. 1998. Lesbian, Gay, Bisexual, and Transgender Friendships in Adulthood, in *Lesbian, Gay, and Bisexual Identities in Families*, edited by C.J. Patterson and A.R. D'Augelli. New York: Oxford University Press, 122–54.

Weiss, L. and Lowenthal, M.F. 1975. Life Course Perspectives on Friendship, in *Four Stages of Life*, edited by M.F. Lowenthal, M. Thurner and D. Chiriboga. San Francisco: Jossey-Bass, 48–61.

Wellman, B. 1992. Men in Networks: Private Communities, Domestic Friendships, in *Men's Friendships*, edited by P.M. Nardi. Newbury Park, CA.: Sage, 74–114.

Wengraf, T. 2001. *Qualitative Research Interviewing: Biographic Narratives and Semi-structured Methods*. London: Sage.

Werking, K. 1997. *We're Just Good Friends*. New York: Guilford Press.

Weston, K. 1991. *Families we Choose: Lesbians, Gays, Kinship*. New York: Columbia University Press.

Westwood, S. 1984. *All Day, Every Day: Factory and Family in the Making of Women's Lives*. London: Pluto Press.

Westwood, R.I. and Rhodes, C. 2006. *Humour, Work and Organisation*. London: Routledge.

Wharton, A.S. and Bird, S. 1996. Stand By Your Man: Homosociality, Work Groups, and Men's Perceptions of Difference, in *Masculinities in Organizations*, edited by C. Cheng. Thousand Oaks, CA: Sage, 97–114.

White, A.M. 2008. *Ain't I a Feminist? African American Men Speak Out on Fatherhood, Friendship, Forgiveness, and Freedom*. New York: University of New York Press.

Whitney, C. 1990. *Uncommon Lives: Gay Men and Straight Women*. New York: Plume.

Williams, C.L., Giuffre, P.A. and Dellinger, K. 1999. Sexuality in the Workplace: Organizational Control, Sexual Harassment, and the Pursuit of Pleasure. *Annual Review of Sociology*, 25, 73–93.

Williams, C.L., Giuffre, P.A. and Dellinger, K. 2009. The Gay-friendly Closet. *Sexuality Research and Social Policy*, 6(1), 29–45.

Willis, P. 1977. *Learning to Labor: How Working Class Kids Get Working Class Jobs*. Farnborough: Saxon House.

Wilton, T. 2004. *Sexual (Dis)Orientation: Gender, Sex, Desire and Self-Fashioning*. Basingstoke: Palgrave/Macmillan.

Winstead, B.A., Derlega, V.J., Montgomery, M.J., and Pilkington, C. 1995. The Quality of Friendship at Work and Job Satisfaction. *The Journal of Social and Personal Relationships*, 12(2), 199–215.

Wood, J.T. 1993. Engendered Relations: Interaction, Caring, Power, and Responsibility in Intimacy, in *Social Context and Relationships*, edited by S. Duck. Newbury Park, CA: Sage, 26–54.

Wood, J.T. and Inman, C.C. 1993. In a Different Mode: Recognizing Male Modes of Closeness. *Journal of Applied Communication Research*, 21(3), 279–95.

Woods, J.D. and Lucas, J.H. 1993. *The Corporate Closet: The Professional Lives of Gay Men in America.* New York: The Free Press.

Worth, H., Reid, A. and McMillan, K. 2002. Somewhere Over the Rainbow: Love, Trust and Monogamy in Gay Relationships. *Journal of Sociology*, 38(3), 237–53.

Wright, P.H. 1969. A Model and a Technique for Studies of Friendship. *Journal of Experimental Social Psychology*, 5(3), 295–309.

Wright, P.H. 1978. Toward a Theory of Friendship Based on a Conception of Self. *Human Communication Research*, 4(3), 196–207.

Wright, P.H. 1982. Men's Friendships, Women's Friendships and the Alleged Inferiority of the Latter. *Sex Roles*, 8(1), 1–20.

Wright, P.H. 1984. Self-referent Motivation and the Intrinsic Quality of Friendship. *Journal of Social and Personal Relationships*, 1(1), 115–30.

Wright, P.H. 1985. The Acquaintance Description Form, in *Understanding Personal Relationships: An Interdisciplinary Approach*, edited by S. Duck and P. Perlman. London: Sage, 39–62.

Wright, P.H. and Scanlon, M.B. 1991. Gender Role Orientations and Friendship: Some Attenuation, but Gender Differences Abound. *Sex Roles*, 24(9–10), 551–66.

Yoshikawa, H., Wilson, P.A.D, Chae, D.H. and Cheng, J.F. 2004. Do Family and Friendship Networks Protect Against the Effects of Discrimination on Mental Health and HIV Risk among Asian and Pacific Islander Gay Men? *AIDS Education and Prevention*, 16(1), 84–100.

Zaleznik, A. 1997. Real Work. *Harvard Business Review*, 75(6), 53–62.

Zorn, T.E. 1995. Bosses and Buddies: Constructing and Performing Simultaneously Hierarchical and Close Friendship Relationships, in *Under-Studied Relationships*, edited by J.T. Wood and S. Duck. Thousand Oaks, CA: Sage, 122–47.

Index